Zero Trust Architecture

Cindy Green-Ortiz, CISSP, CISM,

Bran

Hank Hensel, CCIE No. 3577, CISSP

Patrick Lloyd, CCIE Enterprise No. 39750, CISSP

Andrew McDonald

Jason Frazier, CCSI

Cisco Press

Zero Trust Architecture

Cindy Green-Ortiz, CISSP, CISM, CRISC, CSSLP, PMP, CSM

Brandon Fowler, CCNP Security

David Houck

Hank Hensel, CCIE No. 3577, CISSP

Patrick Lloyd, CCIE Enterprise No. 39750, CISSP

Andrew McDonald

Jason Frazier, CCSI

Copyright© 2024 Cisco Systems, Inc.

Published by: Cisco Press

ScoutAutomatedPrintCode

Library of Congress Control Number: 2023906699

ISBN-13: 978-0-13-789973-9

ISBN-10: 0-13-789973-4

Warning and Disclaimer

Trademark Acknowledgments

Special Sales

For information about buying this title in bulk quantities or for special sales opportunities (which may include electronic versions; custom cover designs; and content particular to your business, training goals, marketing focus, or branding interests), please contact our corporate sales department at corpsales@pearsoned.com or (800) 382-3419.

For government sales inquiries, please contact governmentsales@pearsoned.com.

For questions about sales outside the U.S., please contact international@pearsoned.com.

Feedback Information

At Cisco Press, our goal is to create in-depth technical books of the highest quality and value. Each book is crafted with care and precision, undergoing rigorous development that involves the unique expertise of members from the professional technical community.

Readers' feedback is a natural continuation of this process. If you have any comments regarding how we could improve the quality of this book, or otherwise alter it to better suit your needs, you can contact us through email at feedback@ciscopress.com. Please make sure to include the book title and ISBN in your message.

We greatly appreciate your assistance.

Vice President, IT Professional: Mark Taub

Alliances Manager, Cisco Press: Arezou Gol

Director, ITP Product Management: Brett Bartow

Executive Editor: James Manly

Managing Editor: Sandra Schroeder

Development Editor: Ellie C. Bru

Senior Project Editor: Mandie Frank

Copy Editor: Chuck Hutchinson

Technical Editors: Tom Diederich, Joseph Muniz, Brock Pearson

Editorial Assistant: Cindy Teeters

Designer: Chuti Prasertsith

Composition: codeMantra

Indexer: Erika Millen

Proofreader: Donna E. Mulder

CISCO.

Americas Headquarters
Cisco Systems, Inc.
San Jose, CA

Asia Pacific Headquarters
Cisco Systems (USA) Pte. Ltd.
Singapore

Europe Headquarters
Cisco Systems International BV Amsterdam,
The Netherlands

Cisco has more than 200 offices worldwide. Addresses, phone numbers, and fax numbers are listed on the Cisco Website at www.cisco.com/go/offices.

Figure Credits

Pearson's Commitment to Diversity, Equity, and Inclusion

Pearson is dedicated to creating bias-free content that reflects the diversity of all learners. We embrace the many dimensions of diversity, including but not limited to race, ethnicity, gender, socioeconomic status, ability, age, sexual orientation, and religious or political beliefs.

Education is a powerful force for equity and change in our world. It has the potential to deliver opportunities that improve lives and enable economic mobility. As we work with authors to create content for every product and service, we acknowledge our responsibility to demonstrate inclusivity and incorporate diverse scholarship so that everyone can achieve their potential through learning. As the world's leading learning company, we have a duty to help drive change and live up to our purpose to help more people create a better life for themselves and to create a better world.

Our ambition is to purposefully contribute to a world where

- Everyone has an equitable and lifelong opportunity to succeed through learning

- Our educational products and services are inclusive and represent the rich diversity of learners

- Our educational content accurately reflects the histories and experiences of the learners we serve

- Our educational content prompts deeper discussions with learners and motivates them to expand their own learning (and worldview)

While we work hard to present unbiased content, we want to hear from you about any concerns or needs with this Pearson product so that we can investigate and address them.

Please contact us with concerns about any potential bias at https://www.pearson.com/report-bias.html.

About the Authors

Cindy Green-Ortiz

Cindy Green-Ortiz is a Cisco senior security architect, cybersecurity strategist, architect, and entrepreneur. She works in the Customer Experience, Global Enterprise Segment for Cisco. She holds the CISSP, CISM, CSSLP, CRISC, PMP, and CSM Certifications, along with two degrees—a BS-CIS Magna Cum Laude and AS-CIS with Honors.

She has been with Cisco for 6+ years. Cindy has been in the cybersecurity field for 40 years, where she has held D-CIO, D-CISO, and Corporate Security Architecture Leadership roles, founding two technology businesses as CEO. Cindy is a Cisco Chairman's Club winner (Club Cisco). She is an active blogger for Cisco and has published whitepapers for Cisco and the US Department of Homeland Security. She has spoken to many groups, including PMI International Information Systems & Technology Symposium-Cybersecurity Keynote; Cisco SecCon, and Cisco Live. Cindy is President Emeritus and serves now as the treasurer of Charlotte InfraGard and cofounder of the InfraGard CyberCamp. Cindy lives in Charlotte, North Carolina, with her amazing husband, Erick, and their two wonderful daughters. Cindy and her family love to travel and see the world.

Brandon Fowler

Brandon Fowler is a technical leader for Cisco Customer Experience Professional Services. He holds both CCNP Security and ITIL v4 foundation certifications. Brandon joined Cisco in 2018 with more than 12 years of experience across enterprise networking and security domains. For the past 8 years, his focus has been on identity, access management, and segmentation with expertise across multiple industry verticals, including retail and distribution, hospitality and entertainment, financial services, and healthcare. Additionally, he has helped to develop some of Cisco's current Zero Trust service offerings. Brandon also helps mentor and advise other employees within Cisco and enjoys being challenged and learning new technologies. In his personal time, he enjoys working on cars, photography, and video gaming.

David Houck

David Houck is a security architect, mentor, and advocate. He has been working with Cisco Customer Experience since 2011. David leads delivery teams in implementing solutions globally to financial, energy, retail, healthcare, and manufacturing organizations that focus on identifying and meeting technical and business outcomes. He has presented on the value and implementation of Cisco solutions globally to customers, partners, and internal audiences.

David has worked in networking and security since 2005, with experience in service provider voice, infrastructure, ISP operations, plus data center design and operation before coming to Cisco to focus on security solutions and architecture. He enjoys mentoring to provide experiences and opportunities to see others flourish.

Hank Hensel

Hank Hensel is a senior security architect working for Cisco's CX Security Services providing security consultation, assessment, and design advisory services to Cisco's US and international customers.

Hank has worked more than 30 years (7 years at Cisco) in leadership positions in IT systems, cybersecurity, design, and integration. Hank's areas of expertise include security and infrastructure, project management, disaster recovery, business continuity, risk analysis and mitigation, data mapping, data classification, and cybersecurity infrastructure design. Hank has displayed his expertise and leadership in several different industries, including international banking and finance, healthcare, pharmaceutical, energy, renewable energy, oil and gas, passenger and transit rail, manufacturing, mining, wet infrastructure, chemical, nuclear enrichment, public sector defense, municipality and state infrastructure, and law enforcement. Hank's expertise and extensive training in networking, security, and strong focus with industrial control systems allow him to engage in nearly all areas of a customer's operations, policies, and practices. Hank holds CCIE (# 3577), CISSP, GICSP, and CMMC-RP, and other certifications.

Hank practices Cisco's core values in all customer engagements, which have directly contributed to his consistent project successes in every engagement he has been involved in. Hank's success can be attributed to these values and their consistent culmination by being recognized as a "Trusted Advisor" in nearly every engagement he has been a part of for Cisco.

Hank's role of trust and deep experience extend beyond customer relationships to new service offerings development and Cisco team support. Hank was the original developer of the current CX advisory segmentation service offering that has been in use for the last seven years and has contributed to the development of the new CX advisory Zero Trust service offering. Finally, Hank is currently contributing to building a consulting service offering for the renewables energy sector.

Patrick Lloyd

Patrick Lloyd is a senior solutions architect for Cisco's Customer Experience Security Services team. He focuses on identity and access management, including segmentation, network access control, identity exchange, and identity integration in the Northeast United States and Canada region.

Patrick has worked in technology delivery at Cisco for 13 years, ranging from stints in the technical assistance center (TAC), working as a routing and switching design engineer, security design engineer, and solutions architect. His focus is guiding customers through introducing visibility and identity exchange to minimize business risk and lateral attack vectors. Previously, Patrick worked in higher education and defense industries in system administration and operational roles.

Patrick has extensive experience in integrating identity into various industries, including healthcare, manufacturing, finance, and defense. Utilizing Cisco technologies and the methodologies covered in this book to build a layered security model, Patrick has architected segmentation architectures, including smart building architectures, for more than 100 customers.

Patrick's technology focuses span from TrustSec for segmentation, analyzing traffic flow with Cisco Secure Network Analytics/Stealthwatch for development of segmentation policies, implementing firewall and advanced malware protection, and securing critical building systems through policy and segmentation while maintaining availability.

Patrick resides in Durham, North Carolina, where he teaches self-defense and is a student pilot when not consumed with technology.

Andrew McDonald

Andrew McDonald is a Cisco network and security architect; he works in the Customer Experience, Security Advisory team for Cisco. He specializes in leading delivery teams creating network segmentation and Zero Trust designs and implementation plans.

He has been with Cisco for more than 22 years, working as an escalation engineer, network consulting engineer, systems integration architect, and security architect. Andrew has worked with global customers in all industry verticals and at every level, from front-line support engineers to C-suite executives across multiple technical disciplines. Andrew has worked in the networking and communications industry for more than 40 years. In 1981, he started as a telecommunications technician for Digital Equipment Corporation, where he developed an entry level into a lifelong career.

Jason Frazier

Jason Frazier is a principal engineer with the Network Services group in Cisco IT. In his current role, Jason focuses on Zero Trust technologies, Cisco DNA, operational excellence, automation, and security. Jason has deep knowledge of networking technologies, including programmability, enterprise network architecture, and identity.

Jason joined Cisco in 1999. He is known throughout the company for his work ethic, passion, loyalty, and drive. Jason currently holds nine patents. For Cisco Live, he is a veteran speaker, hackathon coordinator, blogger, booth orchestrator, or anything called for. Jason is also the author of Cisco Press books.

Jason has been happily married to his wife, Christy, for 22 years. Their oldest son, Davis (16), is Jason's best friend. Jason is also wrapped around the finger of their daughter, Sidney (14). Most nonwork time is spent doing something with or for his kids. He likes to spend time on a bike, when possible. Jason and family like to travel when they can. As a computer engineering graduate of NC State University, Jason and his family enjoy Wolfpack sporting events as well.

About the Technical Reviewers

Tom Diederich

Tom Diederich is a Cisco ONEx Community Storyteller. He joined Cisco's ONEx communities team in 2021. He has a bachelor's degree in journalism from The Ohio State University and maintains an active "Secret" level security clearance with the US Department of Defense.

Joseph Muniz

Joseph Muniz is the director of business development for security solutions at Microsoft and a security researcher. He is driven by making the world a safer place through education and adversary research. Joseph has extensive experience in designing security solutions and architectures as a trusted advisor for the top Fortune 500 corporations and US government.

Joseph is a researcher and industry thought leader. He speaks regularly at international conferences, writes for technical magazines, and is involved with developing training for various industry certifications. He invented the fictitious character of Emily Williams to create awareness around social engineering. Joseph runs thesecurityblogger.com website, a popular resource for security and product implementation. He is the author and contributor of several publications, including titles ranging from security best practices to exploitation tactics. Joseph's latest title, *The Modern Security Operations Center*, was released in 2021, and he has a title on virtual private networks.

When Joseph is not using technology, you can find him on the futbal field. Follow Joseph @SecureBlogger.

Brock Pearson

Brock Pearson has been a thought leader in the cybersecurity industry as a consultant or educator for more than 22 years. He has worked for multiple firms, assisting Fortune 500 organizations, plus federal, state, and local government agencies in their quest to protect their data, systems, and computing environments. Within his consultative capacity, Brock has developed and executed cyber program strategies (people, processes, and technologies) and has assessed, enhanced, and transitioned those services to managed security services as necessary. Brock has primarily been engaged in the heavily regulated industry verticals including financial services, healthcare, and utilities. As an educator, Brock has developed and delivered enablement programs globally for two of the largest SIEM and UEBA products in the cybersecurity tooling space.

Dedications

To my beloved husband, Erick Ortiz-Alvarenga, every day is a blessing, and I am truly grateful for all your love and support. To our daughters, Angela and Anna, what a bright future you have. Know that are both loved and supported to reach your dreams. You both inspire me every day! To my Uncle Roger Green and my Aunt Joan Green, you bring me joy and always have a great story from back home. To my parents in heaven, Howard Green, and Nancy Salyers Green, I would not be where I am without your courage to strive for knowledge.

—Cindy Green-Ortiz

To my parents, Nick and Sherry, and my brother and sister-in-law, Derek and Melissa, who have always supported me and helped me become who I am today, I am forever grateful. To my mentors, teachers, and everyone else who has helped in small or large ways throughout the years, thank you for everything that you have done to impact my life and help me get to where I am today.

—Brandon Fowler

For all who teach, inspire, and mentor us. Those who provide the shared human experience of fueling the drive for learning and improvement. A world without these experiences and the people who dedicate themselves to share these experiences never progresses. Take the time to remember, recognize, and celebrate those who have contributed to who and where you are today. Be responsible and kind enough to share of yourself and share that experience with others.

—David Houck

To my wife (and dance partner), Catherine, and our daughter, Katrina, with love. In life, the accumulation of meaningful knowledge and experience does not happen by accident. It is sought and pursued over time throughout our lives. Thank you for your grace in encouragement, support, and especially patience with my long hours and travel over the years.

—Hank Hensel

To my parents, without whose support I never would have pursued dreams that seemed well beyond the reach of many. To the friends and family who supported me through some of the best, worst, and weirdest times we've been through together, your support and guidance are what made this book possible. This never could have been done without you.

—Patrick Lloyd

To my lovely wife, Sharon, for all her support through late-night troubleshooting, weekend cut-overs, long and frequent travel schedules, and listening to me talking about networking for the last 35 years. Also, to my two rotten kids, Charlie and Emily, who suffered through much the same, along with endless droning from "the troll hole" (my home office). No wonder neither of them went into IT. Finally, to my mother and father, who taught me the value of hard work and integrity.

—Andrew McDonald

To my wife, Christy Frazier, I love you so dearly. As the years go by, they just get better. Thank you for always supporting me. As I stand by your side, I am the luckiest man in the world. To my son, Davis Frazier, I am so excited to see you shaping into the man you are becoming. You are the best friend a dad could have. To my daughter, Sidney Frazier, there are no limits for your potential. I will forever be wrapped around your finger.

—Jason Frazier

Acknowledgments

With 40 years in this field, I have too many to thank for your help, guidance, and support. To name but a few, I would like to give special recognition to my friend-sister Patty Wolferd Armstrong, my lifelong mentor Denis McDuff, my Cisco mentors and colleagues: David Ankeney, Demetria Davis, Bill Ayers, Jr., Justin Taylor, Brian Conley, Jim Schwab, Michele Guel, Zig Zsiga, Cesar Carballes, Jason Penn, Chris Mula, Guilherme Leonhardt, Maurice DuPas, Aunudrei Oliver, and this authoring team, who have seen me at my best or at my worst and have helped me navigate life or work's ever-changing landscape. I am ever grateful to my high school science teacher, Mrs. Demchek, and my piano teacher, Edrie Ballard, who set me on my path.

—Cindy Green-Ortiz

I would like to recognize first my high school teacher, Wayne Whaley, who encouraged me to enter Cisco Networking Academy courses in high school and exposed me to the world of computer networking. Additionally, I want to recognize the managers and mentors that I have had along the way who gave me opportunities to prove myself and have helped guide and support me in my career through the years: Bo Osborne, Danielle Desalu, and Guilherme Leonhardt.

To the colleagues and mentors such as Ranjana Jwalanieh, David Houck, Cindy Green-Ortiz, Chris Roy, Dan Geiger, Daniel Schrock, Tim Corbett, Aaron Cole, and countless others who have over the years provided support, friendship, and a place to vent during the more frustrating moments this career can bring, a big thanks to all of you.

—Brandon Fowler

Many people play roles in our lives that impact us on our journeys. I would like to recognize some of those who have had the greatest impact on my journey:

> Teachers: Ben Poston, who taught me rigor; Preston Wannamaker, who helped me embrace failures

> Leaders: Danielle Desalu, who gave me opportunity and visibility; Guilherme Leonhardt, who tempers my rough edges

> Mentors: Maurice Spencer, who selflessly pushes me forward; my late grandfather, Mel Houck, who challenged me to always ask how and why

> Friends: Jim Kent, who supports me in the best and worst of times; Chris Brady, who inspires me to take new paths and find fulfillment

—David Houck

I must give special recognition to my father, Ron Hensel, who taught me to see the world like an engineer. To not only understand how things work but also systematically seek to understand why things work. Based on your lessons, in my career, I have been able to solve most any problem by using both analytical and creative thinking.

—Hank Hensel

In a technology career spanning multiple decades, one does not reach apexes in technical knowledge without exposure and guidance from some of the best managers, mentors, and sounding boards in the industry. It has been my privilege to work with some of the most fantastic people who guided me through a long career in the industry, and sometimes pushed me beyond my limits to grow:

My friend and colleague, Chris Mula

My mentor and first manager at Cisco, Kenneth Huss

My sounding board and hardest working person I've ever met, Courtney Carson

The multitudes of mentees and engineers who have questioned my ideas, forced me to rethink solutions, and offered the spark that turned into the designs contributing to this text.

—Patrick Lloyd

I was incredibly lucky to stumble into this industry in its formative years. In the days when we used the telephone network to carry data, I was given a wonderful opportunity to learn, grow, and evolve with the industry. Along the way there were a few people who stood out and gave me the chances I needed to succeed. First, I would like to thank Chip Duval for handing me a multiplexor, a spool of cable, and a book and said, "Make this work." Second, I would like to thank one of my first managers, Frank Ignachuck, who said, "If you need to be managed, I will manage you." I never needed to be managed after that. Lastly, I'd like to thank one of my customers, Jeff Toye, who gave me a chance to prove myself where others would not have. These lessons in self-learning and reliance helped me build a career where after 40 years, I still learn something new every day. Thank you for the opportunity.

—Andrew McDonald

I must acknowledge three special people in my life. My grandfather, Darrell Smith, taught me how to be a man. My grandmother, Joyce Smith, taught me patience and love. I miss you both dearly, though you are still with me every day of my life. To my mother, Rhonda Frazier, you are a rock of wisdom, teaching me relentless passion and drive.

—Jason Frazier

Contents at a Glance

Contents

Icons Used in This Book

Router

PC

Cisco ASA 5500

Cisco Nexus
9300 Series

Workgroup
Switch

Database

Route/Switch
Processor

Virtual Server

IBM Mainframe

Server Farm

Cisco Nexus
9500 Series

Storage Array

Network Cloud,
White

File Server

Command Syntax Conventions

The conventions used to present command syntax in this book are the same conventions used in the IOS Command Reference. The Command Reference describes these conventions as follows:

- **Boldface** indicates commands and keywords that are entered literally as shown. In actual configuration examples and output (not general command syntax), boldface indicates commands that are manually input by the user (such as a **show** command).

- *Italic* indicates arguments for which you supply actual values.

- Vertical bars (|) separate alternative, mutually exclusive elements.

- Square brackets ([ ]) indicate an optional element.

- Braces ({ }) indicate a required choice.

- Braces within brackets ([{ }]) indicate a required choice within an optional element.

Preface

Where does the idea start to write a book?

For me, there were many signposts along the way. Years ago, when I was young, I knew that books were my way to see the world and to think in a different way. Without them, I would have never ventured from deep in the mountains far from the world outside. I was always a natural scientist, experimenting on anything and everything. Taking apart most things and putting them back together—well, almost. Writing a book was always a thought in my young mind.

Fast-forward many years, I have worked with this group since joining Cisco six+ years ago. With them, we have been solving problems, helping people, and making a difference every day around the world. To say that this is what drives me is an understatement.

The needs of my customers and my teammates drove me to want to start this effort. Understanding the concept of Zero Trust was something I was presenting, speaking, designing, and advising about—over and over. Everyone having a varied understanding.

The only way I could think to solve the issue of getting everyone on the same page was to set out the concepts in writing. It started as a small idea, and then it kept growing. My mentors all said, "You should write a book!" The idea became a reality.

After I approached everyone on this writing team one by one, we formed a tightly bound group, strengthened by the need for the information to be put on paper and standardized in way that was easier to understand and, most importantly, repeatable.

Thank you to each of my coauthors for making this dream come together. It would have never happened without you!

I hope this book helps you, the reader, and makes a difference on your journey.

—Cindy Green-Ortiz

Prologue: Jason Penn, Cisco Director, Customer Experience

"Zero Trust is going to be super easy," said no one ever. While this quote is clearly said in jest, the reality is that Zero Trust is a complex topic, dealing with complex technologies being implemented in complex environments. However, as I tell my children, just because something is difficult does not mean that it's not worth doing and, most importantly, doing well.

I once had a security executive tell me that the security industry might be the only industry where you can buy more and more products but never really feel as though you're achieving better and better results. Even 10+ years later, there is a lot of truth in that statement. To me, this is the crux of what Zero Trust really is—namely, weaving together a grouping of security technologies to increase your security posture, increase your visibility, decrease your response times, and generally feel as though you're using security tools to get better at protecting your critical corporate assets. Wouldn't it be nice if the tools worked for you, instead of the other way around?

In the modern day of "work anywhere," cloud-native/hybrid cloud/multicloud, and so on, there is a seismic shift in the way we access and consume applications, data, and infrastructure. At the same time, the normal adversaries (nation-state, hacktivists, hobbyists) are still out there, but getting better and more aggressive. Which is why I believe the Zero Trust framework is critically important and should be looked at seriously.

Okay, so you're clearly interested in Zero Trust as a concept (you've made it this far into the book anyway). What led you here is probably a common set of questions, such as

- What really is Zero Trust?

- How and where do we start this journey?

- What does success look like?

- When are we done?

- What do we have in our portfolio already?

- What are we missing?

- What do we have that is possibly duplicative?

These questions are valid and common, and they warrant real thought and inspection. And as is typical with these types of initiatives, the answers will vary from company to company based on business objectives, risk tolerances, compliance considerations, and a myriad of other variables that are unique to your company, your industry, and your situation. Which essentially means that you are going to want to create a workable plan that addresses your specific needs. *Workable* being the operative word. A plan that "boils the ocean" is no plan at all.

I have spent many years as a security practitioner, specifically helping organizations with their current and future states, gaps, and strategic direction. In that time, I have learned the value of having a realistic plan that is directionally accurate but also flexible. Not flexible to the point where you rewrite it every year, but flexible enough to nudge the direction or timelines based on the current situation, whatever that may be.

Additionally, I find great value in a plan that allows more frequent, small victories. A plan where it is possible to report forward progress and keep people interested. Hence, the earlier comment about not "boiling the ocean"; biting off too much in a single sitting will inevitably result in frustration, failure, and eventually a loss of funding.

This book is intended to be a guide on how to navigate the entirety of the Zero Trust journey, from concept and planning to a phased approach to execution, across multiple different industry sectors. It is written to face the realities head-on and provide practical examples that are based in experience and that can be used to enlighten your journey.

I hope that you enjoy the topic, the guidance, and the love and experience that went into creating this book. The authors are truly passionate about Zero Trust, so much so that they used their spare time to write a book about it. Talk about dedication!

Foreword: John Strong, FBI Special Agent in Charge, Retired

"Change is the only constant in life." We have all heard this maxim that is credited to the Greek philosopher Heraclitus. In my 30-plus year career as an FBI Special Agent, I saw many examples that supported this. I learned that if you are slow or unwilling to evolve with the changing threat environment, you are eventually going to lose. The threats we face are always evolving. In the cyber world, they are doing so at breakneck speed. If your organization isn't recognizing and effectively reacting to these changes, your security stance is becoming less effective every single moment—and your risk is growing.

From its start in 1908, the FBI developed over the years into the world's premier law enforcement agency. When I joined in 1990, the Bureau had well-honed training and tactics to solve many sophisticated federal offenses. We were good. Some, including me, said we were the best. But we were inflexible. Slow to adapt to the growing threat of terrorism. Reactive.

Events like the Oklahoma City bombing and 9/11 were game changers for the organization. It was no longer acceptable for the FBI to arrive after the crime was committed and solve it. The only stance acceptable to the American people was a Bureau that was proactive and could stop these events before they happened. Since those terrible events that occurred over 20 years ago, the FBI has morphed into a much more intelligence-driven and proactive organization that is prepared for the dangers we face today. It wasn't a pain-free or linear transformation, but we got there. To keep pace with the cyber, terrorism, and traditional criminal threats of today and tomorrow, the FBI has to continuously evolve and adapt to meet the challenge.

Likewise, your business security posture has to evolve with the threats you face before you have your game-changing event. We have gone from the days of locks, fences, and cameras protecting the crown jewels of our organizations to securing them in the cloud. The workplace is no longer static. The public health threat posed by COVID-19 put us on the express lane to a work from anywhere world where fewer and fewer work from "the inside." The insider threat no longer comes predominately from within. Even hackers have changed with the times. We have moved from the destructive teenaged hackers in the basement to sophisticated cyber-criminal cabals using commoditized tools and ransomware as well as state-sponsored hacking organizations. Even that difference has become blurry, as some hackers working for governments will use those same skills and tools in their own criminal endeavors while off duty.

Once someone with authorized access to your systems decides to steal or sabotage, how far can they get? A criminal who has compromised an employee's credentials, can they run amok? A hacker who has slipped in through the cracks, are they lurking in the shadows of your systems? Do you know? Are you sure?

Trusting a device merely because it is within the "corporate fence line" or connected through a VPN no longer creates a solid security posture. If you are not implementing Zero Trust as part of your security plan, you are leaving doors open, which could lead to the loss of your most precious data. Are you ready to secure those doors? If you are, it's *probably* not too late.

During the last quarter of my career, I proudly served as the Special Agent in Charge of all FBI investigations in North Carolina. The Tarheel state is home to many large corporations, including some high-tech powerhouses. We knew that we couldn't effectively protect the citizens and corporations across the state without the assistance of our private sector. We drew upon this wealth of resources and teamed with corporate security professionals from across the state in a public-private partnership known as InfraGard. That's where I had the honor of meeting and partnering with dedicated security experts like Cindy Green-Ortiz.

Cindy served as the president of the Charlotte InfraGard chapter, where she led the effort to share threat intelligence and industry best practices to close security gaps. Being elected to that position by her peers showed the high esteem in which those professionals held Cindy and her leadership. I found their confidence in Cindy to be well-founded.

Cindy not only addressed the concerns of the day. She also had a focus on the future. By dedicating her time, talent, and vision, Cindy was instrumental in inspiring and motivating young minds during the annual, weeklong summer cyber camp for STEM-focused high school students cosponsored by InfraGard and the Charlotte FBI field office. Those talented young people are part of the next generation to take on the cybersecurity challenge. I couldn't have asked for a better partner than Cindy.

Zero Trust fits today's work environment and aligns with the principle of least privilege. It's the latest evolution of security for IT infrastructure and data in today's cloud-based, location-agnostic workplace.

How focused is your organization on the management and monitoring of credential usage? Four out of five network attacks involve the use or misuse of credentials. Are you comfortable that those people and devices that are fully vetted have access to all the data they need, yet only the data they need, to perform their jobs effectively? Have you done all you can to limit the "blast radius" of malevolent access to your systems?

I commend you for starting your journey toward Zero Trust with this book. Zero Trust is flexible in its design and can be tailored to meet unique and specific needs in your security strategy and give you robust ROI.

Your attention now will make it much less likely that you will be calling my former colleagues at the FBI about being hit by a ransomware attack or some other compromise of your organization's crown jewels. Keep up the good fight!

—John Strong, Special Agent in Charge, FBI (Retired)

Introduction

The goal of this text is to provide the reader with tried-and-true methods to implement Zero Trust Architecture throughout an organization based on the combined 85 years of security and architectural experience across all authors. These architects and engineers work together daily across tens of organizations, hundreds across their respective careers, to migrate organizations toward a consistent and replicable Zero Trust Architecture for sites throughout the world. Throughout this experience and the design of a Zero Trust Architectural process, observations of where organizations are most successful have been factored into this text. In addition, discussions entailing where common mistakes are made, or assumptions made that have been proven, generally, false are found throughout.

While there is significant debate throughout the security world regarding the effectiveness of Zero Trust and how aspects of Zero Trust may differ between organizations and their own idiosyncrasies, this text is meant to provide a broad recommendation and guidance to assist organizations, architects, and engineers on their journey toward Zero Trust. Considerations made when evaluating these assumptions and mistakes typically include an organization's business behavior, industry, and capabilities. Additional considerations also include the best ways to mitigate organizationally unique risks, and analysis that can only be done within the organization. This analysis must consider unique facts and insights to best align the proper recommendations within the Zero Trust methodology for an organization's specific needs.

Goals and Methods

This text is meant to be our attempt to articulate what we, the authors, have seen work in the hundreds of customers that we've worked with over the years who are pursuing similar Zero Trust goals. With the continuous changes occurring in the industry related to Zero Trust, and the components that are seen as making up the Zero Trust concept, this reference serves as a point-in-time baseline for what we believe is the most practical approach for most customers.

In a manuscript written to guide customers, the 80/20 rule always must apply. The goal pursued here is that methodologies within this book will assist 80 percent of customers' work toward their Zero Trust goals with minimal variation on the methods stated here. For the 20 percent of customers who have already gotten to a point in their pursuit of Zero Trust that renders much of what is in this text as ancillary to their goals, the hope is that this text might serve as a reference model for operations and engineering—specifically, for how to continue to improve or operate the Zero Trust Architecture.

Throughout the text, we use a fictional customer made up of use cases from across industries, with the names and concepts changed to better illustrate problem statements with Zero Trust solutions. Not only do we hope that this method will aid in your learning, but we hope that it will provide a relatable technology and business concept definition, while protecting the innocent customers who have made very relatable decisions or mistakes.

Many will notice that broader concepts are used throughout the text with some avoidance to state the singular be-all-and-end-all technologies that must be present to accomplish a goal or milestone. This approach is purposeful. As Zero Trust evolves, and it continues to do so every day, products will change, but their functionality and business-aligned goals will remain the same. This is the pattern we've observed throughout tens of years in the industry, and with the hope that many of us will have tens of years more.

Who Should Read This Book?

Zero Trust Architecture (Networking Technology: Security) is for network cyber-security engineers and architects. The primary audience is for network cybersecurity engineers and architects who are responsible for creating a framework based on a set of principles assuring monitored and managed least-privilege access security controls to remediate and mitigate advanced cybersecurity threats. The secondary audience is other networking staff members who have interests in mature least-privilege cybersecurity access strategies in relation to their specific corporate business environments.

This book should be read and used by intermediate to advanced readers. Because of the methods explored in the content, industry experts could reference this book.

Strategies for Implementation of Zero Trust

The key to pulling the organization's teams together will be an executive sponsor who has broad oversight across business units and any areas of the organization that may be affected by the application of the Zero Trust journey. The executive sponsor should be positioned to influence the participation of the disparate teams required for the project and have direct ownership of outcomes. This may entail an executive at the C-suite with mandates from the board of directors, may be a team of executive managers, or may be a singular senior manager with broad influence and authority. Regardless of the person or team, due to the changes in ongoing operations, configurations, and differentiated access, the executive sponsor must have the authority to accept changes to policy and prevent access to individuals while shielding operations staff. At the same time, this executive sponsor must have the influence and connections within the business to socialize and gain buy-in from across the organization. Preparing for and driving toward the implementation of Zero Trust requires broad support and involvement from a wide range of teams within the organization. In addition, programs should account for key performance indicators of the business, providing a metric for evaluating how the program is working and what improvements will be needed to get the program off the ground. Both aspects are critical to the success of the program.

How This Book Is Organized

Although this book could be read cover to cover, it is designed to be flexible and allow you to easily move between chapters and sections of chapters to cover just the material that you need more work with.

The book is organized into 11 chapters and one appendix and covers the following topics:

- **Chapter 1, "Overview for Zero Trust (ZT)"**—This chapter starts by providing an historical overview of Zero Trust. Next, we provide an introduction into Cisco's five Zero Trust capabilities to present the scope of a Zero Trust security infrastructure. Finally, this chapter begins a fictional organization's use case that will be used as you read to give practical examples of each chapter's discussion topics.

- **Chapter 2, "Zero Trust Capabilities"**—This chapter further defines and explores the previous chapter's introduction of Cisco's Zero Trust Capabilities: Policy & Governance, Identity, Vulnerability Management, Enforcement, and Analytics.

- **Chapter 3, "Zero Trust Reference Architecture"**—This chapter presents the Zero Trust Reference Architecture and then breaks down the overall architecture into distinct practical service area locations. Typical service areas explored in further detail includes campus, branch, core network, WAN, and cloud.

- **Chapter 4, "Zero Trust Enclave Design"**—This chapter deals with how the application of a Zero Trust model to an architecture will vary in its construct between different layers of the network, including branch, campus, WAN, data center, and cloud.

- **Chapter 5, "Enclave Exploration and Consideration"**—In this chapter, we discuss and analyze some of the so-called gotchas, or unique attributes, for organizations and industry verticals, and call out considerations.

- **Chapter 6, "Segmentation"**—This chapter examines the aspects of communications before attempting to restrict objects, which is key to a successful Zero Trust segmentation-based deployment.

- **Chapter 7, "Zero Trust Common Challenges"**—This chapter covers many common challenges encountered while implementing Zero Trust.

- **Chapter 8, "Developing a Successful Segmentation Plan"**—As an organization strives to develop a plan of how to classify and segment endpoints while maintaining business as usual, this chapter helps organizations plan for the future of Zero Trust.

- **Chapter 9, "Zero Trust Enforcement"**—This chapter examines a practical plan for how an organization might align with a stepwise approach and ensure that when an enforcement mode for a security-based mindset is reached, an organization can have confidence that as much due diligence as possible has been done to be successful.

- **Chapter 10, "Zero Trust Operations"**—This chapter covers the fundamentals of what should happen when a Zero Trust environment enters a steady operational state, the network and assets are still monitored, and traffic is logged and audited.

- **Chapter 11, "Conclusion"**—Utilizing the five core principles of Zero Trust presented here is a great starting point. However, continuous improvement and reuse of each principle throughout an organization's journey will be key to the ongoing success of Zero Trust.

- **Appendix A, "Applied Use Case for Zero Trust Principles"**—This appendix provides use case examples of an organization's journey that will be key to the ongoing success of Zero Trust.

Chapter 1

Overview of Zero Trust (ZT)

Chapter Key Points:

- This chapter provides an overview for the journey of achieving Zero Trust.

- We include a review of the origins and evolution of what today is known as Zero Trust.

- We discuss the foundational Zero Trust Capabilities that need to be present in an organization to achieve Zero Trust in relationship to the many compliance frameworks that teams will have to navigate.

- We provide a detailed guide on how to run a successful Zero Trust Segmentation Workshop.

- Finally, we discuss organizational dynamics that may require a shift in architecture mindset to create a greater focus on reducing risk and protecting what is valuable to any organization.

Zero Trust Origins

Although many ideas do not start by needing to solve a problem, the concept of achieving Zero Trust did. According to the FBI, "at around 8:30 p.m. on November 2, 1988, a maliciously clever program was unleashed on the Internet from a computer at the Massachusetts Institute of Technology (MIT)."

This cyber worm was soon propagating at remarkable speed and grinding computers to a halt. "We are currently under attack," wrote a concerned student at the University of California, Berkeley, in an email later that night. Within 24 hours, an estimated 6,000 of the approximately 60,000 computers that were then connected to the Internet had been hit. Computer worms, unlike viruses, do not need a software host but can exist and propagate on their own. This worm did not stop at UC Berkeley; it was pervasive across the then-connected devices on the Internet.

"*The New York Times* soon confirmed and publicly reported that the culprit was a 23-year-old Cornell University graduate student named Robert Tappan Morris. Morris was a talented computer scientist who had graduated from Harvard in June 1988. He had grown up immersed in computers thanks to his father, who was an early innovator at Bell Labs. At Harvard, Morris was known for his technological prowess, especially in Unix; he was also known as a prankster. After being accepted into Cornell that August, he began developing a program that could spread slowly and secretly across the Internet. To cover his tracks, he released it by hacking into an MIT computer from his Cornell terminal in Ithaca, New York.

"At the same time, the Morris Worm inspired a new generation of hackers and a wave of Internet-driven assaults that continue to plague our digital systems to this day. Whether accidental or not, the first Internet attack 30 years ago was a wake-up call for the country and the cyber age to come."

The pursuit to resolve the worm attack vector supported by having excessive trust in the environment began with and is credited to Stephen Paul Marsh at the University of Stirling, which covered the concept that is now Zero Trust in his doctoral thesis, "Formalizing Trust as a Computational Concept," in April 1994. In his view, Marsh explores the word *Trust* as it relates to human interaction, its subjectiveness, and a way to formalize it for digital applications using mathematical and other logical, objective concepts.

Marsh further explores that, in 1994, agents being developed assumed an implicit trust and that this assumption is both "unreasonable and misguided." He relates to the example of the 1988 "Internet Worm," commonly known as the Morris Worm, which exploited trust across multiple vectors, such as through the **rexec** and **rsh** command services within Unix systems, as well as through bugs within the **sendmail** SMTP service and **finger** command, which allowed for remote code execution. Because these systems were built with the idea that the users or administrators of both the source and destination systems trusted remote connections, these vulnerabilities were easily exploited and allowed the worm to propagate to 10 percent of Internet-connected computers within 24 hours. Marsh provides this as a beacon of the security issues that the concept of implicit trust brings and the reason to understand and define it, such that it can be leveraged appropriately within a digital context to improve security.

The concept of Zero Trust was further explored, and its application was refined, through the Jericho Forum in 2003. The Jericho Forum, being convened internationally for the specific purpose of defining and promoting a decreased network perimeter, was seen as the first stepping stone to forming a centralized body for defining secure architectures for organizations worldwide.

The Jericho Forum, which merged into The Open Group Security Forum in 2014, sought to answer the question of how to move past the limitations of the common architecture of a hard-secure perimeter with that of a soft-flat interior. This practice focused on placing security resources at the perimeter, assuming trust could be assumed as true once inside the network.

The specific driver for this need to focus on rearchitecting the network was research indicating that most attacks originated from within the network. While the perimeter may have been difficult to cross through conventional means of attack, like zero-day exploits, the use of social engineering, phishing, and physical means—such as malware-infected flash drives—allowed attackers the opportunity to gain access to a network with enough determination and planning. Once inside, the movement of a threat could be unfettered due to the mistaken idea that anything within the network is inherently trust-worthy. Naturally, as networks grow, they become more exposed to evolving threats, with ransomware as an example. As a result, an increase has been consistently observed in the number of attacks. The Zero Trust Historical Timeline is depicted in Figure 1-1.

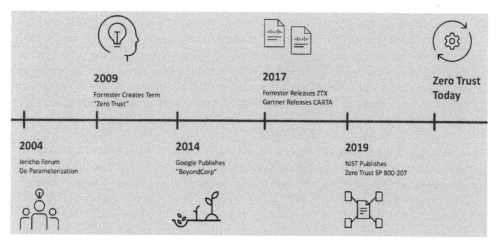

Figure 1-1 *Zero Trust Historical Timeline*

All organizations are targets. Security posture and detection capabilities are minimum requirements. The value of data moves from its ability to be resold to others to instead being sold back to its original owner. Considering these advancing threats, additional entities began their work to contribute to the idea of Zero Trust. In 2009, John Kindervag of global market research company Forrester helped popularize the modern basis of Zero Trust. He defined Zero Trust as a strategy to simplify the application of security. His approach hinged on the assumption that everything—users, data, systems—should be treated as untrusted, and thus the concept of applying security should be more efficient-ly designed and implemented. While the idea holds that it is easiest to assume everything is untrusted and grant access once determined otherwise, the application of this principle was far more complex. Many of the tools necessary to perform this work either did not exist in 2009, or network architectures were not built with the idea that separation inside the trusted interior would be required.

The effort helped spur additional action from technology companies to recognize the issues presented by the Jericho Forum and Forrester. With this, a new generation of development for tools, processes, and best practices occurred. One of the earliest derived examples comes from Google, which in 2009 began its initiative to move to a new security model, dubbed BeyondCorp. BeyondCorp sought to instantiate the core components of Zero Trust across Google's entire organization. From this effort, Google provided insight into the lessons learned to help others move forward within their organizations. Technology vendors also began developing tools and software to help address challenges such as visibility and control within networks.

Planning for Zero Trust

The largest undertaking for many organizations is the amount of work required to understand their business, tools, capabilities, and plan for implementing Zero Trust. This understanding must be combined with an exploration of how the business processes can be integrated with technology used to secure it. Completion of these factors ensures that the process complements the business as opposed to hindering it. This process comes in the form of a workshop involving major stakeholders throughout the business, under the guidance of a broader goal to secure all aspects of the organization. Key to this workshop is the goal of all major stakeholders understanding the business in more depth. For most organizations, siloed operational approaches result in a siloed understanding of the impact of an undertaking such as Zero Trust. Remaining in this mindset will hinder organizations from securing the business with a Zero Trust approach, due to limited perspective. Up to this point, the visibility of endpoints, connections, services, and applications has been explored; however, understanding the business and the potential impact of Zero Trust has taken a back seat to discovery. A common mistake many organizations make is skipping this understanding of risk and potential impact. By doing so, the first impact to business as usual with an inability to understand the perspective of the stakeholders impacted will make the stakeholders leery of future impacts. Often, losing the buy-in from stakeholders critical to the success of the Zero Trust journey will doom the project to failure.

Discovery Zero Trust Segmentation Workshop

The first step to understanding the business and business units that make the organization a success is to have representation from all business units present in a single workshop. The focus of this workshop needs to start out with why the need for Zero Trust pertains to the business. A common mistake many organizations make is assuming stakeholders from throughout the business understand regulatory, oversight, and contractual obligations that the organization must secure the business and impacts if they do not.

With the evolution of the Zero Trust terminology and its application to technologies and processes well outside of the core principles documented here, many participants may come with assumptions on their role to play in the pursuit of Zero Trust. Therefore, a baseline of understanding the goal and how all business units are critical stakeholders to the success of that goal is key to setting out in the right direction.

Commonly, we at Cisco see that organizations attempt to host a workshop for all major business units to be represented in, while also allowing for business-as-usual to continue distracting key players and limiting overall success. This workshop, given its impact on the business through planning for enforcement and application of differentiated access between systems within the business, should be considered a mission-critical priority.

Defining the Zero Trust Discovery Workshop Purpose

Detailed discovery, analysis, and understanding are critical activities in designing and implementing Zero Trust for any business. Figure 1-2 provides a framework for doing so. Discovery can typically be conducted as a series of workshop sessions that break down business goals, core services functions, and cybersecurity goals into tangible operational and technical requirements. These operational and technical requirements should integrate closely with the endpoints, controls, and processes determined in the preceding discovery process. The requirements should also be applicable in such a way that they align with a policy, either existing or in development, that aims to continue to enable the business and business entities while protecting them at the same time.

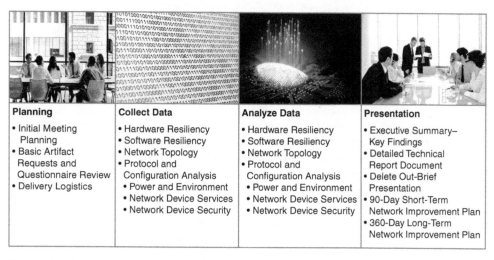

Planning	Collect Data	Analyze Data	Presentation
• Initial Meeting Planning • Basic Artifact Requests and Questionnaire Review • Delivery Logistics	• Hardware Resiliency • Software Resiliency • Network Topology • Protocol and Configuration Analysis • Power and Environment • Network Device Services • Network Device Security	• Hardware Resiliency • Software Resiliency • Network Topology • Protocol and Configuration Analysis • Power and Environment • Network Device Services • Network Device Security	• Executive Summary– Key Findings • Detailed Technical Report Document • Delete Out-Brief Presentation • 90-Day Short-Term Network Improvement Plan • 360-Day Long-Term Network Improvement Plan

Figure 1-2   *Discovery Workshop Activities*

Through these workshops, key stakeholders from across the business are brought together to identify functional goals, objectives, and benefits versus risks of utilizing the mapped-out tools and capabilities to limit the risk exposure and potential exploitation. Additionally, discovery workshops identify a company's "current-state" of existing or planned/inflight cybersecurity capabilities. Organizations that run these workshops gain a significantly better, more cohesive understanding of the inner workings and interactions between business units. This understanding can minimize time to resolve access-related issues and bolster company culture by understanding the interrelationships and reliance of business units on each other. The expected outcomes of this sort of workshop are defined in the following subsections.

Defining Participation in the Discovery Workshop

The most common question organizations have when planning for a discovery workshop is who should be involved and to what capacity. It is fully understood that a re-architecture and rethinking of how the foundation of business communications occurs is a massive undertaking. However, this undertaking's critical aspect is considering who has the appropriate knowledge to be required and who can be excluded. Given the potential impact to an organization by bringing critical knowledge into a singular workshop, considerations must be made for running the business, which include timely follow-up when gaps in knowledge arise. Commonly, four categories of attendees are required to be present in the Zero Trust workshop:

- **Principle stakeholders:** Principal stakeholders are the owners of a given business unit and the business processes that allow it to generate revenue. While titles of these participants vary wildly across industries, these stakeholders can be defined as those who are responsible for profit and loss margins related to the business unit, especially in times of risk exploitation. Rarely does this include individual contributors, but rather focuses on managers-of-managers who oversee budgets to be allocated to resolving risk to the business. These resources should understand the business unit as it pertains to the overall organization and be able to make commitments related to their teams and what the team is willing to support related to the Zero Trust architecture journey. This commitment may involve resources such as people, systems, endpoints, or time.

- **Cross-functional subject matter experts:** Most organizations have cross-architectural subject matter experts who understand technologies as they are architected to support multiple business units. Domain administrators, for example, may understand technologies such as DNS, DHCP, NTP, certificate authorities (CAs), and other capabilities that are crucial to the success of the business. While planning for the potential application of enforcement mechanisms that could be applied, a subject matter expert who can speak to the potential impact or how the protocol works related to the organization would be a crucial member of the workshop.

- **Key strategists and decision makers:** The application of a new framework for the business is a major undertaking, as discussed throughout this chapter already. Executive buy-in for and participation in the workshop, specifically in the form of C-suite or delegated representatives, are key. These resources provide the authority to guide the entirety of the team on the strategy that should be pursued. This authority makes them key to helping ensure participation of business units where clarification or buy-in may be hindered due to organizational politics.

- **End-user/Audience experience representatives:** The application of the Zero Trust framework to the endpoints present on the network implies a need for those who support the endpoints to be ready for any potential challenges they may need to face. As part of this readiness, ongoing risk assessment should be done to consider what the potential impact to users will be when controls or configurations are added or changed on the network. These additions and changes will occur throughout the evolution and life cycle of both Zero Trust and the endpoint. Therefore, this end-user experience representative should be involved early in the process to set the stage for future, inevitable changes. In addition, this risk should be understood by end-user representatives to ensure they can bring feedback and preparatory steps back to users to limit overall impact. Communicating with users on what to expect is critical whenever an impact may exist. Representatives should also be included who support applications and headless devices that do not have a user logged in to them. While these endpoints may not have a consistent user to observe changes graphically, this does not negate the criticality for devices that are reliant upon these systems from understanding changes to their access.

Goals and Risks of the Zero Trust Architecture

As the priority in the workshop, a definition of Zero Trust should be agreed upon with attendees. Due to the nature of Zero Trust within the security industry, many participants within the workshop may come with an expectation or impression of what Zero Trust is, what it means to them, and whether they are already compliant with their interpretation.

In some cases, buying in may be required to determine whether the expected outcome is feasible to the business. One major focus of the workshop should be to differentiate between feasibility related to effort applied and feasibility based on impact to the business, because the two will often be conflated. In many scenarios, business units describe feasibility as it relates to how little effort needs to be implemented to accomplish any level of outcome. Make no mistake, additional effort will be required to apply processes, tools, and capabilities that enable the business to be more aligned with a Zero Trust Architecture. However, the result of doing so is minimization of risk and exploitation at the cost of effort to align the business with these protection mechanisms.

Results of Discovery Processes Already Executed Upon

Based on the goals agreed upon within the workshop, several factors then need to be aligned to the execution of the plan. Creating an actionable plan to ensure that efforts decided upon can become a reality ensures Zero Trust does not become "vaporware" or a set of products to sit on a shelf. The major assumption for this stage in the Zero Trust workshop is that attendees can create a set of executable next steps for implementing mechanisms to move the Zero Trust journey forward. This effort must be balanced with the assumption that attendees have the authority and willingness to allocate resources, budget, and time to these next steps, in the name of accomplishing the organization's Zero Trust goals.

Typically, this endeavor is enabled via the executive sponsorship for the workshop, having top-down authority to impart attendees with the authority to determine risk to their business and allocating individual contributors to help mitigate those risks. This involvement of executive sponsors has a downstream influencing effect, enabling next steps to be executed upon. This downstream effect may impact budgets from the staffing and technology perspectives. With executive involvement, the expected result is an allocation and buy-in to the need for increased budget and resources to realign to the Zero Trust architecture goal. It should not be understated that planning, testing, and implementing a Zero Trust architecture will not go without impact on daily operations to the business, and this impact should be addressed in earnest before attempting to deploy an architecture framework that can never be a success.

The Definition of Success and Benefits

Only after the exploration of goals, capabilities, discoveries, and activities already accomplished has been completed can planning for realistic timelines and projects begin. Within this stage of the workshop, processes that have been determined as critical to success should be broken down into granular outcomes. Each process should have a definition of the benefit and contribution to success that the outcome contributes to the overall Zero Trust goal. Far too often organizations will focus on broad goals and massive undertakings before being able to articulate the benefit to the organization that the goal was fulfilled. For example, for most organizations, an understanding of endpoints or how they interact should be the primary goal pursued. A significantly better approach would be to break down visibility into consumable areas, defining goals such as understanding all endpoints connected within the organization's smallest office.

These undertakings also must be attached to timelines or other metrics that define their success. In the case of device discovery, the metric of success may be based on sites, based on number of unique device types in relation to the larger number of total endpoints, or may be the discovery of endpoint types belonging to a business unit. Regardless of the approach, a timeline for when the accomplishment should be completed must be a discussion point tracked and adhered to for measuring success. This success metric should be agreed upon across business units to determine dependencies and plan for allocation of staff and resources to the broader goal.

A Practical Approach to Success and Future Needs

In its most basic sense, the practice of segmentation is to identify an object and separate it from the context of other objects. To determine how and where to apply network segmentation that supports Zero Trust, discovery activities are required to understand a business's services and subsequent functions. Identification of a company's core business services is one of the first steps in identifying where and when segmentation can be applied. However, an often-overlooked aspect of anything Zero Trust or segmentation related is the change that the implementation of these new technologies and methods will have on operations and troubleshooting. While networking and security projects are typically run out of their respective teams, which serve as escalation points, the first line of interaction for end-user challenges is often a help desk that must be able to work through the problem as it relates to the architecture.

A roadmap for how much can be implemented to change the network and make it more Zero Trust compliant while accounting for operational considerations must exist and be planned for. Going along with the methodology found in Chapter 6, "Segmentation," defining the gaps in technology implementation, and then testing the remediation to those gaps should both be done over a reasonable amount of time to ensure that the help-desk staff can train subject matter experts (SMEs) on the technology. These SMEs should also be involved in the testing to gain firsthand experience in understanding the design goals. This effort may slow down implementation of the gap-filling technology, or even take resources away from daily operations response, but will ensure that the technology enables the business, as opposed to consuming it with escalations. All these aspects should be discussed in the workshop with buy-in from respective parties gained.

A roadmap for how the business will need to change over time is also fundamental to a successful Zero Trust journey. Focusing on business core services, most organizations can be broken down into a sum of their parts:

- Operations functions cover the largest part of a company's focus on cybersecurity because these functions fulfill a company's business mission. Segmentation can be critical to meet adequate stewardship and regulatory obligations for a company's mission fulfillment and its customer's goods or service needs.

- Management functions include a company's administration of personnel and resource functions.

- Marketing functions provide exploring, creating, and delivering value to meet a company's customer needs in terms of goods and services.

- Strategy functions execute plans and actions on how a company competes in its targeted market, as well as overall growth of the company.

- Finance functions provide for the acquisition of funds, management of operational spending, management of income from customer-provided goods or services, and investment into the overall growth of the company.

- Technology functions design, implement, manage, and operate technology, tools, equipment, and facilities used by the company's employees, partners, and customers.

Among these core services, traffic discovery must focus on mapping out communications that occur between systems on a company's network, while keeping in mind critical reliance on those systems. Critical reliance may include financial reporting, marketing of products or services, and people management. Nontechnical teams involved in the workshops can help understand these processes and critical reliance, providing a schema for discovery of traffic and applications that may be potentially affected by application of controls on the network.

Technical tools can, often temporarily, be deployed to analyze existing traffic patterns on a company's network. These tools map this traffic to specific systems and help understand the type of information that may be communicated between these systems. Network taps, NetFlow collection appliances, endpoint traffic analytic applications, and firewall log parsing, for example, should all be done for a time span that allows for as much unique information as possible to be gathered. This will often happen in conjunction with or after identity discovery. During the workshop, both identity discovery and traffic mapping should be planned for on the future roadmap, with buy-in from stakeholders obtained.

Commonly, businesses will go into a "change freeze," preventing any changes from being made on the network well ahead of their "busy season." The busy season is the best time to capture this information to understand how devices, tools, applications, and the like interact with one another during the highest volume time. This way, tracking and telemetry can be collected for most elements in an application ecosystem. Some elements may be accessed only monthly or even quarterly. Executing traffic discovery in overnight or less utilized hours may not gather critical functionality with the highest impact to the business. Financial reporting that runs only at the end of the quarter or fiscal year, for example, is critical to business operations and should be captured to ensure it is not impacted by Zero Trust remediation efforts and policy application. This understanding should be socialized within the workshop and mitigating efforts planned for should the traffic discovery tools have an unplanned impact.

Traffic discovery, with an end goal of segmentation, must also include an understanding of the context for the communications that occur between these systems. To accomplish this, traffic discovery must include interviews with the previously mentioned business resource personnel to form the context of what is being communicated between systems, the purpose of these systems, the sensitivity of the data stored or processed by the systems, and data for the operation of the company. Another key discovery point is to map and understand the fallout from impact if these systems or data become compromised or unavailable. This segmentation discovery to understand context is typically called a top-down approach. This top-down approach is described in Figure 1-3 in a descending manner.

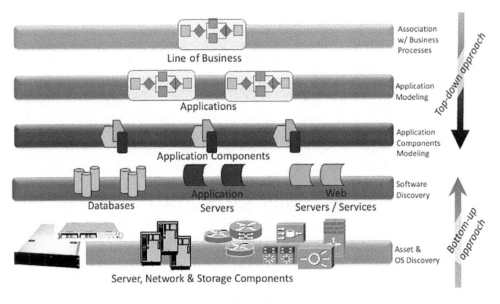

Figure 1-3 *Practical Top-Down Design Example*

It is important that both the top-down approach and the bottom-up approach are included to complete a full exercise of segmentation discovery workshops. It is using both discovery approaches that validation of findings and segmentation recommendations are accomplished. As illustrated in the preceding paragraphs, a singular direction for the design may not suffice to understand the full context of data within the network. While personnel are working with lines of business to understand their applications and use cases, this information should be cross-referenced with traffic discovery to validate the intercommunications that occur for the application. This may extend out either the planning phase or discussion phase of the workshop to gather, analyze, and cross-reference this information with the business unit representation, but will lead to a much more robust understanding of applications to minimize service disruption.

Artifact Gathering for Successful Workshop Outcomes

Segmentation discovery workshops are a critical part of planning cybersecurity and segmentation of critical networks. These workshops enable the alignment of stakeholders, users, partners, and inevitably customers through the exploration of the scope for segmentation and how it is to be applied across the company's infrastructure. Workshop discussions should enable collaboration of decision-making stakeholders, explore technical and procedural feasibilities for Zero Trust, identify budget considerations, and finally provide a structured roadmap for the implementation of segmentation findings. After the foundation is laid for understanding the business, there will come a time when technical artifacts will be required to align with business goals and functionality. These technical artifacts will differ depending on the core component and/or phase in which organizations find themselves. The artifacts may include any of the following:

- Policy documentation as it relates to the types of endpoints allowed on the network. This should include what access they should be provided, data that may be stored on the endpoint, restrictions related to the interactions of endpoints with data and tools, and required analysis of data for loss prevention and similar functionalities.

- Identification flows for how endpoints and users are identified on the network. This should include their use cases, where they are authenticated or referenced against, and what access requirements exist for various groups within the organization.

- What requirements endpoints must have to join the network and be provided their expected amount of access. This may include software for evaluating spyware, malware, or virus infections, standard endpoint provisioning policies or information, tool sets for evaluating these requirements, and responsibility matrices determining who must validate compliance.

- Restrictions to be placed on endpoints related to various use cases, specific to each endpoint's access requirements.

- Locations, identification, and information gathered for analyzing, storing, and maintaining the aforementioned information for future review and investigation, where need be.

The application of Zero Trust is not done in a vacuum, however. Artifacts and understanding of the business should also focus on business-related goals and be seen as enabling the business as opposed to hindering it. Specifics on subjects or topics to be covered during discovery workshops are most often defined by a company's specific industry and business delivery strategy outcomes.

Exploring the Business to Secure It

During workshop discovery interviews, types of questions asked and output from discovery sessions can vary depending on the type of company and its method of product or services delivery. Even though some of the following may have been identified during artifact gathering and reviews, for the purposes of validation and expanding on understandings, discovery workshop interview questioning and discussion are required. Examples of questioning and discussion points should include

- What are the company's security goals?

- What are the current security strategies?

- How are these goals currently being met with current technologies and processes?

- What security controls are in use today? This should include controls applied to infrastructure, security, systems, users, and partners.

- Does their use and the processes for use align with Zero Trust core principles? Can it?

- How are goals not being met?

- What security technologies are under consideration or are in-flight to be implemented?

- Are there areas of security policies that do not meet their stated security goals?

- What regulations or standards does the organization or business unit abide by to maintain a successful operation?

- How are endpoints currently prevented from communicating between one another, and where do these policy enforcement points sit? This is commonly a reference to the artifacts previously gathered.

- Are there any initiatives, technologies, or contracted services within any of the collective business units that are explicitly intended to move toward Zero Trust methodology?

- Are all business divisions or departments aligned to the stated security goals? If not, how do they differ? Where they differ, can they be brought back into a common alignment? How or why not?

- Are all partners, vendors, suppliers, or other third parties aligned to the stated security goals? If not, how do they differ?

- Are all clients, customers, and affiliated customers aligned to the stated security goals? If not, how do they differ?

- Prevention of data loss due to employee attrition

- Minimization of impact of potential threats to data, such as malware and ransomware

In translating these business requirements into technical requirements, SBC Healthcare has produced the following technical goals, with further implications defined within each:

- Identify endpoints using AAA to a Cisco Identity Services Engine cluster.

  - **Implication:** Each network access device will need to be configured with AAA configurations, which will allow for the authentication, authorization, and accounting of endpoints as they join the network. This configuration will need to be factored into the current configuration templates used by SBC Healthcare and be validated through internal review processes to ensure no impact on endpoints will occur.

- Profile devices joining the network to validate their contextual identity.

  - **Implication:** A process must exist for definition of known endpoints expected on the network and resolution of devices unable to be identified correctly. For those devices not identified correctly, operations will need a methodology to investigate whether this is related to the device, the network access device through which the endpoint joined the network, or the upstream ISE authentication server.

- Apply restrictions for how electronic medical record devices access the Internet.

  - **Implication:** A process will need to be put in place to determine an endpoint's needs for external access, or potential needs based on its functionality and features currently implemented. For features that could be implemented in the future, a separate process for reevaluation should exist to evaluate what changes are being made to the device's access, including additions and subtractions. This process should dictate where enforcement of this access should be implemented, with a preference on enforcement of denied traffic being done as close to the source of the communication as possible. Where resolution of the IP to a domain name can occur, and where identity can be consumed to identify who attempted to access the resource, it should be done.

- Control east/west traffic flows between clinical endpoints and building Internet of Things (IoT) endpoints.

  - **Implication:** Like the process that evaluates what access an endpoint needs to external resources, a separate process needs to be implemented to evaluate how the endpoint interacts with devices within the network. This process should consume identity as applied to devices, where capable, and aim to map out communications related to ports, protocols, and groupings of endpoints. The enforcement mechanism should be as close to the source as possible.

- All network access devices should be within the support life cycle of the vendor to minimize downtime and supportability costs.

■ **Implication:** As part of the asset management policies that SBC Healthcare implements, end-of-support milestones should be noted and tracked related to not only endpoints, but the network access devices through which they connect. Based on this information, planning for refreshing these network access devices can be undertaken, and this planning can be integrated into the technical and business goals the network access device is participating in.

Zero Trust Organizational Dynamics

Organizations are at a crossroads: either they are interested in pursuing Zero Trust or are not convinced Zero Trust is a "real thing." Challenges may exist in recognizing the real problem that the organization needs to address by implementing a Zero Trust Strategy. No one product, tool, or solution can be installed and turned on that causes the organization to be able to say that Zero Trust has been accomplished. Solutions or critical infrastructure may need to be implemented before an organization is ready to fund or staff these tools, solutions, or infrastructure. Common behaviors and ways to include or bring along stakeholders in the journey forward are typically encompassed by the following.

"We have a plan"

"My group OWNS Zero Trust" or "We've got this" are common viewpoints for organizations that believe that Zero Trust will be fleshed out five years from now and a common industry strategy documented. Unfortunately, not only will organizations with this mindset be too late to prevent a critical impact on business as usual, but this mindset also leads to no action. Kicking the Zero Trust can down the road when business usually relies on it will only result in catastrophe.

When multiple teams or focus groups lead the plan, many competing, siloed Zero Trust strategies form, which leads to the pieces not working together. Organizations trying to navigate these issues within their company to achieve Zero Trust find a labyrinth of challenges. Primarily, a singular definition of Zero Trust is rarely seen. A champion, typically a senior leader, needs to be named and in charge of Zero Trust as an initiative to unify groups that play critical roles in Zero Trust. Several groups commonly are involved in the concept of Zero Trust. These groups include but are not limited to Network, Security, Applications, Governance, and Senior Leadership. In the end, they all need to be working together.

Please note that this leader should have enough authority within the business, collaboration acuity, and budget to influence teams around them. This leader will have to be ready to face obstacles and be able to move forward, despite the challenges. Success is best illustrated by the anecdote of aligning teams to work together with everyone in the same boat, rowing in the same direction.

Competing Teams

Sometimes challenges are based on past practices. For example, it is common for organizations to have a leadership team that tends to fund only the network programs, and not security programs or the opposite. This situation may be an outgrowth of the different challenges in the business, such as enabling only growth-type projects, not protective control projects, that lead to a short gap in funding.

However, the Zero Trust champion being high enough up in the organization to drive distributed policy throughout teams will typically assist in overcoming this challenge. As noted previously, social acuity is key for this champion, and influence over budget is also crucial. Budget challenges exist in all organizations. It is up to the Zero Trust champion to navigate and make the initiative a priority for the broader business. In the end, to make Zero Trust a reality, all teams will be required to work together to make Zero Trust a possibility in their organization.

"Problem? What problem?"

One of the most significant challenges occurs when teams do not believe a Zero Trust Strategy is needed or a problem exists. Organizations that do not recognize Zero Trust as a "real thing" do not recognize gaps in their security posture, which are typically the most concerning. The term *Zero Trust* was quickly grabbed by marketing departments as interest rose and was applied to nearly any product that would be involved or sometimes even peripherally associated with the concept of Zero Trust. In addition, much of this messaging centered around how a sole product would apply Zero Trust to an organization with a click of the button. Unfortunately, the truth is that no such product exists today. When Zero Trust acceptance is driven within an organization, a strategy is necessary to help move past the marketing and allow people to understand the key aspects of Zero Trust. One strategy is to reiterate that Zero Trust is an architectural strategy, not a product strategy, meaning that the principles must be incorporated into the design and deployment for every project and those principles tailored to the organization based on its risk acceptance, technological maturity, and available resources.

"We are going to the cloud and the cloud is Zero Trust by default"

Somebody else's data center is commonly perceived as the solution to the problem of Zero Trust. Organizations typically tend to believe that by going to the cloud, they will automatically implement Zero Trust. This is not true. Throughout this book we discuss ways to apply Zero Trust at every layer of an environment. The architecture design methodology we explain in this text is meant to be implemented at every layer of the organization, whether that be in the cloud, data center, campus, branch, affiliate, or endpoint.

Solutions, tools, and infrastructure must be developed with Zero Trust in mind when an organization is moving to or is in the cloud, just like when moving data centers. In the cloud, organizations must bring their own tools, solutions, and security, as documented in the cloud vendor's shared responsibility model. Visibility into the environment is needed to ensure that proper infrastructure exists to support a Zero Trust journey in public cloud environments. Understanding the flows of applications and endpoints becomes significantly more important. As many providers are leading organizations to believe, it is impossible to "flip a switch" and turn on Zero Trust.

Cisco's Zero Trust Capabilities

Cisco developed Zero Trust Capabilities to assess environments and their readiness to migrate from traditional segmentation into Zero Trust Segmentation. Cisco used and aligned to many different frameworks and methodologies to create these five pillars. We find that organizations with these capabilities can move to a Zero Trust strategy. Without the capabilities outlined in this chapter and explored in more detail in Chapter 2, "Zero Trust Capabilities," organizations will struggle to fully adopt a strategy. Everything considered in a Zero Trust architecture should fall inside one of these five Zero Trust Capabilities or pillars. One capability may occupy more than one of these pillars. For example, anti-malware software may not only detect and manage vulnerabilities inside the vulnerability management component but may also enforce policy and act inside the enforcement component.

Zero Trust is a mindset, a way of operating an organization to demand that every exchange is justified against an evolving security policy. The journey to Zero Trust does not start when an organization has all the components, products, services, or policies. It begins when an organization first engages with planning. The goal is to reduce risk to the organization while balancing the needs of the business to act against known and unknown threats. Cisco's Zero Trust Capabilities are depicted in Figure 1-4 and outlined in the following sections.

Figure 1-4 *Cisco Zero Trust Capabilities*

Policy & Governance

The Policy & Governance pillar dictates what information must be captured from any identity on the network and what access it should have. This pillar addresses policy and governance that control information and systems through enforcement points to the intended destination. Based on the Zero Trust Capabilities outlined throughout this book, an organization can begin to map out what its needs for the network are and how each of the capabilities can be implemented across the organizational structure. While policy is specific to the organization and its business functionalities, commonalities can be found in the need to allow only corporate assets onto the network and provide them access to business-critical resources while segmenting off areas where unauthorized contextual identities might sit, such as guests, contractors, and even high-risk devices.

Policy & Governance is a function of the buy-in that is gained from executive leadership, propagated down to individual contributors, but is abided by all in the organization.

Identity

The Identity pillar addresses contextual identity, including WHO is on WHAT device, WHERE in the network they connected from, HOW they connected and to which medium, and WHEN they connected. This pillar addresses any tool used in classifying systems, services, assets, transport identity, or users.

When the policy is in place and signed off, approaches to the Identity pillar can vary throughout the organization. Identity can be an inconsistent aspect of the Zero Trust journey given the number and variability of identity across users, devices, organizations, and detection mechanisms. In general, some mechanism to enable enforcement of contextual identity to authenticate and then be authorized based on aspects of that contextual identity must exist.

The authentication when an identity is connecting a device to the network should be actively pursued via methods such as 802.1X when a device supports it and the RADIUS protocol, or via a centralized web auth portal where a device has an active user interacting with it but without the ability to provide a network-based identity. Either method should be combined with a centralized authentication method or database where identities reside, to add an additional point of integration, ensuring the identity can be manipulated based on its change in context. This may include Lightweight Directory Access Protocol (LDAP), Microsoft Active Directory, a public or private certificate authority, multifactor authentication mechanisms, an asset management database, mobile device management system, or customized database consumed via Open Database Connectivity (ODBC) or similar protocols.

Where a device is "headless" or has no active user with the ability to acknowledge or provide authentication information, MAC Authentication Bypass can be used to present the device's "burned-in" identity to the network; however, this approach should be considered a fallback option due to the easy ability to spoof this identity. To make up for the inherent vulnerability of spoofing, the authentication method should always be combined with the authorization condition of "profiling," or the ability to use protocols common to the participation of any device on the network to determine what the device is, adding additional confidence that the device is what it presents itself as by adding in aspects that are harder to spoof or manipulate.

The results of this condition, being one aspect of the contextual identity, should be a classification or enforcement mechanism that can be used to validate the endpoint on the network, such as a VLAN push ensuring the device is in the right "segment" of the network, or a downloadable access control list (ACL), TrustSec tag, or combination therein that can prevent access for the device as it communicates on the network. Typically, devices for which there is less confidence in the information provided to the network identifying them in a definitive manner will have more restrictive and/or higher quantities of authorization restrictions applied as opposed to devices that have definitive identities that are verified through more advanced or trusted means.

This identity also needs to be considered when devices are newly purchased, acquired, or merged into the network with an explicit onboarding process being performed, easing future needs to rediscover endpoints as part of the initial identification phase. As part of the policy, not only should considerations be taken for which devices are currently on the network to access restricted resources critical to the business, but how to ensure that future devices present an identity that is conducive to determining what access they require when introduced onto the network. This policy typically results in a discreet onboarding process, detailing what purchasing, devices, configurations, and policies are all acceptable for devices that are to be used on the network and have access to restricted data in any form.

Does the organization have policies that will allow for enforcement mechanisms? That capacity can dictate the architecture of the network and may determine how demilitarized zones (DMZs) are architected and which identities must be placed in them, as opposed to having access to the organization's crown jewels.

The contextual identity of an entity on the network will become the second most critical pillar because it infuses all the rest of the capabilities with a subject to which they can be applied. Without an identity, enforcement or vulnerability management cannot be applied to a single construct and cannot fulfill their roles in the journey.

Identity must be contextual. It must consider not only the person who owns, manages, troubleshoots, or retires a device, but also needs to consider what that device is, to better make an informed decision on what level of risk is acceptable for that device to be on the network. A cell phone in a manufacturing plant, for example, may not need access to robotic control mechanisms or CAD drawings, whereas an industrial PC may.

Therefore, identity must consist of who or what currently uses, manages, troubleshoots, or owns the entity in question. What database can we use to identify this "who" and validate that their credentials, primary or secondary, are trusted in accordance with the policy and requirements to be on the network? By whom is the device being introduced onto the network? Many devices will need access to the network and be unable to actively interact with it to provide a definitive credential for who is currently connecting the device. What information do we have about the device that can be combined with who is attaching the device to the network to make a better decision on what access this device will need?

Where is the entity connected to the network? Many organizations now have flexibility in where users can work from, whether it be an office, home office via virtual private network (VPN), or branch site. There is a country or locality that an entity can be expected to connect from via whichever method they connect through. For devices connecting through a VPN head end, there is a general expectation that they will connect through a head end closest to them, or at the very least within the country. When an entity attempts to connect from a location outside of its baseline, such as an infrastructure device attempting to connect over VPN, or a user connecting from a country halfway around the world, this can be factored into the considerations of the contextual identity. In a similar fashion, the closer a user is to a resource, the more access to that resource it could be provided, such as the example of a surgeon needing access to critical medical information while in the operating room, or robotics repair technicians needing access to schematics when working on the robotics control systems.

When is the entity connected to the network? While many organizations provide for 24-hour connectivity of most devices on the network and staffing commonly present in office buildings or campuses to monitor the network in an ongoing fashion, exceptions occur for devices connecting to the network that should be considered suspicious based on the entity's common baseline behavior. If an executive rarely works outside of an 8 a.m. to 8 p.m. schedule and is seen accessing the network at early hours of the morning, an investigation may be warranted, which can be further determined by the other aspects of contextual identity. If the executive had a major presentation for the APAC region, for example, had left early in the day to return, presented both the correct primary and secondary credentials, and was connecting from their office on their corporate PC, less scrutiny of the login may be warranted. If the user used only a single credential from a site in China on an open-source mobile platform, additional scrutiny needs to be considered and potential restrictions applied to the session.

How is the entity connected or attached to the network? In a software defined segmentation architecture, environments with standard design principles of access, distribution, core, and wide area network structures, dictate that there are inherent areas that should not have certain entities connected due to it being a violation of the policy or logic. There are plenty of devices that should rarely, if ever, be seen in certain mediums. An Apple iPad, for example, may not ever be expected to connect to the wired network. Should it be observed on the wired network, considerations need to be considered for whether this is what the device presents itself as, whether the methods used to place it on the unexpected medium are allowed, and whether a valid business case should allow for this connectivity as part of the overlay policy.

Vulnerability Management

Devices are continuously evaluated for their threat to the network by reviewing security posture, device health, and application health. In addition, this Vulnerability Management pillar considers who owns, manages, troubleshoots, and uses the device in question as part of its vulnerability management equation. The Vulnerability Management pillar includes systems structured to monitor, manage, and mitigate vulnerabilities.

For every device that is connected to a network, regardless of the user owning, managing, using, or troubleshooting it, there is an inherent risk posed by having the device present on the network. To minimize this risk, an analysis of how the device behaves as opposed to how it is expected to behave while on the network needs to be done. This analysis is highly reliant upon the contextual identity of the device, considering the authentication information or profiling information related to the device, to ensure context can be factored into this risk analysis. As part of this analysis and minimization of the risk the device poses to the network, IP schemas can be used to place all devices that have not been analyzed or that are considered higher risk into segmented areas of the network, such as a quarantined VLAN or quarantined IP subnet. While IP addresses are structures that typically do not serve as a unique identity, the proper architecture and layout of IP subnets can integrate with the contextual identity to indicate that a device is unknown based on a lack of information relating to its contextual identity.

In addition to where the device sits and how it "looks" to the network from the perspective of the profiling engine, active interrogation of a device can help determine what risk it poses to the network, including whether it has open ports or protocols that are outside of normal operating expectations, whether it has installed anti-X software that is also up to date, and what information the device is exchanging with endpoints within the network as well as outside of the network. Understanding the "posture" of the device not only can assist with ensuring that the device belongs on the network and what access it requires to the network, but also can assist in decisions relating to change management, such as when a network access device with this type of device can be changed or disconnected; what information should be maintained in relation to endpoints, devices, and data workloads within the network; how to classify devices for more effective enforcement; and how to ensure that when enforcement is applied it is applied in such a manner that redundancy exists to maintain business continuity.

While contextual identity is the bedrock of understanding what is on the network and where it is located so that enforcement can be applied to it, how does an organization know whether the application of an enforcement mechanism is going to prevent the device from performing its key business function? Understanding the potential vulnerabilities that a device poses to the network is a key aspect of the Zero Trust journey and must be done before attempting to move to future capabilities, including enforcement. While vulnerability prevention and remediation have been thought of in the legacy connected world, vulnerability management should also include the understanding of what resources a device connects to internal and external to the network. Developing a baseline of which resources a device connects to allows variations within that baseline to be detected and understood if a new feature or functionality of the contextual identity was enabled. Meanwhile, the understanding of this communication pattern can be used as the basis for an enforcement policy to be applied, preventing this communication outside of the known required ports and protocols.

The Vulnerability Management pillar also incorporates the more commonly known tool sets required in a vulnerability management program, such as authenticated vulnerability scanning and the tracking and reporting of those vulnerabilities for remediation. The authenticated scanning tool provides the critical ability to query systems connected to the network to ascertain whether they are currently vulnerable to a known vulnerability. These tools use a database of Common Vulnerabilities and Exposures (CVE) maintained by the MITRE organization. The goal for this database is to catalog publicly disclosed vulnerabilities and make them readily available in a consistent format. When effectively used, an authenticated vulnerability scanner can help manage risk by providing visibility relating systems to known vulnerabilities and their necessary remediation. When published by MITRE, these vulnerabilities utilize a Common Vulnerability Scoring System (CVSS) to provide an estimation of the risk and impact. The issue with the CVSS score is that it is published as a base score using the base metrics formula that relates to the foundational aspects of the vulnerability, such as access vector and complexity to exploit. To ensure the most efficient remediation of vulnerability risk, these scores must be adapted through the modification of the temporal and environmental metrics provided by the CVSS to obtain a complete view of risk to a particular organization. The temporal metrics account for details such as whether a proof of exploit is available, the level of remediation available to deploy, and the level of confidence regarding the vulnerability. The environmental metrics then adapt the score further by adjusting for the use case of the system by an organization. This includes factors such as the distribution of vulnerable systems as a percent of the whole, the level of anticipated damage to the system or organization because of a successful exploit, and the impact to the CIA triad of confidentiality, integrity, and availability. This adapted score can then properly inform organizations on the most efficient use of resources in mitigating risks from identified vulnerabilities.

Enforcement

Controls and enforcement are based on contextual identity. The Enforcement pillar includes enforcement points, enforcement policy, and the methods of implementing those policies.

While determining identity and vulnerabilities within the network should undoubtedly be considered the "critical path" for Zero Trust, enforcement through a variety of mechanisms is the goal. The art of enforcement is ensuring that the correct methods of enforcement are applied in the correct areas to minimize risk that vulnerabilities can be exploited or that contextual identities are introduced into the network that are unable to be accounted for. This enforcement needs to be layered and present throughout the network, and in areas where the vulnerabilities inherent to the devices participating in that area of the network can be best controlled in the most effective manner. It is important to remember that while the goal for security is to remove vulnerabilities to limit risk, this is not always possible due to business limitations. The use of proprietary niche systems commonly produced by smaller companies may not have the necessary support for timely updates but are otherwise difficult to replace due to market limitations.

Enforcement mechanisms related to cloud access, denial-of-service prevention, data loss prevention, domain spoofing, email spoofing, or exploitation of devices to prey on their vulnerabilities or connectivity can be applied to prevent exploitation. Applying these enforcement mechanisms as close to the destination of the potential exploitation is key to ensure that before a contextual identity is exploited, that vulnerability is managed, and limits are applied to what can be exploited without significant alarms being sounded. These alarms take the form of the Analysis pillar, and understanding the baseline expected behavior of a given contextual identity.

This Enforcement pillar is typically defined by an enclave in which a contextual identity originates to determine the policy that allows for the enforcement, identity mechanism used to identify the device, expected flow for the device, and therefore how it can be restricted. Mechanisms exist to enforce this policy throughout the organization, including cloud, remote access, guest, or DMZ-focused areas, building management areas, standard corporate access, and business-critical data centers. These mechanisms should be prudently applied based on the full contextual identity. Where heterogeneous endpoints exist in each of the common enclaves in which enforcement is being applied, an evaluation of risk based on the contextual identity should be applied to the decision-making process of which level of enforcement and gradual increase in the level of enforcement.

After due diligence, understanding of the contextual identity and the vulnerabilities it may pose to the network and correlating that with an overlay policy to determine how access can be modified, enforcement can be used to prevent unnecessary communication patterns, based on this understanding. This enforcement can take many forms, spanning from the application itself and securing login, through TrustSec tags local to the VLAN, downloadable ACLs for communication across VLANs, and firewall rules for communication outside of the local site or by using a Virtual Routing and Forwarding (VRF) layer 3 segmentation control.

This layered enforcement mindset ensures that a singular device is not overloaded with the breadth of enforcement needs for a given contextual identity. This ensures that a single point of failure does not exist, thus preventing or allowing access, upon device failure, to resources that are considered unneeded or potentially risky.

Analytics

The Analytics pillar provides a mechanism for insight into the digital environment by tracking what entities are accessing, via what transport, what device, and what methodology.

Contrary to popular belief, a secure network is never as secure as it could be, and there will always be new endpoints, users, use cases, and business functions that require updating the overlay policy, discovering new devices, determining their traffic flow needs and vulnerabilities, and enforcing these policies accordingly. The modifications of this policy, as well as validation that the policy is working as expected, are found in the Analytics pillar of Zero Trust. Analytics, both analyzing device behavior and the policy it hit when it came onto or changed its disposition on the network, are fed into all other pillars to validate the functionality of those pillars and improve how they are applied to contextual identities.

The analytics capabilities should consider information gathered from the each of the other pillars, such as using the identity to validate against an asset management database to determine whether a device present on the network was retired and dormant for months and has been reintroduced onto the network recently. While everything may look in accordance with that identity, further analysis applied will indeed show it to be out of the ordinary. The same goes for being able to build lessons learned and valuable information relating to device behaviors, user behaviors, and success or failures related to each to ensure false positives and true negatives can be more easily noticed. External feeds or information on these devices and their expected behavior, or behaviors seen in the wild that go against expected behavior, also need to be part of this analysis.

The Zero Trust journey is cyclical in nature with a need existing not only for ongoing analysis and understanding of the devices on the network and how their access may change throughout their life cycle, but also understanding and analysis of new devices or contextual identities that will inevitably be added to the network over time. This analysis feeds the rest of the Zero Trust pillars in that understanding of devices and contextual identities may influence changes to the overlay policies, may add more information to be used in the identification of devices and users, may uncover previously unknown or undetected vulnerabilities, or may determine when enforcement needs to be restricted or loosened to allow an identity to fulfill its business function.

The analysis therefore should be fed from all information available to be gathered on the network, ranging from application logs, to switch counters, syslogs from devices throughout the network, and identity accounting information. This information then needs to be aggregated, analyzed, sorted, and presented in an effective manner based on the business goals an organization has, which often require further analysis of the data and its conclusions to modify and get the correct data per those goals. We discuss types of solutions that support these capabilities throughout this book.

Summary

Armed with the knowledge of how a Zero Trust implementation is done and in what sorts of phases, these methodologies and considerations need to be applied in the form of a workshop with key stakeholders. The workshop aims to ensure that all stakeholders are on the same page, understand the goals and risks of the Zero Trust journey, and understand their part in making the journey a success. Gathering artifacts and information on how business units and devices interact, determining a device communication baseline, and planning for control mechanisms should all be outcomes of the workshop. While organizations and verticals may have unique goals for their Zero Trust journey, the workshop unifies the vision for all resources who will be part of the planning, designing, implementing, and operating of the Zero Trust implementation. Therefore, it is important to also ensure that questions asked and answers provided can be agreed to by all parties involved, either directly or indirectly.

With competing priorities, budgets, and organizational dynamics, a Zero Trust goal, strategy, and implementation plan are necessary. With evolving threats, newly introduced endpoints, and a need to protect business continuity, organizations must align and be ready to progress in the implementation of Zero Trust.

References in This Chapter

- The Morris Worm, FBI, www.fbi.gov/news/stories/morris-worm-30-years-since-first-major-attack-on-internet-110218
- Stephen Paul Marsh, "Formalizing Trust as a Computational Concept," University of Stirling, April 1994, www.cs.stir.ac.uk/~kjt/techreps/pdf/TR133.pdf
- Jericho Forum, https://en.wikipedia.org/wiki/Jericho_Forum
- Computer Security Resource Center, "threat," https://csrc.nist.gov/glossary/term/threat

Chapter 2

Zero Trust Capabilities

Chapter Key Points:

- This chapter provides an overview of the five pillars of Zero Trust, including how to overlay policy, being identity-led, providing vulnerability management, enforcing access control, and providing visibility into control and data plane functions.

- We provide ways to identify what Cisco defines as Zero Trust Capabilities and where to start looking in the organization for these capabilities.

- We also provide an extensive reference, or "dictionary of capabilities," that can be used for many efforts within an organization.

- Capabilities outlined in this chapter may be broken down further, but for the purposes of achieving Zero Trust, the book focuses on the critical capabilities needed.

- We establish a foundation to build Zero Trust into an organization.

The cornerstone to creating a Zero Trust strategy is to identify the capabilities of an organization using a focused process to identify how well a capability is addressed by reviewing technical administration capabilities, functional cross-organizational process capabilities, and overall adoption of the capabilities.

By reading and referring to this chapter of the book, you will be able to identify what Cisco defines as Zero Trust Capabilities as well as where to start looking within an organization for these capabilities. The organization will need to review its requirements related to policy creation and fulfillment, along with what is deemed critical infrastructure, to define the overall risk tolerance for issues or gaps.

After a risk tolerance level is established for the organization, an assessment of the available capabilities should be performed. Risk assessments are often performed by an outside organization to remove critical biases and to enable all parts of the organization to consume the findings of the assessment. Priorities and gaps that are identified should establish a strategy for going forward and a roadmap for a Zero Trust–driven organization.

Following chapters in this book outline use cases, methods, and best practices to implement Zero Trust, as outlined in this critical foundational chapter.

Cisco Zero Trust Capabilities

The pillars of the Cisco Zero Trust Capabilities, as outlined in Figure 2-1, represent various capabilities that are necessary for a successful Zero Trust strategy. These capabilities are not all inclusive but function as the minimum required set of capabilities necessary. Some organizations may need more specific capabilities relevant to their unique use cases.

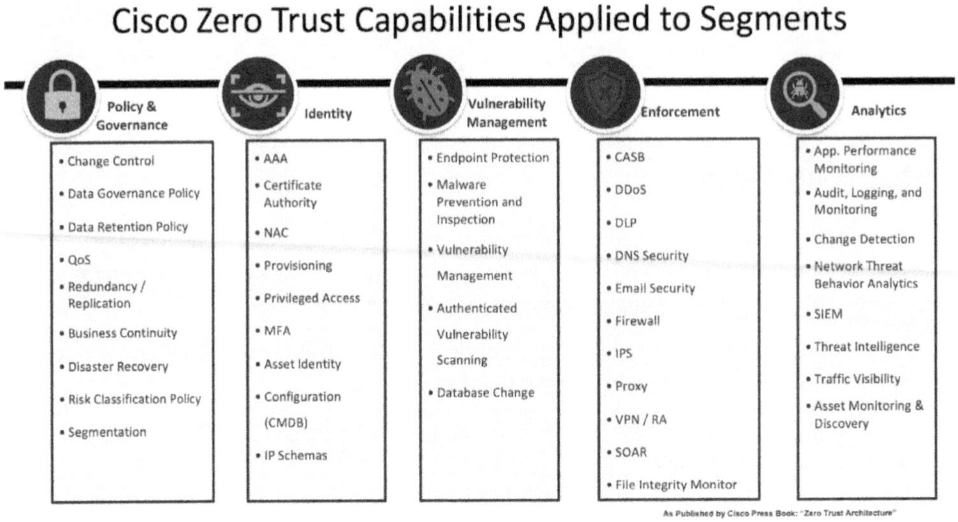

Cisco Zero Trust Capabilities Applied to Segments

Policy & Governance	Identity	Vulnerability Management	Enforcement	Analytics
• Change Control	• AAA	• Endpoint Protection	• CASB	• App. Performance Monitoring
• Data Governance Policy	• Certificate Authority	• Malware Prevention and Inspection	• DDoS	• Audit, Logging, and Monitoring
• Data Retention Policy	• NAC		• DLP	• Change Detection
• QoS	• Provisioning	• Vulnerability Management	• DNS Security	• Network Threat Behavior Analytics
• Redundancy / Replication	• Privileged Access	• Authenticated Vulnerability Scanning	• Email Security	• SIEM
• Business Continuity	• MFA		• Firewall	• Threat Intelligence
• Disaster Recovery	• Asset Identity	• Database Change	• IPS	• Traffic Visibility
• Risk Classification Policy	• Configuration (CMDB)		• Proxy	• Asset Monitoring & Discovery
• Segmentation	• IP Schemas		• VPN / RA	
			• SOAR	
			• File Integrity Monitor	

As Published by Cisco Press Book: "Zero Trust Architecture"

Figure 2-1   *Cisco Zero Trust Capabilities*

This chapter develops your understanding of each capability and what that capability can be used for within an organization to move toward developing a stronger security posture against would-be attackers. We begin with the Policy & Governance pillar because it establishes what can or cannot be done within the organization. We then move to the Identity pillar, which establishes the identity of not only users but also devices, transport, and many other object types. It cannot be understated how important Identity is to establish a stronger security posture.

The Vulnerability Management pillar enables organizations to identify, track, and mitigate known vulnerabilities to reduce organizational risk. The Enforcement pillar capabilities are what traditionally are thought to be security operations center (SOC) or network operations center (NOC) tools; however, as the team reviews these capabilities regarding Zero Trust, you will see that these capabilities extend beyond these groups and are used or managed by multiple teams throughout the organization. In the Analytics pillar, we review how an organization can see what is happening to objects and what is acting upon them inside and outside of the environment.

Having well-established governance, identity stores, vulnerability management, enforcement, and visibility capabilities enables a Zero Trust strategy.

Policy & Governance Pillar

Finding the right balance of security and business enablement is a crucial requirement for any Zero Trust strategy. The primary category to help achieve this balance is the Policy & Governance pillar of Cisco's Zero Trust Model. With the Policy & Governance pillar, an organization may establish how tightly the entire organization is governed, how long information is retained, how the organization will recover in an emergency, and how important sets of data are managed from group to group. Organizations also need to focus on their industry, their regulations, the organization and its business goals, and their customers' risk tolerance levels. The Policy & Governance pillar focuses on key factors that must be established to enable the Zero Trust journey.

Change Control

It is necessary for many organizations to have change management services. Many use the Information Technology Infrastructure Library (ITIL) change management process. ITIL is an accepted approach to managing Information Technology services to support and enable organizations. ITIL enables organizations to deliver services. Frameworks such as ITIL help establish architectures, processes, tools, metrics, documentation, technology services, and configuration management practices.

Changes must be coordinated, managed, and details disseminated to relevant parties. A unique characteristic of Zero Trust means that changes will occur end to end within the environment, so special care must be paid to ensure smooth forward progress. As a critical part of the change process, testing provides the ability to ensure that production deployments in support of Zero Trust can be accomplished in a timely and effective fashion.

Data Governance

It's critical to classify data and to understand where it is stored and how it is monitored for compliance to organizational policies. Some examples of data classifications are personally identifiable information (PII), Electronic Protected Health Information (ePHI), Payment Card Information (PCI), Restricted Intellectual Property, and Classified Information. Data governance also includes a well-defined and maintained configuration management database that contains where all data stores are located, who owns them within the organization, along with data classification, labeling and storage, and access requirements.

Data Retention

Data retention is dictated based on organizational and regulatory requirements. After an incident, the ability to determine the cause of an outage or breach is critical information that must be retained both for restoration of service as well as audit purposes. Data retention must consider data at rest, how long the data must be stored, and when the data should be purged to limit organizational liability. The legal and compliance teams of the organization manage policy requirements on what data an organization must retain and for how long.

Quality of Service (QoS)

Quality of service, including the marking and prioritization of key traffic in times of micro or long-term congestion, is a key component of availability to ensure that control plane traffic continues to flow to ensure Zero Trust capabilities function as intended. QoS provides for preferential treatment of traffic to meet defined policy requirements to ensure that critical functions necessary for security and business functions continue without undue impairment. Without this safeguard in place, organizations run the risk of congestion on the network having unpredictable impacts to traffic and the solutions that rely on that traffic.

Redundancy

Redundancy is necessary to maintain availability and is part of a Zero Trust strategy. Critical components of the ecosystem are required to be duplicated by many frameworks, standards, regulations, and laws. Redundancy can have multiple aspects: control plane redundancy is necessary for the functioning of capabilities, whereas data plane redundancy is necessary to ensure that business functions continue unimpeded.

Replication

Replication involves the duplication and the encryption of key data stores to backup storage arrays and offline storage backups, which provide a restoration path in the event of partial or complete loss of an environment due to ransomware. Software automation is necessary to ensure that the proper environments are replicated to proper locations. Without replication automation, errors are inevitable, and critical data stores may be overwritten, creating a large-scale outage requiring full restoration of one or many databases.

Auditors, regulators, or governing bodies routinely validate these controls. The key point to note is the regulations, standards, or laws are the minimum of replication that should be in place for the organization. Protecting an organization's data is its top concern. Without protective controls—that is, encryption and locations around these replicated data stores—there can be no data integrity, confidentiality, and in the end availability; therefore, a gap in Zero Trust is created.

Business Continuity

Confidentiality, integrity, and availability are the foundation of all security programs and are necessary in a Zero Trust strategy. Business continuity relies on a well-executed Zero Trust strategy. The development of business continuity teams and business continuity documentation that can be accessed by the critical teams in the event of a crisis is a cornerstone to business continuity. Please note that a business continuity plan (BCP) should always be protective of human life first, in all cases. Ensure teams are safe at the outset of plan activation and throughout the event. A well-developed communication plan will assist in locating and checking in on those associated with the organization. The plan should also be protective of what is shared publicly to provide a level of protection to recovery efforts.

The second most important step is maintaining the integrity of data in the middle of responding to a business continuity event. Maintaining data integrity may seem trivial to some of those responding to a critical event, but that is exactly when an attacker will attack. Ensure "temporary" controls or measures do not expose the organization to issues with data integrity along with availability. Some ransomware attacks may activate the business continuity plan and be the cause of an organization-level outage. Restricted or intellectual property may be at risk.

Work out these scenarios in advance and partner with your nearest fusion center and other government entities to respond to these critical types of events. Tabletop exercises may expose gaps, but putting teams through BCP drills reveals how prepared teams are to respond and may uncover shortcuts that could expose the organization's critical data stores.

Disaster Recovery (DR)

Typically, a disaster recovery event is activated as soon as a problem has been detected, but many times the business continuity plan (BCP) should be activated. After the BCP team assesses the situation, recovery efforts are officially started. The DR plan may include many of the same contacts from a leadership perspective as the BCP does, but the DR plan focuses on recovering a solution, a set of solutions, or the critical infrastructure of the organization.

The scope of any DR event may be assessed and categorized as minor, or it could go more broadly. At first, the event may impact only one aspect of the business or even one solution, but this is where teams should not have tunnel vision and should consider other systems and environments that could be also impacted. Activating the proper process and notifying the right level of leadership is a function of the business continuity plan based on impact and risk. It is important that proper criteria have been established for DR planning, primarily the criticality of the system to the organization and impact upon daily functioning and therefore the acceptable limits of data loss and recovery time. This is normally classified into two categories, recovery point objective (RPO) and recovery time objective (RTO). RPO defines the amount of time acceptable for transactional data loss. Stated another way, RPO is the amount of data or work that will be unrecoverable after a system failure. RTO, on the other hand, is the amount of time it takes to restore the system and data back to normal. These are minimum variables that should be defined for each system where it is determined that DR capability is required.

DR plans go hand in hand with the business continuity plan. With proper controls as defined in the "Policy & Governance" section of the book, disaster recovery should be achievable and complete. Development and testing of a DR plan are part of the standup procedures for new environments. Each environment must define a method of recovery prior to "production go-live" events so the definition of what constitutes a successful recovery can be worked through and can be checked off as complete during an actual DR event or during a DR test. If the plan is not created after the application has been purchased, many installation requirements are forgotten, neglected, or known by only a handful of individual team members. Testing of the DR plan is required for both new and old ecosystems. The adage still holds true: "If there is no testing, there is no DR plan." Adding to that, without a business continuity plan and a disaster recovery plan, there cannot be a valid and implemented Zero Trust strategy.

Risk Classification

Risk classification helps inform multiple other capabilities such as data governance, business continuity, and redundancy. This includes classifying the risk for data as well as capabilities. For data, risk must be assessed to understand the criticality of the data to the organization. For capabilities, risk must be classified to understand what impact to the organization may occur if that capability ceases to operate as expected.

Risk classification structures should be developed with compliance and legal teams to ensure that the business is protected and to ensure business continuity. Having a Zero Trust mindset as these classifications are developed or updated will go a long way to provide greater protections and controls put in place, while at the same time enabling the business.

Identity Pillar

Identity is a concept to represent entities that exist on a network and is analogous to what an entity *has* or *is*. Sometimes, entities may offer a configured or known credential, while other times they do not. Identity alone is not enough to gain access to data. Determining identity is a fundamental process of authentication. Organizations using an identity alone as a basis to grant access to an object from a central authority are not aligning to a full Zero Trust strategy, because full context of the identity has not been established. As an example, possessing a driver's license as identification does not allow anyone on an airplane. Someone or something must verify the identification matches the entity attempting to use the license against valid confirmation information.

Authentication, Authorization, and Accounting (AAA)

What is meant by the phrase "Triple A"? In simple terms, *authentication* is a validation of the "who" or "what" of an entity, *authorization* is the set of resources or data to which the authenticated entity can access, and *accounting* is the record of interactions that occur throughout the operation.

The first step for any entity accessing the network is to authenticate. This step requires that the entity requesting authentication—be it a person, computer, or any number of other networked devices—must provide details about itself in at least one form. These details may be provided directly by the entity, for example, using a username and password, a certificate, or a MAC address provided by the entity.

Authentication can be accomplished using multiple criteria, which is referred to as multifactor authentication. The process of authenticating does not imply the permissions to which the entity may interact. Take, for example, an ATM: anyone can walk up to one with a valid debit card and insert it into the machine. With the proper PIN code, the user will authenticate, but the possession of the card and PIN code does not explicitly provide details to which accounts that person should have access, which leads to the second "A," authorization.

Authorization involves taking the identity of the authenticated entity and, in combination with other conditions, determining through a defined policy what level of resource or data access should be provided. Depending on the policy engine in use, these conditions can become quite granular. Some examples of additional conditions for authorizing network access might include device health or posture, a directory service group membership, time and day variables, device identity, or device ownership. Going back to the ATM example, after authentication, the customer is provided access to their accounts after a policy engine makes the necessary determinations, such as permission to view and interactions allowed with each account.

Finally, accounting is a way to record the actions an entity on the network takes for audit purposes. This includes documenting when the entity attempts to authenticate, the result of that authentication, and what interactions are made with the authorized resources and ends after the entity disconnects or logs off from the network. This accounting data is crucial for both troubleshooting and forensic purposes. In troubleshooting, it provides valuable data to help identify where in the process of AAA the entity is encountering a problem, such as why they are not getting authorized to expected data or resources. For forensic purposes, it provides the ability to understand when an entity accessed the network, what actions were taken, and when it disconnected or if it is still connected to the network.

AAA Special Conditions

It is also important to mention the challenges for AAA brought about by the rapid increase in Internet of Things (IoT) devices. In most cases, these devices operate in a more rudimentary fashion when it comes to network connectivity and may not be capable of providing a username and password for authentication, much less a certificate. In some cases, while these capabilities may be available from the device, a lack of suitable management may make use of these features not technically feasible. In either case, it is important to ensure that alternatives are available to authenticate and authorize these devices effectively and safely. Commonly, this will mean using the MAC address to authenticate the device against a database, and authorization will follow a similar set of conditions as for other entities. There are numerous efforts underway to improve the interaction of IoT devices, especially regarding enterprise networks, such as the Machine Usage Description (MUD) attribute, which provides the purpose of the device to the policy engine. Ultimately, though, these devices can be more easily spoofed when authenticated through MUD or MAC address-based paths, so caution must be taken. This lower level of confidence in positive identification and authenticating the entity in detail means special thought and care must be taken when assigning authorization to resources or data.

Certificate Authority

An alternative but slightly higher overhead for identifying devices uniquely within a network is the ability to present a certificate. A certificate, simply put, is a unique identity issued to a user or endpoint, which relies on a chain of trust. This chain of trust consists of a centralized authority being the root of the trust, and branches in a tree-like structure providing for distributed trust the world over. Issuance of a certificate to endpoints or to users provides for an "I trust this authority, and therefore I trust this entity" ability.

Certificates are typically considered a stronger method of authentication because of the ability to both prevent exportation of the identity and providing for the ability to validate the identity presented within the certificate against a centralized identity store—for example, Active Directory, which is the Microsoft Directory Store; Lightweight Directory Access Protocol (LDAP), which is an Open-Source Directory Store; or Azure Active Directory Domain Services (Azure AD DS), which is cloud-based.

By blocking the private aspects of the certificate from being exported, the certificate cannot be shared with another user or even another device, making it a secure identification mechanism. In addition, like directory service attributes, alternative names and attributes can be added into a certificate that can be used to uniquely identify an endpoint and what access the device should be provided on the network.

Certificates are typically exchanged with the policy engine via Extensible Authentication Protocol–Transport Layer Security (EAP-TLS). These certificates can be assigned to either the endpoint or the user itself. The combination of user and machine certificates creates a unique contextual identity. This contextual identity provides differentiated access based on the attributes associated to the type of identity, whether that be user, application, or machine.

Network Access Control (NAC)

A network access control system provides a mechanism to control access to the network. There are many solutions available to provide this Zero Trust Capability to maintain control of who or what accesses the network for any organization. The NAC system needs to have the ability to integrate with the other Zero Trust Capabilities, described within this chapter. The NAC system will directly participate in the Policy & Governance, Identity, Vulnerability Management, Enforcement, and Analytics pillars. Policy & Governance must influence the configuration of the NAC system.

After a device is purchased, onboarded, and identified, there needs to exist a database and policy engine to validate the identity using AAA (see the previous section). This policy engine should contain

- Integrated authentication into a directory service

- Endpoint posture for vulnerabilities

- Ability to control endpoint access via policy

For example, with identity, there is a reliance upon Directory Services, or a certificate authority, which requires that the NAC system integrate with the identity store to determine and enforce AAA. NAC should utilize this identity to link vulnerability into the contextual identity, then apply and enforce controls, and then log these actions locally or to an integrated system, such as a Security Information and Event Management (SIEM) system. Logging events being generated in the NAC system requires collection of what was done and why to be able to better analyze devices on the network and their potential security implications to the network.

Provisioning

Provisioning is a process to acquire, deploy, and configure new or existing infrastructure throughout an organization based on Policy & Governance. Provisioning heavily impacts the decision-making process when implementing a Zero Trust strategy. Provisioning happens in multiple phases across multiple groups in the environment. All stakeholders must understand the importance of a unified policy and process.

Organizations define their own needs to meet specific requirements. A comprehensive Zero Trust strategy requires a wholistic approach that addresses the flexibility needed in the process and while maintaining tight controls that enforce the policies of the organization and regulating bodies. Proper provisioning practices dictate that a common form of tracking and visibility of access needs should be documented during all stages of the infrastructure life cycle. The following sections detail some Provisioning policy enforcement categories to consider.

Device

Some common device types range from printers, computers, IoT, OT, specialty equipment, and managed, and not managed. Groups responsible for creating, maintaining, and executing these functions exist in almost every facet of an organization. Devices need to respect the presence of Zero Trust controls in any physical, logical, or network environment.

User

Users can exist in many parts of the organization but, unlike devices, should all be controlled within a defined role within the organization. User identities created for third parties must map to a role with the organization. Access for devices, people, and processes relies on these role-based user accounts. These accounts may represent multiple roles for differing functions. Zero Trust relies upon user identity, which is an important attribute in aligning policy to an action. "User" is a component of the Zero Trust Identity Capability for user attribution, assignment, and provisioning and builds a foundation for establishing trust.

People

A Zero Trust strategy should inform and guide all onboarding and offboarding processes within an organization of each entity. People have the potential of becoming soft targets and therefore vulnerabilities to the organization. Security threat awareness, training, and testing help build resilience within the people who work for the organization. The scope of provisioning as it relates to people applies not only to those with access to systems. Provisioning of users, devices, access, services, assets, and many other important aspects of provisioning are affected through these processes. Zero Trust controls attempt to apply attribution to any interaction with people throughout the organization, third parties, or partners. These concepts can branch out to encompass interactions with any asset by a person to any connection.

Infrastructure

The Identity of infrastructure objects defines what an object is, what an object needs to function, and relates the object to what are valid activities of the object to support the organization.

Infrastructure provisioning processes create the pathways through which access to objects occurs. Administrators need to define what protections are needed to enable the use of the infrastructure to support the user community and the functions of their role. Administrators tasked with supporting the infrastructure mediate how and when provisioning steps interact with services and flows.

Services

Services enable an application or a suite of applications to support and allow users to fulfill their defined user role within the organization. Without services, there is no point in giving a user access to an application. The services attribute for Identity capabilities is used to define access attributes for users to be able to execute critical functions assigned to their roles.

Service Identity provisioning processes interrelate devices, users, people, and infrastructure to further build contextual identity capabilities. Documenting the access requirements and restrictions associated to devices, users, people, and infrastructure creates policy that can be directly enforced by Zero Trust. Services rely on consistent and accurate identity information derived from provisioning to define these policies in an effective manner. Access denial and access acceptance are attained through the documentation of these identifiers and classifying what is allowed to utilize the service and under what conditions the service is being requested.

Privileged Access

Privileged access is elevated user access required to perform functions to support and manage systems. Privileged Access can be found within any portion of the infrastructure, including network appliances, databases, applications, operating systems, cloud provider platforms, communications connectivity systems, and software development. Privileged access should follow the concept of "least privileged access" and should be limited to a very small population of users. Types of users leveraging privileged access include but are not limited to database administrators, backup administrators, third-party application administrators, treasury administrators, service accounts, and systems administrators, along with network and security teams.

Privileged access introduces higher risk to data, availability, or controls. Privileged access may be leveraged by attackers to cause the most damage to an environment, ecosystem, or proprietary information, making this type of Identity what an organization should highly guard, monitor, and control.

To monitor and control privileged access, solutions are available to control this higher level of access, with timers to allow access, and stronger controls, including the logging of changes made while leveraging privileged access levels of Identity. It is recommended that organizations audit the use of privileged access on a routine basis with management oversight and signoff. Many regulations and laws require privileged access controls be put in place within an organization, with demonstrable compliance to external auditors on a routine basis. Teams should review the requirements for their organization based on regulations and legal team guidance.

Multifactor Authentication (MFA)

Multifactor authentication is the practice of leveraging factors of what a user knows (i.e., password), what a user has (i.e., managed device or device certificate), who a user is (i.e., biometrics), and what a user can solve (i.e., Captcha with problems); it is a foundational principle of Zero Trust. These aspects allow for many interpretations, and therefore, the Policy & Governance pillar needs to address the requirements of MFA within a given organization that are pushed out to all users of the environment.

Classical usernames are identifiable through email addresses, and passwords may not be well configured by users or are reused on many systems, making them easily vulnerable to brute-force attacks. By leveraging additional factors of MFA, organizations increase their resistance to attack; however, strong onboarding/offboarding of employees, interns, and contractor processes with monitoring and auditing is required to maintain control of identity stores and MFA factors and to limit unauthorized access.

In some cases, organizations may want to move to a true "passwordless" access control methodology using only device certificates to increase convenience to the user population. It is recommended that organizations review this method with legal teams and regulating bodies prior to moving to a true "passwordless" approach. For example, for most operating systems, after the user logs in to the machine, a supplicant is presented a certificate as an authentication mechanism to a policy engine. Are a user login and a device certificate enough for the organization and the regulations with which they are required to comply? These challenges to defining MFA may occur, so organizations should be specific on whether MFA is two or more of the same factors or a unique combination of factors. These details need to be specified by the organization via Policy & Governance.

Asset Identity

Asset identity is a method, process, application, or service that enables an organization to identify physical devices that interact with the organization with certainty of the actual real device type, location, and key attributes.

Organizations need to be able to identify all unique assets operating within their ecosystems. Based on the identity of the asset, the metadata adds context that will drive Policy & Governance requirements for the asset type involved or the specific asset that is necessary for a Zero Trust strategy implementation. Examples of assets that are critical for identification are not limited to servers, workstations, network gear, telephony devices, printers, security devices, and low-powered devices.

More difficult to identify are assets that include devices that do not respond to requests for unique identity like low-powered devices. These devices may not have a supplicant, or even conform with standardized RFCs dictating the format, frequency, and protocol for responses. In these cases, unique asset attributes need to be used to identify the endpoint. Passive abilities are available to identify an endpoint and have been built into standards used to manufacture devices. The unique MAC address embedded into a device's network interface card (NIC), for example, has the first 24 of 48 bits reserved to uniquely identify the manufacturer of that endpoint against a known database of registered and reserved organizationally unique identifiers (OUI). The MAC address is a data element in standard configuration management databases.

Configuration Management Database (CMDB)

A configuration management database is an important repository of critical organization information that contains all types of devices, solutions, network equipment, data center equipment, applications, asset owners, application owners, emergency contacts, and the relationships between them all.

Whether the attribute used is the MAC address of an endpoint, a serial number unique to an aspect of the endpoint, or a unique attribute assigned to the endpoint or combination of its properties, a CMDB or an asset management database (AMDB) should exist to ensure that devices, services, applications, and data are tracked and provide critical information to respond to important events or incidents.

The information contained within the CMDB ensures that solutions may reference the data in the CMDB to control access to only authorized objects. Discreet onboarding processes are required to support a Zero Trust strategy. A description of exactly what needs to be known when an endpoint is put onto a network, with roles, responsibilities, and with updating requirements, is part of a mature organization's Zero Trust profile.

The use of a consistent onboarding process will ensure an optimized and efficient onboarding process can be practiced. This consistent onboarding process ensures that similar provisioning practices are followed across unique vendors, and configurations are applied in a consistent way to identify entities within the network. While variations may occur in devices, even from the same vendor, consistency in identifying the device in alignment with an onboarding process will lead to a notable change in security posture. Critical elements to review when differentiating devices or device types include

- Firmware versions

- Base software versions

- Individual hardware component revisions

- Organizational unique identifier (OUI) variation for NICs

Internet Protocol (IP) Schemas

The Internet Protocol schema provides identification of services or objects via unique IP addresses. Necessary to any Zero Trust Segmentation program is having an IP address schema or plan to enable communications from workload to workload, within and outside of an ecosystem. Organizations should not focus specifically on the IP address to create a Zero Trust Segmentation strategy, but rather use an IP schema as another tool in an administrator's toolbox to assist in identification of workloads and/or objects.

Another consideration is whether an organization should use provider-independent (PI) or provider-aggregated (PA) IP space to improve the security profile, while potentially adding an additional benefit of the organization easily moving from one provider to another.

Most organizations prefer to go with a provider-independent IP space. As stated in the technical paper "Stream: Internet Engineering Task Force (IETF)":

> a common question is whether companies should use Provider-Independent (PI) or Provider-Aggregated (PA) space [RFC7381], but, from a security perspective, there is minor difference. However, one aspect to keep in mind is who has administrative ownership of the address space and who is technically responsible if/when there is

a need to enforce restrictions on routability of the space. This typically comes in the form of a need based on malicious criminal activity originating from it. Relying on PA address space may also increase the perceived need for address translation techniques, such as NPTv6; thereby, the complexity of the operations, including the security operations, is augmented.

Best practices to create a stable IP space environment include implementing an addressing plan and an IP address management (IPAM) solution. The following sections detail the three standards of IP addressing spaces that can be used to create or combine to create an IP Schema.

IPV4

Internet Protocol version 4 addresses, better known as IPv4 addresses, enable workloads to communicate over public mediums utilizing a standardized 256-bit addressing standard. It is well known that the world is running out of IPv4 addresses, and this has become a driver for organizations to move to IPv6.

IPV6

IPv6, with its standardized 128-bit address, is expected to be almost inexhaustive with the ability to assign an address to every square inch of the earth's surface. This direction to implement IPv6 is difficult and should not be entered into without a well-vetted plan. This is further complicated by a need to map out significantly more address space within IPV6, typically a 56- or 64-bit allocation to a given organization, and the flows between endpoints within the address space.

To begin, a directional plan to move to IPv6 has become a legal matter and requirement for some organizations in recent years. Workload communication over IPv6 is becoming necessary, especially when working with public sector agencies. Working on a Zero Trust migration and an IPv6 migration in the same program is a daunting task. A recommendation would be to develop a roadmap to making incremental improvements over time. As part of these incremental improvements, and especially as organizations start to roll out IPv6 greenfield, a mapping of communication for how endpoints interact with each other across their respective communication domains is highly recommended. While most engineers and administrators inherited the design or design standards for IPv4 networks, organizations have a unique opportunity related to IPv6 and its ability to be part of a security strategy.

Each workload that gets an IPv6 address and can communicate over IPv6 also has a unique identity that can be associated back to IPv6. With such as a massive address space available within IPv6, identity can be tied back to the addressing, or at least associated as another tool in the network engineering toolbox.

Dual Stack

In many cases organizations need to use IPv6 address space in a "dual stack" implementation that includes IPv4 addresses, as well as IPv6 addresses to enable a transition.

In the case that a transition must be managed as a dual stack, this process requires double the work for administration teams. Implementing dual stack requires that each workload gets an IPv4 and an IPv6 address and can communicate over IPv4 or IPv6. This dual stack process can create a high degree of administrative overhead, including mapping out addresses, designing recognizable subnets or network architectures, and managing network devices by applying the same identity and policies to two separate addresses. Being in this dual phase of implementation tends to go on for several years or is a permanent method to manage the organization's IP address issues.

Vulnerability Management Pillar

The Vulnerability Management pillar refers to the Zero Trust capability to identify, manage, and mitigate risk within an organization. Effective implementation of vulnerability management requires well-defined Policy & Governance practices that are integrated into the solutions used to manage vulnerabilities. A Vulnerability Management organization needs to be established within the organization using best practices, such as the ones found in the Information Technology Infrastructure Library (ITIL) or those provided as part of the NIST Cybersecurity Framework. Many regulations, laws, and organizational policies rely on effective Vulnerability Management processes to classify known risks, to prioritize these risks for mitigation, to enable leadership to own these known risks, and for response to regulating bodies.

Endpoint Protection

An endpoint protection system not only provides the capability to detect threats such as malware but also provides the ability to determine file reputation, identify and flag known vulnerabilities, prevent the execution of exploits, and integrate behavioral analysis to understand both standard user and machine behavior to flag anomalies. It may also provide some level of machine learning, which can attempt to prevent zero-day malware or other endpoint attacks by monitoring for attributes that are common for malware, relying less on published intelligence data.

Endpoint protection should be able to monitor the system to detect malware and track the origination and propagation of threats throughout the network. Each individual endpoint protection agent has a small view of the environment in which it is connected. However, when data is aggregated between devices and combined with network-level monitoring, it is possible to provide a more complete picture of how a piece of malware enters, propagates, and impacts a network.

Endpoint protection should be able to provide a clear picture as a piece of malware enters and begins to spread through the network. Systems that can run endpoint protection will begin to detect and restrict the actions of the threat, while at the same time beginning to generate alarms. Systems will begin taking retrospective actions to understand where a malicious file originated. This in turn provides the ability to aggregate this data across all the protected endpoints and network monitoring systems, making it possible to illustrate the entry point and impacted systems until its detection.

In other considerations around the endpoint, the protection must extend beyond the endpoint itself. An example of this would be that it is rare to find any enterprise network that does not have Internet of Things (IoT) or operational technology (OT) endpoints. These endpoints may be part of a building management system, such as thermostats or lighting control features, or programmable logic controllers running conveyer systems in a warehouse. The commonality between IoT and OT is that both will be unable to utilize endpoint protection applications, and therefore administrators must rely more heavily on all the other controls available to provide protection. It may be difficult at first to understand how an endpoint protection application on a desktop could help protect a thermostat, but this capability comes down to the forensics being available in these systems.

Malware Prevention and Inspection

Malware is one of the most prevalent threats facing organizations. Due to this widespread usage of malware and its targeting of businesses for monetary gain, organizations cannot solely rely on malware prevention to occur at the endpoint. This is especially true when considering the number of IoT and OT endpoints that cannot run endpoint protection systems. Therefore, it is imperative that malware prevention be layered throughout the ecosystem, deployed on dedicated appliances, or in combination with other security tools. As discussed with endpoint protection, these network-level malware prevention and inspection capabilities must be able to integrate and work in concert with other systems to provide the greatest possible benefit. If the ecosystem can detect malware, it can then communicate this with connected endpoints to alert them of both the presence and type of malware to allow each endpoint to act against the threat. In addition, inspection systems can alert administrators to the threat and begin response efforts if the systems are unable to address the threats automatically.

An additional strength provided by malware prevention and inspection systems is the ability to have a central control point for scanning and blocking of malware. By placing a malware prevention and inspection system prior to a manufacturing network with OT endpoints, for instance, it allows for greater risk mitigation for those business-critical endpoints that are incapable of running their own malware prevention tool sets. As data moves in and out of these segments, malware can be quickly identified, and other connected systems and administrators can begin to take action to remove the threat to keep the organization running. Defense-in-depth means that malware prevention and inspection must occur as often as possible and be well integrated to the overall security ecosystem of an organization to achieve Zero Trust.

Vulnerability Management

Vulnerability management systems fulfill the role of identifying when exploits are possible on a system due to misconfigurations, software bugs, or hardware vulnerabilities. As technology advances in capability, software must become more complex to provide the features that can take advantage of these additional capabilities. At the same time, this software is being developed too quickly to maintain quality, leading to mistakes or oversights, known as bugs or vulnerabilities. From a security viewpoint, there are many instances where these bugs do not pose a problem, but as complexity and the pace of development increase, the quantity of bugs will increase as well, and it is inevitable that some of these bugs will be exploitable. Proactive discovery of these exploits and the ability to remediate before they can be leveraged by an attacker is of paramount importance to protecting an organization. The larger the organization, the greater the importance of a vulnerability management system to allow administrators to quickly ascertain the health of software deployed and identify these exploits as soon as they are made known.

The number of applications that are installed in an organization may not be always known. It is common for the count of applications to be well into the thousands, requiring operations staff to try to identify when each of these applications may be vulnerable to an exploit. Visibility, automation, and AI are required to support and scale vulnerability management teams due to the sheer number of objects within an organization. Vulnerability management systems provide the ability to scan the network and endpoints consistently and reliably against a database of known threats that is continually updated. These systems provide the automation and scale necessary to look across thousands of endpoints and their applications to understand what software is present, the vulnerabilities within that software, and to monitor the remediation efforts as patches or other upgrades are undertaken.

A vulnerability management system should also provide the ability for administrators to quickly understand and prioritize the vulnerabilities present. It is not enough to just rate the threat from a vulnerability based on its impact but should also factor in how often attackers are leveraging the exploit, the level of complexity to exploit, and the number and criticality of the systems that are vulnerable. Zero Trust strategies rely on context for decision-making, and vulnerability management is no different. If the particulars of an organization cannot be factored into the exploit analysis, administrators run the risk of spending precious time remediating exploits that would realistically have minimal to no risk to the organization and delay actions against those threats for which they are truly vulnerable. Some of these lower-risk items may be already appropriately mitigated and should be tracked, along with other mitigated risks, as part of a residual risk database. Residual risk is a method to track any remaining risk after evaluation of security controls and mitigations are completed because it is not possible to completely remove all risk in most scenarios.

Authenticated Vulnerability Scanning

Authenticated vulnerability scanning, where a vulnerability scanner is provided valid credentials to authenticate its access to the target system, is a major component of a well-rounded vulnerability analysis program supporting a Zero Trust strategy. On its face, vulnerability scanning seems logical: scan the network and look for known vulnerabilities that could be exploited so that the organization has visibility into what should be fixed. Authenticated vulnerability scans, though, are a bit less obvious to some, with frequently posed questions like Why should I bypass security I already have in place? Or does it really matter if there is a vulnerability where I have security mitigations like multifactor authentication in front of my application? It's important though to separate the concept of authenticated vulnerability scanning from penetration testing. For the latter, allowing access through authentication controls would defeat the purpose, but the goal of authenticated vulnerability scanning is to gain better visibility into an organization's current level of risk. Authenticated vulnerability scanning is just another layer of a defense-in-depth strategy that allows a closer look at the vulnerabilities in an application that may otherwise be protected only by a username and password. Most security professionals would agree that relying only upon a username and password would be unwise, which highlights why authenticated vulnerability scanning must be a part of any Zero Trust strategy.

These authenticated scans remove the blind spot and provide insight into the true level of risk of an application or system. Once an attacker has made it onto a system, even if the account compromised has minimal privileges, other exploits may easily allow for additional actions to be taken utilizing the initial target as a jump point. Common exploits include privilege escalation or the ability to gain further visibility to other assets for pivot opportunities to spread deeper into the network, or to more critical systems. By implementing authenticated scans, these vulnerabilities can be more easily identified, and fixes or mitigations can be assessed to ensure that the risk to the organization is both understood and minimized or eliminated, if possible.

Systems such as multifactor authentication or passwordless authentications that rely upon hardware security keys can make the implementation of authenticated scans more difficult. It is important to thoroughly evaluate the scanning tools to be used to ensure that they are successfully navigating these hurdles and performing full authenticated scans against the potential targets. Some scanners may report a successful scan, dependent on configuration, even if part of the authentication fails or the entire scanning session does not maintain authentication. It is therefore imperative that the scanning platform is accurately assessed and that threat feeds are updated and regularly reviewed to ensure that configurations meet the vendor best practices and are providing the visibility expected by the organization. In certain cases, it may be appropriate to leverage multiple scanning platforms or related tool sets, such as endpoint protection systems, dependent on network and application architecture.

Unauthenticated vulnerability scanning essentially provides a "public" view of potential vulnerabilities that may exist on the scanned system. This view represents what a malicious attacker would have access to without user credentials. These scans typically discover fewer vulnerabilities because they don't have access to user-level services.

Database Change

Acting as critical repositories of data regularly accessed by both employees and customers, databases are some of the most important knowledge repositories of an organization and may be commonly referred to as the "crown jewels" of the organization. The content of these databases can vary greatly, such as internal employee data for HR teams, product designs, customer data generated from an ERP system, company financials collected for accounting and executive teams, and system audit logs utilized by IT teams.

The scope and breadth of these databases means that many tend to be both very large in size and numerous in count for most organizations. Both their criticality to the smooth functioning of an organization, as well as their size and scope, can make them enticing targets for an attacker and are critical for organizations to ensure the integrity and confidentiality of the data stored. Data integrity and confidentiality are critical for ensuring that business decisions are made from sound data sources. By controlling risk and unauthorized access surrounding databases, the organization is protected from fines being applied by regulating bodies. Database change monitoring is therefore a critical component of Zero Trust to ensure that data is reliable and available when needed.

A Zero Trust strategy must incorporate robust monitoring of database systems to monitor for unexpected changes to any database, whether it be malicious or inadvertent to identify threats both due to a targeted attack as well as misconfigurations or other user errors that might introduce problems into the database or its operation. These monitoring systems must be able to quickly detect the changes in behavior and help to take action to ensure that any impact to the organization is minimized as much as possible. Monitoring database changes can also help to act as a check and balance for other security controls, such as monitoring for the source IP address of an administrator accessing the database and alert if that connection attempt does not take place from a jump box authorized for such a connection.

The selected database change monitoring tool must be able to correlate across multiple databases regardless of their type or location, providing alerts based on the actual usage patterns of the organization to their data rather than the individual database itself. It must also provide an appropriate reporting mechanism that can direct alerts into the organization's chosen ticketing system when human intervention is necessary to further analyze or respond to a detected event. Some systems may also provide other features such as data insights regarding volume and context of data within each database, which can assist with audit scoping. Other features may also include the ability to classify the data stored based on regulatory labels, policies, and vulnerability notifications for the database software itself. Database change solutions may integrate with privileged identity systems to control access end to end with controls applied to specific database fields.

Enforcement

Enforcement is the ability of an organization to implement Policy & Governance rules using solutions, methods, and attributes to restrict and control access to objects within the organization. The ability to enforce policy is a key result of Zero Trust. Building on the Security Capabilities of Zero Trust covered in this chapter, the Enforcement pillar builds controls over the concepts described in Policy & Governance, Vulnerability Management, Identity, and Analytics.

Cloud Access Security Broker (CASB)

A Cloud Access Security Broker typically sits between a specific network and a public cloud provider and promotes the use of an access gateway. These gateways provide information about how the cloud service might be used, and also govern access as an enforcement point. CASBs attempt to provide access control through familiar or traditional enterprise security approaches.

Further, CASBs are typically offered in an X-as-a-Service model at the front door to a cloud presence. This capability allows movements of workloads into a cloud-hosted model while helping to track and manage entity behavior. CASBs can also help to monitor what data flows in through the network-to-network interconnection (NNI). One example of this enforcement control is to allow only encrypted traffic into specific zones.

A CASB can also be useful in dealing with "shadow IT." Due to the ease of setting up a tenant or subscription on a cloud provider, many business units may decide to bypass normal IT processes to obtain cloud-based services on their own, leaving IT with a massive blind spot. CASBs can help by monitoring traffic between an organization's network and cloud service providers to bring these out-of-standard groups into focus and allowing for IT to remediate. This same visibility also allows for some reporting capabilities on the usage patterns of cloud systems by the organization.

Distributed Denial of Service (DDOS)

A denial of service (DoS) or distributed denial of service (DDoS) is a cyber attack that is used to attack an organization by denying access to critical resources. This kind of attack may negatively impact customers, employees, businesses, or third parties given the scope. DoS attacks can originate from anywhere. These attack vectors represent the inability for a targeted system to be used the way in which it was intended.

For networks, intended use relies on a working control plane and a working data plane. The interruption of either could impede the system from working as expected or designed. Most systems that attempt to offer any sort of protection in this area are based on the ability to realize an attack via a signature, which defines the patterns observed in another organization. If the organization is the first to observe the attack "in the wild," then the organization needs solutions to help redirect the traffic to minimize impact via a "sandbox" or other attack response process.

When multiple systems are networked together toward a target, this is known as distributed denial of service (DDoS). The primary difference between a DoS and DDoS is that the organization being targeted may be attacked from many locations at one time. Typically, DDoS attacks are more difficult to mitigate or remediate when compared to single-source DoS attacks.

Data Loss Prevention (DLP)

Data loss prevention is an enforcement point that controls and prevents the loss, misuse, or ability to access data or the intellectual property of an organization. Data is the "crown jewels" of the organization and must be protected using many capabilities and controls.

DLP programs control information creation, movement, storage, backup, and destruction. When the organization maintains inventories of data at rest, having visibility of where this data goes and where the data is allowed to go must be monitored. This data movement implies visibility over networks, static devices, mobile devices, and removable media. Also, DLP programs control what and how data will be retained or destroyed. Strategies for DLP should be developed and approved before technology solutions are employed to control the data.

Domain Name System Security (DNSSEC)

Domain Name Systems (DNS) represent how humans or machines interact with one another. DNS translates domain names to IP addresses so Internet resources can be used. DNSSEC is a protocol extension to DNS that authenticates and/or inspects DNS traffic to maintain policy or protect systems from accessing resources they should not be allowed to access. A DNSSEC system can also be used to protect attackers from manipulating or poisoning responses to DNS requests.

Email Security

Email security represents the ability of an organization to protect users from receiving malicious emails or preventing attackers from gaining access to critical data stores or conducting attacks (for example, ransomware attacks.) Email security typically complements any ability to prevent data loss by monitoring outbound email.

Email is a common threat vector that enables attackers to communicate to end users who may not have security threat awareness practices at the top of their minds. It is important to remove malicious emails using security solutions prior to an end user interacting with the email to reduce risk to the organization.

Firewall

A firewall is a network security device that monitors incoming and outgoing boundary network data traffic and decides whether to allow or block specific traffic based on a predefined set of security rules. The general purpose of a firewall is to establish a barrier between computer networks with distinct levels of trust. The most common use of a firewall is to protect a company's internal trusted networks from the untrusted Internet. Firewalls can be implemented in a hardware-, virtual-, or software-based form factor. The four types of firewalls are as follows:

- **Packet Filtering:** Packet filtering firewalls are the most common type of firewalls. They will inspect a data packet's source and destination IP addresses to see if they match predefined permitted security rules to determine if the packet should be able to enter the targeted network. Packet filtering firewalls can be further subdivided into two classes: stateless and stateful. Stateless firewalls inspect data packets without regard to what packets came before it; therefore, they do not evaluate packets based on context. Stateful firewalls remember information of previous packets and can then make operations more reliable and secure, with faster permit or deny decisions.

- **Next Generation:** Next-generation firewalls (NGFWs) can combine traditional packet filtering with other advanced cybersecurity functions including encrypted packet inspection, antivirus signature identification, and intrusion prevention. These additional security functions are accomplished primarily through what is referred to as deep packet inspection (DPI). DPI allows a firewall to look deeper into a packet beyond source and designation information. The firewall can inspect the actual payload data within the packets, and packets can be further categorized and stopped if malicious data is identified.

- **Network Address Translation:** Network Address Translation (NAT) firewalls map a packet's IP address to another IP address by changing the packet header while in transit via the firewall. Firewalls can then allow multiple devices with distinct IP addresses to connect to the Internet utilizing a single IP address. The advantage of using NAT is that it allows a company's internal IP addresses to be obscured to the outside world. While a firewall can be dedicated to the purpose of NAT, this function is typically included in most other types of firewalls.

- **Stateful Multilayer Inspection:** Stateful multilayer inspection (SMLI) firewalls utilize deep packet inspection (DPI) to then examine all seven layers of the Open Systems Interconnection (OSI) model. This functionality allows an SMLI firewall to compare a given packet to known states of trusted packets and their trusted sources.

Intrusion Prevention System (IPS)

An intrusion prevention system is a hardware- or software-based security system that can continuously monitor a network for malicious or unauthorized activity. If such an activity is identified, the system can take automated actions, which can include reporting to administrators, dropping the associated packets, blocking traffic from the source, or resetting the transmission connection. An IPS is considered more advanced than an intrusion detection system (IDS), which can also monitor but can only alert administrators.

An IPS is utilized by placing the system in-line for the purpose of enabling inspection of data packets in real time as they traverse between sources and destinations across a network. An IPS can inspect traffic based on one of three methods:

- **Signature-based:** The signature-based inspection method focuses on matching data traffic activity to well-known threats (signatures). This method works well against known threats but is not able to identify new threats.

- **Anomaly-based:** Anomaly-based inspection searches for abnormal traffic behavior by comparing network activity against approved baseline behavior. This method typically works well against advanced threats (sometimes referred to as zero-day threats).

- **Policy-based:** Policy-based inspection monitors traffic against predefined security policies. Violations of these policies result in blocked connections. This method requires detailed administrator setup to define and configure the required security policies.

These IPS inspection methods are then utilized in single or layered combination methods on one of the system's platforms:

- **Network Intrusion Prevention System (NIPS):** A NIPS is used in the previously mentioned in-line real-time method and is installed strategically to monitor traffic for threats.

- **Host Intrusion Prevention Systems (HIPS):** A HIPS is installed on an object, which can typically include endpoints and workloads. Inspection of inbound and outbound traffic is limited to this single object.

- **Network Behavior Analysis (NBA):** An NBA system is also installed strategically on a network and inspects data traffic to identify anomalous traffic (such as DDoS attacks).

- **Wireless Intrusion Prevention System (WIPS):** A WIPS primarily functions the same as a NIPS except that it is specialized to work on Wi-Fi networks. The WIPS can also identify malicious activities directed exclusively on Wi-Fi networks.

IPS security technology is an important part of a Zero Trust Architecture. It is through IPS capabilities and by automating quick threat response tactics that most serious security attacks are prevented. While an IPS can be a dedicated network security system, these IPS functions can also be incorporated in firewalls such as the NGFW and SMLI systems.

Proxy

A proxy acts as an obfuscation and control intermediary between end users and objects to protect organizational data from misuse, attack, or loss.

Proxies are deployed in several circumstances, but for most organizations, there are two primary use cases. One is a proxy to the Internet, where the proxy is placed in-line between the corporate user community and the Internet. These proxy services are often combined with other control capabilities to provide secure web gateway, email security, DLP and other outbound traffic, to the Internet traffic controls. This set of controls can be located on-premises or could be cloud-based. Policy enforcement controls can then be employed on all outbound Internet traffic. Policy enforcement through a proxy can then impact which sites and services can be accessed, whether files can be transferred, what user identity attribution can be gleaned, or which network path is taken, to name a few.

The second common use case is a reverse proxy, where control is placed in front of offered services (that is, intranet and/or Internet) where the proxy acts as an intermediary between application front-end services and the user community. Reverse proxy services often supply load balancing, encryption off-loading from application front ends, performance-related caching, and AAA of sessions and users.

With the current evolution of general network architectures, where users and services can be located anywhere, the function and location of a proxy have an important role in a Zero Trust Architecture. Corporate users cross a boundary to communicate with Internet-based cloud and SaaS services on a routine basis. Internet-based users cross a boundary to access private cloud and corporate data center services. These boundaries are not only key policy enforcement points, but they are also opportunities to derive attribution from endpoints, users, and workloads. This attribution can be used to determine the current posture of the objects involved in the connection request.

Virtual Private Network (VPN)

A virtual private network is a method to create an encrypted connection between trusted objects across the Internet or untrusted networks and is an important method to be leveraged in Zero Trust Architecture designs. VPNs take many forms, from carrier-provided Multiprotocol Label Switching (MPLS) services to individual user-focused remote access (RA) VPNs.

If we look at this solution from a security controls perspective, VPNs can provide general traffic isolation and routing controls, which reduce the attack surface through broad control over where network packets can be forwarded. Remote access VPNs may also help organizations categorize use cases and policy definitions that may exist to identify users, endpoints, and functional groups.

If an organization were to make a full accounting of its various VPN deployments, it would document organizational constructs such as how MPLS VPN and Virtual Routing and Forwarding (VRF) may be deployed to isolate traffic across business units, divisions, or subsidiaries. It also would account for vendor, partner, and customer access mechanisms along with service and application access requirements.

Security Orchestration, Automation, and Response (SOAR)

Security orchestration, automation, and response or SOAR is set of solutions that enables an organization to visualize, monitor, and respond to security events. A SOAR is not a single tool, product, or function. The intention of a SOAR is to automate routine, repeatable, and time-consuming security-related tasks. The SOAR ties disparate systems together to provide a more complete picture of security events across multiple security platforms. A SOAR is used to improve an organization's ability to identify and react to security events.

From a Zero Trust perspective, these capabilities can also be used to enable, update, and monitor Zero Trust policies across the entire security ecosystem. For example, orchestration capabilities utilized to tie vulnerability management systems with network access controls could allow for policy adjustments to be made based on discovered endpoint vulnerabilities where connecting devices with known vulnerabilities are no longer allowed to connect to the network until remediation occurs. Also, automation could be used to provide unattended remediation services to devices that have been flagged as untrustworthy.

File Integrity Monitor (FIM)

As an enforcement control applied to a Zero Trust architecture, a file integrity monitor provides the ability to detect potentially nefarious changes made to the files or file systems supporting services and applications. FIM capabilities are typically applied to server platforms but can be deployed across any platform with an accessible file system. File change detection and alerting could be used in a Zero Trust Architecture to affect the trust status of a system that has experienced recent changes. Zero Trust policy may direct sessions to be limited and/or restricted completely to or from systems where unexpected file changes have occurred.

To realize Zero Trust capabilities from this control, organizations must expend effort in setting baselines for known and expected behaviors. Administrators will then need to define which categorizations of file changes will trigger actions to isolate systems where change has been detected. Change detection policy and change detection alerting must then be translated into response plans and actions. This activity could be arduous and time-consuming but will result in less effort expended chasing false positives. Tying the FIM capabilities into a SOAR architecture can then result in automated isolation and remediation for impacted workloads.

Segmentation

Segmentation is the art of identifying and classifying sets of services, applications, end-points, users, or functional classifications and isolating them from other sets of systems. This isolation is typically accomplished through various techniques that focus on network traffic controls. These sets of controls will vary depending on where they are applied and the classification of the assets being segmented. For example, isolating a corporate intranet from the Internet will require significantly more capabilities due to the scope and scale of business services that need to traverse this boundary. In contrast, isolating building management systems attached to the corporate network from general-purpose corporate workstations would be a "deny any" rule, assuming one can clearly identify building management systems and corporate workstations. The foundational process for identification and classification of corporate assets is essential to creating a Zero Trust Architecture, where defining segments or enclaves is used to establish trusts to other enclaves and sets of controls employed to protect sets of assets within an enclave.

Analytics Pillar

The Analytics group of Zero Trust Capabilities is an extremely important aspect of the Zero Trust deployment process. The need for analytics, like the ongoing need to continue to look for and gain more insight into anything identity based, is constant and ever evolving, with a need to sort through a massive amount of data sometimes likened to "noise" to find the data that indicates what is happening within the ecosystem.

Analytics comes in many forms and can be anything from the analytics associated with changes made to the network that may attempt to overcome the Zero Trust implementation, including tracking users and their actions on the network throughout their time both on and remotely connected to the network. Analytics about what threats are found within the network that provide more insight into how to detect these threats, and, of course how these threats were blocked will all come into play and will help overcome any reluctance that management, business units, operational staff, or administration staff have when it comes to the implementation.

Application Performance Monitoring (APM)

Application performance monitoring is the process of establishing data points on the performance of an application by observing the behavior from user interactions as well as via synthetic testing. These data points can be used to establish a baseline that can then be used to understand when the application is deviating from that baseline and requires investigation.

The data points collected can include CPU usage, error rates, response times or latency, how many instances of an application are running, request rates, user experience, and more. This data can also be utilized to ensure that an application is meeting a specified level of performance or availability as part of a service-level agreement (SLA). A well-rounded APM should be able to monitor not only down to the application code level but also across the infrastructure supporting the application to ensure a complete picture of the health and performance of an application. This means the APM solution setup process will need to include stakeholder decision-making on how to implement monitoring and tuning of the solution for optimal effect in each unique environment.

APM is a necessity for Zero Trust Architectures because users may access an application from various locations using disparate devices that may or may not be managed by the organization. When a user experiences a problem with an application, it is imperative that the operations and engineering teams can quickly understand whether the issue is related to the application itself or if there are factors beyond the organization's control. This data is important to ensure that an unhealthy application is restored to a healthy state or, if outside factors are causing the issue, that the users are informed so they can adjust as necessary to improve their experience. As mentioned, APM can also provide a way to track application performance against a service-level agreement, so Software-as-a-Service offerings can be monitored to ensure that the organization is receiving the level of service they have agreed to with the vendor.

Finally, APM provides the ability to utilize synthetic tests, which are tests that the APM runs to simulate normal user behavior but in a repeatable fashion. These tests can be useful in periods of low user utilization or after a change to an application or its supporting systems to function as a check and balance. The output of these tests may help an organization quickly ascertain whether the changes made have had a meaningful negative impact to an application and allow for quicker resolution. Due to their repeatability by isolating as many variables as possible, synthetic tests run at regular intervals may also be able to highlight minor deviations that, if left unchecked, can turn into user-impacting issues. This enables the organization to proactively address the issue and keep the application in a healthy state to improve user satisfaction and improve organization efficiency.

Auditing, Logging, and Monitoring

Audit, logging, and monitoring are an ongoing process that takes in the identity and vulnerability assessment of an endpoint and attempts to link or align this assessment with what the user or device is doing on the network throughout its life cycle on the network. The challenge of logging and monitoring is the sheer number of devices and users who access the network on a regular basis, and the need to crunch vast amounts of data to validate and archive what users and devices are doing. In addition to the need for users to administer network devices through command issuance, upgrade, periodic reboot, and similar actions, the organization also must track the behaviors of users and devices as they then connect through the network access devices and the potential responses that are sent back to the actions taken by these devices.

The phrase "signal within the noise" has been used throughout this book without much detail on what that signal is that should be looked for and sorted through. After the identity of a user or device has been determined, the identity's expected behavior is mapped out, actions are taken to determine the potential vulnerabilities that exist within that identity, and enforcement is applied to attempt to prevent that identity from communicating with resources that it is not meant to do so. What could arguably be considered the most ongoing labor-intensive aspect of the equation is now required. This aspect is the need to monitor the behavior of that user or device while validating that this behavior is expected and aligns with security policy.

Change Detection

Change detection is when change occurs within the ecosystem, and that change is detected. Many times, this is not the case because there may be gaps in change detection tools within the organization. Working to close those gaps, even across Shadow IT environments, enables an organization to improve Zero Trust capabilities.

Change detection is just as it sounds. Changes happen. Organizations need to know what was changed, how it was changed, who authorized and/or did the change, where the change was made, and when it was changed. The organization needs to know all changes that occur, for research, response, or regulatory requirements.

For change detection in Zero Trust, if a change is made that violates policies, we want to be able to identify whether automatic alerts will be generated and sent to SOC, NOC, or appropriate personnel, including all of the what, how, who, and when information. Change detection can be very challenging; changes typically occur constantly in IT environments. Changes can include software updates or patches that are frequently applied. Configurations are frequently updated or newly created to support changes. The following types of solutions identify changes or detect unauthorized changes:

- File Integrity Monitoring Solutions
- Syslog
- Messaging
- Privilege access solutions
- SIEM

Network Threat Behavior Analytics

Behavior analytics enables the method of Zero Trust that is to be able to define what traffic is expected in the environment or what traffic is out of norms in the environment. As a part of monitoring, organizations need to focus on not just what they are able to pull into a file that contains activity; organizations also need to analyze that information to make it actionable. When we say "make it actionable," it is important to understand that organizations need to be able to see what traffic is doing in the organization's environment whether in the data center or in the cloud. This is where network threat behavior analytics comes into a Zero Trust strategy.

Informing network behavior analytics with threat information and intelligence is critical to create greater understanding of the traffic in the environment, with current threats that are changing every day, every hour, and every minute. Network threat behavior analytics solutions are only as good as how they have been tuned for the organization.

Most organizations have enormous amounts of data transferring to and from data centers and externally to third parties. It is important for organizations to monitor this activity and define whether it is normal or if the activity is out of the norm. By implementing automation to sort through the alert information, organizations can use their teams to look at what is shown in the anomalies and what are the exceptions. By sorting out the "noise" and by extracting pertinent information, teams are able to respond with solutions to the most important events as they occur, instead of SOC or NOC personnel getting lost in the avalanche of information being collected when trying to track down relevant information.

One of the key takeaways is that organizations must be able to look at their information flow and define what has been compromised or is in a nominal state. This must be done in a structured way due to the level of traffic involved in the environment. Monitoring of network threat behavior analytics is a regular function that must be maintained and updated. It is not a "set it and forget it" set of solutions. For organizations, it is a very important part of any security operations center or any network operations center. The data must be analyzed in many ways. Next, we look at a few key concepts to analyze the data flow.

A common term in network threat behavior analytics is *lateral movement,* or *east-west movement.* When we talk about lateral movement, we must think about what normal traffic is between applications, databases, and endpoints and what is abnormal behavior.

- Does this traffic go to an unknown repository inside the environment or ecosystem?

- Are there communications between servers that should not talk to one another?

- Is database traffic being transferred into a file for exfiltration?

- Is there some kind of nefarious activity going from or to various objects on an intermittent basis or at a high frequency?

- Do communications originate from a compromised endpoint?

Rules should be established in these tool sets to alert key resources to unexpected behavior in the environment. Another form of network threat behavior analytics modeling is looking at *north-south movement,* or *vertical movement,* which is traffic coming into or going out of the organization. Organizations need to ask questions like these:

- Is data moving using standard methods, or are there command and control communications between malware and known threat actors in the world?

- Are there geographic tendencies of the data going to places where the organization is not doing business?

- Are there organizations that should not be receiving information from them?

- Why is data moving out of the organization in large volumes?

- What destinations are receiving traffic from the organizations? Valid or invalid?

These are valid questions to review and monitor, to establish rule sets that conform to the organization's best practices. Organizations should define what actions should be taken when they see abnormal traffic performing outside of the baseline. When looking at this traffic, many times we see a combination of east-west traffic with periodic north-south traffic, to a command and control (C2) host outside of the organization.

In addition to network behavior, the same analytical process can be used by other tools for applications or cloud data. These tools will ingest data available to them using sources such as logs, API data, and other telemetry feeds to define a baseline for user or entity behaviors. As with network behavior analytics, other behavior analytic platforms will likely require a degree of tuning to help adapt the system to each particular organization. An example might be accounting systems that experience increased utilization for reporting during quarter or year-end financial events, where the number and frequency of user visits will increase as data is compiled to support financial reporting requirements. The output from application or cloud behavior analysis tools is similar to those supporting the network, in that they enable security personnel to more rapidly identify variances in access frequency or duration that may require further investigation. An attacker in the network may not be actively exfiltrating data or operating in a way to trigger the network behavior analysis tools but, if actively focusing on high-value systems, could still be discovered by other behavioral analysis platforms. Thus, ensuring that behavioral analysis beyond the network is also addressed helps to alleviate blind spots and prevents a false sense of security.

Security Information and Event Management (SIEM)

A Security Information and Event Management solution enables an organization to ingest enormous amounts of log and audit data from multiple systems and process this information into actionable data on security threats for response.

To have manual review of this data would be both ineffective, and potentially, even counterproductive. Therefore, a well-tuned and maintained SIEM is key to ensuring that the right information is presented in such a manner to be actionable in a Zero Trust Architecture.

A robust SIEM should be able to capture all desired events that are sent from the syslog or other sources and typically requires that the SIEM be designed and implemented in a distributed manner to ensure no blind spots or data gaps exist. It should be able to classify the source of the logs that it receives to add intelligence into the analysis process, with different analysis algorithms being applied to servers as opposed to network devices. A SIEM should have the ability to tag sources of events with some sort of metadata labeling system, giving the ability to add ownership by department, user, use case, or organizational data to the event source. It should be able to sort sources of events into a classification system. It should also support secure transport so that messages sent between systems of interest and the SIEM prevent eavesdropping.

The same need for behavioral monitoring goes for the ability to analyze denials from enforcement actions, such as access control lists or authentication failures. While it may be expected that a device is prevented from accessing the network or a specific device on the network, once enforced, that attempt to access that device should be limited or halted by the source device altogether. When the attempts to access the network or device continue, a threshold should be set indicating abnormal behavior thresholds have been met, which will trigger an alert on the SOC console, which will in turn lead to investigation of the identified issue. This approach can also take into consideration the identity of the device or user attempting to access the network or a certain resource. An alert to a specialized team, such as one that supports the C-suite executive team, would then be sent and prioritized for remediation.

The SIEM should directly integrate to organizational data brokers, such as a CMDB, ticketing system, or other security event monitoring solutions. This integration can provide additional valuable information that enhances the quality of data in the SIEM. Integration may also trigger external activities to occur via ticketing systems or other monitoring systems like in a network operations center.

For example, in many identity-based network access control products, the addition of data into tables, such as local users, or the addition of invalid data into tables to attempt to undertake a SQL injection attack may not trigger a syslog. However, inquiries via the API of the user database table can detect changes and utilize intelligence built into the SIEM to monitor and alert on this invalid data injection attempt.

There is commonly confusion for some on the differences between a SIEM and other seemingly similar tools, such as extended detection and response (XDR) and security orchestration, automation, and response (SOAR) platforms. While the intent for these tools is similar in their goal to aggregate and analyze data from multiple sources, they differ in that SOAR is focused on supporting multiple security tools to coordinate their activity based on one or more inputs. An XDR, on the other hand, concentrates on utilizing collected data from endpoints, which provides a large-scale view of changes to the environment because many security events will either ingress or occur at the endpoint, making it a valuable data stream.

Threat Intelligence

Threat intelligence is information that is collected by incident responders, governments, application vendors, equipment vendors, and many other sources. This intelligence gains more usefulness when it is ingested directly and in real time into the network, security, and application solutions within the organization. The information consists of things such as indications of compromise (IOCs), Common Vulnerability and Exposures (CVEs), IPS rulesets, and other types of information surrounding new or ongoing security events.

The global threat landscape is constantly evolving and shifting. The concept of collecting threat intelligence brings a clear focus into the strategy of Zero Trust. Understanding the environment in which an organization operates—with an eye on what is trusted and what is not—is what creates and tunes threat intelligence for an organization. Relationships between different types of active threats and the associated Internet activity to malicious domains provide deeper insights into patterns of malicious actors' behavior. Keeping an eye on what is happening in the world, the country, the regulating bodies, and the news surrounding the organization can help inform the overall security standing and posture of an organization.

Partnering with key organizations that help connect an organization to its critical infrastructure community is critical. Working with fusion centers, government agencies, and public–private intelligence-sharing organizations helps you to partner with like or disparate organizations that will be important in a crisis. Setting up these relationships when times are good helps to support organizations when times are bad. In the US, organizations like InfraGard (Infragard.org) connect the community and are free to join.

Understanding the organization's risk tolerance and key goals provides "tuning" to the intelligence that needs to be collected. Key questions include

- Have there been changes to security reporting laws that impact the organization?

- Are there new requirements that the organization is required to respond to?

- Has there been a breach of a supply chain organization?

- Does the organization have a robust third-party risk program?

- Do third and fourth parties have a duty to report issues or breaches they have experienced in the contracts the organization has in place?

- In public source news, does the organization observe threats that are impacting the organization, suppliers, governments, or treaty groups?

Taking this observed information and turning it into action requires solutions and tools that keep a constant vigilance over the threat landscape. An organization must have several methods to obtain threat intelligence and digest that intelligence directly into the organization's solutions as well as to the teams and leaders of the organization. Being able to react and respond to critical situations and make correct business decisions based on the threat landscape enables companies to outperform their competition. Public sector organizations or agencies are better able to respond correctly to nation-state actors.

Most sources should be readily and automatically ingested by the processes, solutions, and services with a primary focus on the diversity of threat feeds and methods of intake in the overall solution set for the organization. Firewalls, automated segmentation solutions, anomaly detection solutions, monitoring solutions, endpoint protection solutions, and host protection solutions are examples, all of which need to have active thread feeds and the ability to alert when changes occur that affect the organization.

Traffic Visibility

Traffic visibility is the ability to view the full data activity of an organization at the time of occurrence and the ability to aggregate the traffic to be usable in the future. Many critical infrastructure organizations are required to retain traffic visibility information for extended amounts of time due to laws or regulations. This information should be aggregated into specific systems that support profiling of endpoints, security events, network events, or data analysis information.

Another requirement of traffic visibility is to ensure that there are no blind spots in the organization's span of control. If there are blind spots, there will be issues with compliance to regulation based on industry (for example, PCI, FCC, FFIEC, and many others). When there are blind spots within an organization, they will weaken the organizational posture related to Zero Trust and may even degrade the function of critical capabilities.

Traffic visibility tools are also critical components of determining and creating segmentation enforcement policy.

Asset Monitoring & Discovery

The asset management database is a set of tools that are consistently and reliably updated as assets have been purchased, retired, or, in the case of building the asset management database, currently exist in the network. For those devices that currently exist in the network, a specified amount of information should be set as a standard to be populated, to give those monitoring the analytics for potential threats or security breaches within the network a fair advantage in investigating the endpoint. Policy & Governance should define the attributes that should be collected for each asset type.

Asset management is another key area to ensure that organizations have a standardized life cycle for all assets to provide the most effective and efficient usage of those assets for their intended purpose. The intent of an asset management program is to simplify operations and reduce risk by ensuring that the entire life cycle of the assets is mapped out and approved processes are followed from prior to acquisition up to the point of decommissioning or disposal. This includes standardizing as much as possible, such as configurations that make it easier to track for unapproved changes or modifications to these assets, while also ensuring that new deployments are fit for use. A lack of proper asset management can easily lead to lost productivity as users are unable to access key resources, such as applications, resources, or data repositories. With proper asset management, an organization gains the ability to harden configurations, ensure physical and virtual maintenance is regularly performed, and validate designs, while ensuring that assets are fit for use. While for the purposes of Zero Trust, the operation and configuration of an asset are likely to be the first line of thought, asset management must extend beyond this to include the entire life cycle of an asset, including the evaluation and acquisition, design, operation, maintenance, and replacement or decommission of the asset. The final point of replacement or decommission must also be properly managed to ensure that the asset is appropriately purged of any proprietary or sensitive data to limit risk to the organization.

Summary

In this chapter, we covered the pillars of Cisco's Zero Trust Capabilities, which are Policy & Governance, Identity, Vulnerability Management, Enforcement, and Analytics.

Policy & Governance is the organization's policy and sets the groundwork for how endpoints and data are governed on the network. While this pillar should be strict enough to act as the "badge and shield" allowing for enforcement actions to be taken, it needs to strike the right balance between allowing devices to perform their business purpose on the network while maintaining least privileged access.

Identity is key to applying the policy because it determines the context in which an object and its respective business purpose on the network. Identity provides the necessary context required for solutions to provide effective security controls on the network.

Vulnerability Management evaluates this risk of compromise through the evaluation of device communications, baseline behavior, known vulnerabilities, open ports and responses, and susceptibility to malware infection.

Enforcement considers each of the pillars to prevent access to critical resources within an organization based on a policy. Enforcement employs proactive and reactive control mechanisms.

The Analytics pillar considers information found throughout the other pillars and determines whether threats are actively prevented, whether identities changed throughout their life cycle on the network, and where enforcement actions prevented access to resources that were required for the entity's business purpose. This analysis influences all other pillars to keep up with the changing landscape of Zero Trust and security threats.

References in This Chapter

- É. Vyncke, K. Chittimaneni, M. Kaeo, and E. Rey, RFC 9099, "Operational Security Considerations for IPv6 Networks," August 2021.
- Maya G. "ITIL Change Management Process," ITIL Docs, June 30, 2021, www.itil-docs.com/blogs/news/itil-change-management-process.

Chapter 3

Zero Trust Reference Architecture

Chapter Key Points:

- This chapter describes the aspects of a Zero Trust Reference Architecture and its importance as the first step of a solid Zero Trust strategy for any organization.

- We explain how to apply the reference architecture to various areas of an organization's network, because each will require adaptation based on the organization's business vertical, functional, and regulatory requirements, along with other factors.

- We also address challenges and recommended strategies for each network area, such as branch, campus, data center, and cloud for adapting to a Zero Trust Reference Architecture.

A Zero Trust Reference Architecture mapped to a high-level enclave design provides a target plan for organizing key zones of an organization's functional infrastructure and service area locations. These service area locations in the reference architecture will typically include campus, branch, core network, WAN (wide area network), and cloud. Within these service locations, data traffic flows occur to support all business applications and processes as well as the access by endpoints or other service areas.

A practical reference architecture, as seen in Figure 3-1, will present segmented enclaves based on an enterprise's application services, data accessed and processed by these services, and the endpoints and users who are supported by these applications and data. Each of the previously mentioned service area locations may have unique or common enclaves, depending on associated application services and endpoints. Development of a Zero Trust Reference Architecture, as described in Figure 3-2, enables the organization to align and understand the level of segmentation required.

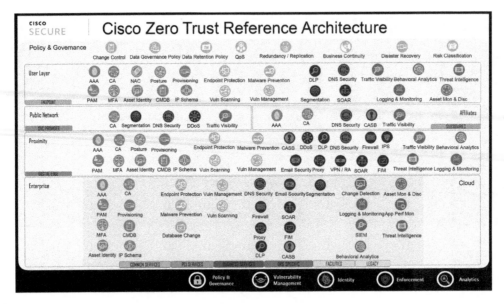

Figure 3-1 *Zero Trust Reference Architecture*

Finally, a Zero Trust Reference Architecture must include elements of protection and risk mitigation control capabilities identified in the five pillars discussed in the preceding chapter. Determination of specific capabilities to be used in enclave segmentation designs should be based on risk and impact mitigation, criticality, application functionality, and possible regulatory requirements for data that may reside or is processed within the enclave.

The following section discusses the campus, branch, core network, WAN (wide area network), and cloud service area locations' architectural scope, types of endpoints typically found within these areas, and general strategy for applying Zero Trust Capability principles.

Zero Trust Reference Architecture: Concepts Explored

Zero Trust focuses on the more granular segments of a network and endpoints that exist in those segments to both assume that a device is compromised before it connects to these networks but also that devices still need the ability to communicate in such a manner that can exclude the devices that are known to be compromised. Devices that have passed the checks related to their business function are provided as-needed access and maintain business as usual. However, the focus on preventing threats from exploiting the network never considered the potential for threats internal to the network to develop and fester in an unregulated area of the network that was focused on connectivity over security.

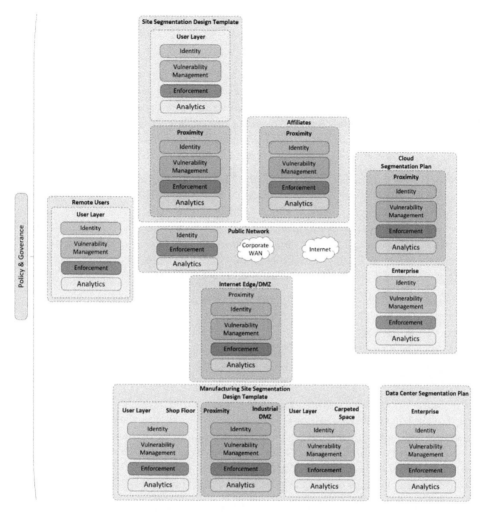

Figure 3-2 *Zero Trust Reference Architecture Overview*

Branch

The branch may be the easiest of use cases that can have policy applied to it but can also be particularly challenging. Commonly, changes of administrative regimes, acquisitions, and mergers allow for varying architectural standards to be allowed to flourish within a given organization. For organizations that have adopted a rule of using a centralized campus or data center in which all critical information is housed, the branch will typically consist of users and various types of devices with local unified communications infrastructure. Adding some complexity, unified communications infrastructure may have a backup in the form of an onsite server connected directly to the core or collapsed core area of the topology.

The branch then communicates to its policy server, typically over RADIUS, via a link back to the data center. This link back to the data center can be private, such as an MPLS connection, a public connection (e.g., Internet service provider), or a combination of multiple links by using a software-defined WAN (SD-WAN) solution and overlays that can be built over a private connection to make it more secure.

Regardless of the mechanism that branch locations communicate through, the branch consists of a minimal number and common set of endpoints from site to site. Common branch functions will typically shape commonalities between similar types, which make it much easier to apply policy to, as compared to a data center or campus network. Throughout the Zero Trust journey, organizations will have an imperative to deploy enforcement mechanisms to endpoints and collect endpoint communications for policy creation.

A branch is the perfect place to start with the Zero Trust mechanism deployment. If the branch has a relatively small number of network access devices, they can be integrated into the policy server to download policy. Combined with a traffic collection or analysis mechanism, such as NetFlow or traffic taps, both mechanisms are used to determine the impact of policy on a set number of devices. When integrating the network access devices into the policy server, it is also recommended that branches be classified in accordance with their business priority, as well as their business impact.

Throughout the identity, vulnerability management, and enforcement stages of an organization's Zero Trust journey, the organization will use the business priority and business impact to deploy policy in a minimally invasive manner. The goal for most organizations is to minimize disruption while applying policy. Utilizing lessons learned from smaller, less business-critical sites can have a significant impact while deploying to larger sites in later phases. In later chapters, more will be discussed related to this classification strategy.

One of the key challenges when conducting a branch deployment of Zero Trust principles is having consumer grade or prosumer grade network access devices, such as switches and routers. This challenge stems from the mindset of designing networks before security was of a major concern. When connecting devices to the network, the network design focus is on how packets can be put on the wire and taken off the wire in accordance with the business case of the location for which it is being designed.

Considerations for security features may not have been a focus when implementing branch networking switches. Due to the low-cost network infrastructures found in branches, organizations may find limitations related to policy enforcement, thus impeding the organization's progression toward Zero Trust.

Branches are a good place for organizations to employ effective identity controls, such as posture. Evaluating endpoint posture will typically be easier in a commonly designed area of the network like a branch, assuming that the largest representation of endpoints is end users accessing the network. The organization can run posture evaluating software, which reports that information back to the policy server to allow for determinations on the status and compliance of the endpoint before granting network access. Posture is normally accomplished with an agent on the endpoint, either as an installed agent, an ephemeral agent, or a scanning function that can audit the endpoint via operating system-provided APIs or similar extensions or hooks. The combination of Vulnerability Management, Identity, and Policy & Governance capabilities can then be used to create an access policy for user endpoints.

Application of branch enforcement core principles enables the Zero Trust policy to be deployed from location to location. After a pattern or design is created, such as that seen in Figure 3-3, policies are created, and enforcement is activated. Reuse of the same policy across branches with similar use cases is quite common. Multiple layers of defense, as a theme to Zero Trust, are crucial at a branch due to the potentially limited features supported by the branch infrastructure. Therefore, policy enforcement must be considered. The organization should ensure both management plane and data plane exploits are protected against. Unauthorized identities should be prevented from accessing network access devices and also prevented from gaining access to peer-to-peer endpoint communication. Only with this level of enforcement can a branch be truly secured given its potential impact to the overall business operations.

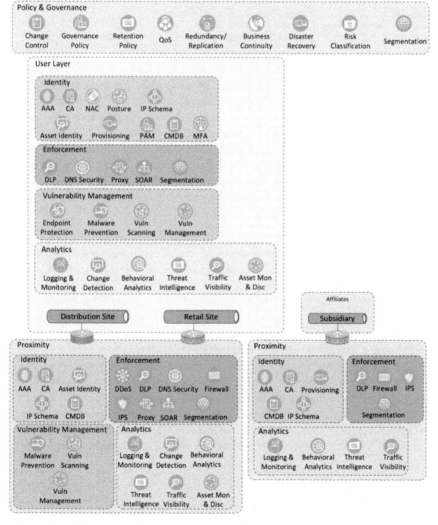

Figure 3-3 *Corporation's Branch Office Zero Trust Reference Architecture*

Campus

Some might consider the campus as the next evolution of the branch network. The campus has many of the same goals when it comes to user connectivity, but it is typically much larger with a larger variety of endpoints, and therefore threats, present on it. Whereas the branch was the starting point for many of the efforts made to move an organization from a connectivity mindset to a security mindset, the campus also can act as a potential starting point. Visibility is typically lacking on the campus and can lead to longer amounts of time to understand connected identities. Before moving to enforcement, significantly larger amounts of data need to be validated. However, the larger makeup of the campus network, larger variety of endpoints, and network design of the campus also bring with them significant advantages. A larger number of access-layer enforcement points, security appliances present, and larger numbers of unique identities can all provide significant advantages in securing the campus.

Campuses are commonly architected according to the need of the business at the time. While best practice would state that a campus should have a definitive access, distribution, and core layer, this is not always the case. In addition to having some architectural idiosyncrasies to work through, campuses often have a mini-data center contained within them that serves as the testbed for new applications and offerings. This configuration results in a need for careful planning related to exceptions to the organization's chosen connectivity model. Due to application of the standard identification mechanisms typically only being applied at the access layer, the assumption that any distribution or aggregation switches exist only in secured areas of the campus building may be incorrect. In turn, this assumption leads to many missed endpoints connected to these unsecured devices and therefore an inability to control the enforcement actions related to these endpoints.

For the campus, identification should start at the access layer, with the assumption that aggregation into the distribution layer will occur for many communications. However, unlike the branch, which commonly has small numbers of access layer devices, the considerable number of access layer devices that are communicating leads to a consideration of potential rogue devices being introduced that may be more difficult to detect manually. Policies and visibility should be robust enough to detect rogue devices being introduced and preventing their connectivity. For many campus use cases, individual users need to have a larger share of wired connectivity ports than others, creating legitimate use cases for the extended access layer to exist. Therefore, where possible, all links between switches on the campus should be authenticated and encrypted in a switch-to-switch fashion, with a technology such as MACSec. The exchange of identifying information from each of the switches within the network allows for trusted communication between them. Subsequent encryption of communications between the switches ensures that any traversal of traffic across the network can be validated and protected from unauthorized entities.

In addition to authentication between switches, campus switches should have validated cabling schemas. Functionalities such as uplinks to other switches or endpoint attachments must have defined groupings of ports. When the groupings of ports to which endpoints are commonly connected are defined, identification and authentication mechanisms can be consistently configured on endpoint ports. Uplink ports may therefore have a separate template for configuration, specifically related to peer authentication configurations. This schema can more easily indicate where devices are attached incorrectly through review and analysis of the device connectivity policy. As a cross-check, the policy server can be used to authenticate endpoints, indicating incorrectly cabled infrastructure devices connected to endpoint ports.

As visibility and connectivity within the campus are successful, the move toward identity-based controls will typically be more robust. In the branch, where the largest grouping of endpoints is PCs, agents could be deployed to the endpoint to determine the posture of the endpoints. These agents could be permanently installed on the endpoint or ephemeral in nature, being installed and uninstalled for each check done. When it comes to IoT-based devices, building management system devices, and non-PC devices in general, the agent approach is not as feasible. Varying abilities to install new software onto an already-resource-constrained endpoint need to be considered, especially for those devices that may have a lack of programming abilities outside of firmware updates. Therefore, an external service, such as an NMAP scanner or dedicated posture scanner, must be used to determine the posture of a given endpoint. This scanner needs to communicate these results to the policy engine and correlate this data to the contextual identity of the endpoint. This posture state information can then be factored in when determining the enforcement action.

The enforcement action also evolves for the campus. The campus is typically more robust than the branch but contains a larger number of endpoints and therefore threats. The campus topology typically consists of multiple VLANs, subnets, and VRFs, giving a natural control point between layer 2 (L2) data link and layer 3 (L3) routing structures. For each VLAN to communicate between each other, there needs to be an associated layer 3 routing point, typically consisting of an L3 switch, router, or firewall. While not replacing the control point that can be applied to the endpoint session, an additional control point can be used to apply subsets of enforcement actions that are static in nature. For the VLAN communication example, VLAN mapping can be undertaken to understand how devices commonly placed in each VLAN need to communicate, and the routing structure configured to allow that communication. If each VLAN has a subnet associated with it, ACLs or firewall policies can be applied between subnets belonging to those structures, while terminating through a router or firewall. VRFs needing a termination point between virtual routing instances have a similar ability to have traffic filters applied when traversing a firewall.

The campus does put a significant amount more effort and onus on the analysis core principle. A sample of this concept is shown in Figure 3-4. The larger number of devices, VLANs, subnets, and VRFs makes for a need to better understand traffic traversal between all these structures and their respective endpoints. Continual analysis will contribute to an ever-evolving policy being applied. The larger number of network access devices, however, also allows for application of the enforcement mechanism in smaller areas of the overall campus network. Traffic monitoring and identity enforcement, for example, can be done on singular switches that still have a larger variety of connected endpoints. This way, singular switches or areas of the network can be analyzed without impacting critical workloads and users. This analysis can illustrate key communications that are common across endpoints, minimizing future downtime. This breaks the campus down into smaller analysis areas, like branch analysis, and allows for lessons learned to be applied much more quickly. Small areas of analysis may also streamline operational abilities if the network topology and enforcement mechanisms can clearly identify where a group of identities commonly exists.

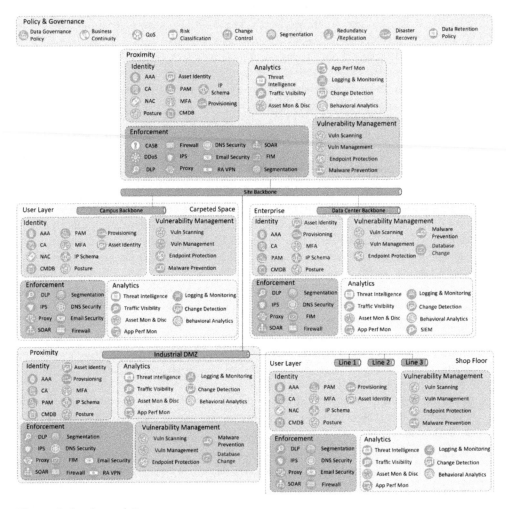

Figure 3-4   *Central Campus*

Core Network

As alluded to throughout the "Branch" and "Campus" subsections, regardless of the topology in which Zero Trust is being applied, there is an inherent reliance on the network and underlying infrastructure. Where the infrastructure is less vast and quantitatively smaller in nature, that is, a single switch or handful of switches existing in a branch, less effort may be required to secure the network. Where a lesser number of switches exists, there is a tendency for more homogeneous endpoints and network access devices to also exist. However, core principles of securing network access devices still exist and follow along with many of the same Zero Trust principles discussed here. The identity of a network access device is still critical, providing it the ability to identify itself to the policy server and any other integrations to which it is configured to send information to.

For most policy servers, this ability comes in the form of an IP address, typically a loopback or dedicated management address on the device. It is also recommended to associate the actual hostname, model, location, function, and any other metadata with the network device's identity to complete the contextual identity portion of this core principle. Some of this information may also be able to be used when applying policy, specifically relating to peer-to-peer authentication or endpoint authentication.

The network device should be configured with enforcement abilities, typically in the form of a peer-to-peer authentication. Enforcement prevents other devices from receiving information from the network device until they have completed their identity exchange. The use of infrastructure access control lists and the ability to determine where a device should be administered acts as the first line of enforcement, preventing unauthorized identities from gaining access to the network device. Controls for prevention of unauthorized identities can consist of a jump host, management network, or common subnet allocated to individuals authorized to administer the device.

The use of a device administration protocol, such as TACACS+, ensures that each command issued to the device is associated with an authenticated identity. The identity is authorized on a command-by-command basis to validate the authorization to make changes to the configuration of the network access device. Integration from both TACACS+ as well as logging capabilities of the network access device into a syslog or SIEM server can provide valuable information for actions taken on or by the device.

Traffic capture abilities via NetFlow or taps for traffic flowing over the device provide for much-needed analysis of endpoint communications, as depicted in Figure 3-5. Key to this communication is how the endpoints communicate with one another while connected to the network access device.

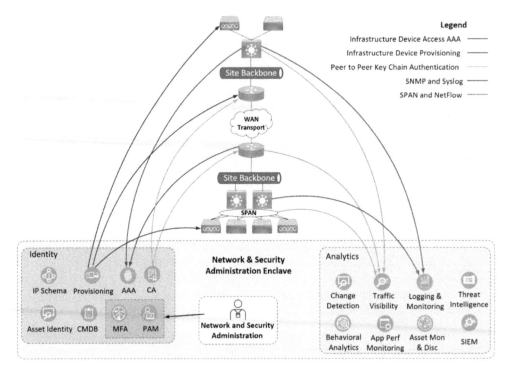

Figure 3-5 *Network Telemetry*

WAN

Unlike the branch or campus network, the WAN is a more hands-off area when it comes to Zero Trust. That said, the WAN continues to have many of the same concepts of Zero Trust as the branch and campus networks, as illustrated in Figure 3-6. This stems from the WAN being in one of two models, either network access devices that are owned by an organization and terminating circuits that are typically leased to them from a service provider, or the model of a fully owned and managed WAN by a service provider. In the case where equipment is owned by an organization, the same concepts apply as did the network:

- Identity of the network access device being synchronized with the policy application/enforcement server.

- TACACS+ being used for authentication of actions being taken on the device.

- Command-by-command authorization when actions are taken.

- Integration into a SIEM for tracking all changes made.

- As-a-service offerings from service providers or partners including web application firewalls or distributed denial of service protection may be available and more suitable than on-premises implementations.

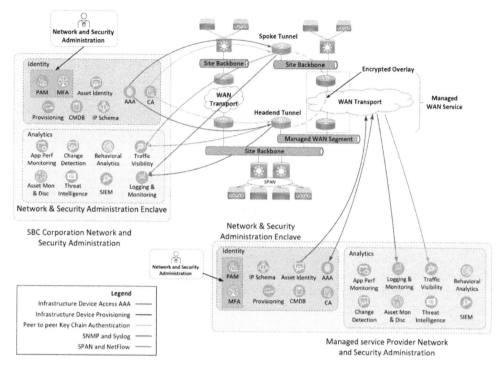

Figure 3-6 *WAN Control Points*

Where a Zero Trust application for the WAN skews from branch and campus networks, the recommendation is to utilize an overlay to protect traffic as it traverses the WAN. This is especially true when the WAN is fully managed and operated by another entity. The greatest source of concern for an organization when it comes to its WAN is the potential for a man-in-the-middle attack. Man-in-the-middle attacks on the WAN are facilitated by the flow of packets through the WAN provider's infrastructure and the owning organization having little visibility of the traversal of that data. In the same way that NetFlow and network taps were recommended for branch and campus networks, WAN providers may use the same mechanisms to understand packet flow and trouble-shoot traversal across the WAN for customer data flows. Given the likelihood of secured protocol traffic being decrypted when built into applications, having a mechanism to universally encrypt all traffic in transit is highly recommended. Utilizing an implementation of SD-WAN, such as the Cisco SD-WAN series of implementations, provides the added benefit of carrying segmentation data in the packet as well, creating a full fabric where policy can be applied.

A fabric overlay, implemented over the top of the WAN, such as Dynamic Multipoint Virtual Private Network (DMVPN), Group Encrypted Transport Virtual Private Network (GETVPN), or IPsec VPN configured in a full mesh allows for securing of traffic flow. Depending on the protocol, exposure of the sender's IP, the tunnel source's public IP, or an overlay-based IP can provide significant flexibility in what information is exposed while in a service provider's cloud. As a bonus to encrypting the links and preventing man-in-the-middle–type attacks, when utilizing segmentation tagging technologies, like Cisco TrustSec, the TrustSec tag can be written directly into the DMVPN, GETVPN, or IPsec tunnel packet, and allow for that information to traverse the WAN. Without these technologies the information from the tag may very well be stripped. This allows for policy application that occurred at one site to traverse the WAN, allowing for additional identifiable information for endpoints to become ubiquitous throughout the network.

Data Center

The data center has always been the nerve center of most organizations. It is where the "crown jewels" are typically stored, and where most of the major servers and applications that run the business and process the data critical to business success exist. Therefore, it only makes sense that a major focus needs to be put on determining what exists in the data center and how it communicates within and external to the data center, and validating that endpoints in the data center belong there. Commonly, devices will be hosted in data centers as opposed to other areas of the architecture, due to the "free" ability to power, cool, and maintain the devices away from scrutiny within smaller branches and campuses. However, there have also been numerous examples of unauthorized servers existing in data centers, hosting P2P file-sharing activity, hosting websites for nation-states, crypto mining, and other exploitative activities where data centers are not the focus of security.

While unauthorized usage should be a major concern for data centers and their operators, the potential for a seemingly innocuous and otherwise authorized endpoint to be used within the boundaries of the data center that then infects the data center through no purposeful fault of the user is an even greater concern. As mentioned in the introduction to this section, securing a data center has always been a relatively straightforward task, when it focused on threats being on the outside of the data center and needing to find a hole to get in. However, when servers exist in the data center that may not be authorized, or even when authorized may host malicious software, apps, or data, it puts an organization at as much, if not more, risk than that from external attackers.

As a prime example of this, the IRS found 1150 servers within its data center of 1811 that were unauthorized, and the threat they presented to the network was immeasurable. One reason why threats from the outside were easier to secure against is the traffic traversal nature of servers communicating to the outside world needing to communicate through a firewall. The firewall then logs at least an IP, hopefully static in nature, that can be used to track activity of the server. When it comes to internal threats posed by virtual servers, the lack of a definitive hardware enforcement point prevents an easy understanding of communications.

While unauthorized usage should be a major concern for data centers and their operators, the potential for seemingly innocuous and otherwise authorized endpoints to be used within the boundaries of the data center also poses a significant risk. As mentioned in the introduction to this section, securing a data center has always been a relatively straightforward task, when it focused on threats being on the outside of the data center and needing to find a hole to get in. However, the common nature of small, portal, fully functional operating systems that can easily be connected without significant visible scrutiny also poses a significant threat to the network. Where servers exist in the data center that may not be authorized, there is the potential to host malicious software, apps, or data, putting the organization at risk as much as, if not more than, that from external attackers.

The challenge with data centers is the mixed nature of the data center and how the continued evolution of the data center impacts what can be monitored and how. The desire to condense data centers, minimizing cooling and power costs, has caused many organizations to use various virtualization models to collapse multiple physical servers into a single physical server. A "hypervisor" or virtual management plane utilizes a single or dual physical network interface card to send traffic for all the respective virtual servers on the physical chassis. While each server may have its own IP address, the lack of ability to apply policy to a physical network port prevents granular policy from being applied. While there may be some ability for the hypervisor itself to be a centralized control point, integrations between the virtual and physical architectures still have many gaps. The inability to track communications of virtual servers within the same hypervisor, or even within the data center, limits the enforcement abilities to limit these workload-based threats. This limitation may be overcome through agents installed on the servers or with hypervisors that act like switches, with the ability to apply policy to the unique virtual machine "sessions" correlated to the virtual network interface card.

Therefore, when it comes to data center topologies related to Zero Trust, many of the same methods apply that have been referred to in this book thus far, just with the additional challenge that the virtualized nature of the data center may impact the ability to fulfill a lot of the need for discovery and enforcement. A sample of a typical data center architecture may be found in Figure 3-7. To prevent against unauthorized servers having access through the data center network, the first requirement of a machine that connects to the data center network is a clear identity that can be presented to the network and used to track activity of endpoints contained therein. The challenge in a data center related specifically to identity is that most servers will either not have a user logged in to them or will have a service account that is used to maintain the login, while individual users are given specific rights to make changes or configure the server respective to their application's needs. This means that a server may either have no specific user identity presented to the network, and therefore needs to consider other aspects of its contextual identity to continue to build the identity it uses to validate its business purpose on the network, or that the same physical or virtual server may have many identities utilizing it, and therefore present multiple identities over a short period of time. Regardless, this contextual identity needs to be aggregated and aligned with the device for analysis purposes.

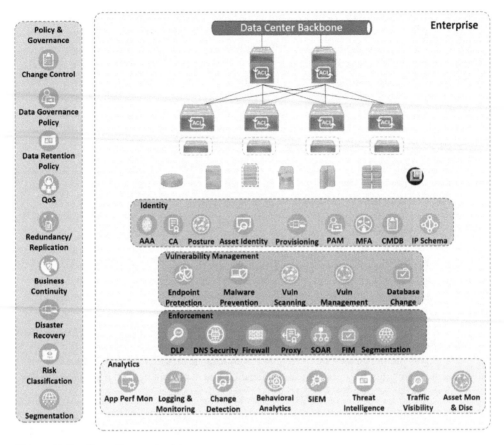

Figure 3-7   *Data Center Architecture*

The second challenge that may happen in the data center regarding endpoints relates to vulnerability management. Once a server can be accurately identified with a contextual identity, it then needs to be validated in terms of its posture and hardening status from internal attacks. While some vendors have made hardening servers a menial task with group policies that can be replicated based on identity, the validation of anti-virus, anti-spyware, or anti-X can be a challenging conversation in many environments due to the perception that running these utilities could slow the processing time of valid workloads, or worse yet, not be supported due to the age of the server. In many environments, monolithic servers and applications live on in infamy due to their massive cost to replace or rewrite the applications residing upon them. This means out-of-support operating systems that no longer have anti-X applications written for them, and for those that can be worked around to force anti-X to work on them, a lack of ability to centrally manage those applications due to their age and own support models.

In these situations, a business case may be able to be made for a longer-term success, which includes rewriting the application, or segmenting the server in such a way that duplicates with its same functionality exist and can process records should that server be compromised while not communicating with one another in such a way that would compromise the shared workload if one were infected in some way, shape, or form. A shared back-end database with read replica-type models, or copies of data synchronized in a snapshot type model, may be of use to ensure that potential compromise in this environment would not inhibit business as usual. In addition, good practices would include asset management policies that define appropriate configurations for out-of-compliance systems such as legacy servers and operating systems, which will help to mitigate risk by having rigorously reviewed hardened configurations and standards.

Once this final challenge is overcome, multiple enforcement mechanisms exist, dependent upon the type of server in question. For virtual servers, both in private data centers as well as public clouds, the use of an on-server enforcement agent or a policy-based gateway is required to apply policy due to the inability of the hypervisor to recognize dynamic policies applied to the switchport itself. This is due to the RADIUS enforcement mechanism, based on a common session ID between the network access device and RADIUS server, with a need to apply that policy to the specific virtual machine in question. This policy gateway could be in the form of another virtual machine that acts as the network access device itself, such as a virtual switch that is onboarded into the RADIUS server, or could be in the form of an aggregation point that all traffic is sent through, which applies policy to all devices. Where a centralized policy enforcement agent was not feasible to the data center design or throughput requirements, agents can be deployed to individual servers, which act as micro enforcement agents and are pushed policies for what traffic the server can send and receive.

For physical servers, the enforcement mechanism requires particular care to be demonstrated in ensuring that data center switches being used support Zero Trust-level enforcement. For many environments, vendor production of switches has focused on specific use cases, like a trading floor with micro-second or pico-second latency or a large data center with massive throughput needs with very few "bells and whistles." With any of these use cases, the addition of security mechanisms to be included in the feature set of the switch may not have been a consideration, or special configuration circumstances may exist. There can be situations when utilizing RADIUS on these servers that there may not be support for a change of authorization. Another case is when using a tagging mechanism such as TrustSec, the tag may need to be statically assigned to the port, port profile, VLAN, or subnet.

Regardless of how enforcement and policy application are done within the data center, overlay and analytics principles hold as they would with any other topology. There is a need for understanding of traffic flow, along with regulatory requirements that apply to the data that exists on the endpoint and how enforcement is applied to the endpoint, regardless of the enforcement mechanism. Logging and analytics of access attempts, in addition to the flow of traffic to and from the server and associated identities of that traffic, need to be aggregated, reviewed, and validated for any potential intrusion or threats to the network. Please find a sample Cisco ACI Fabric Policy Model used to provide Zero Trust Controls in a data center in Figure 3-8.

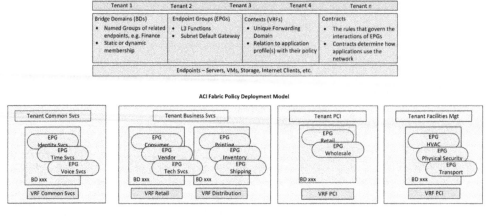

Figure 3-8   *Cisco ACI Fabric Policy Model*

Cloud

Most organizations treat the cloud as an environment that may or may not have the same level of controls, visibility, or security enforcement. A relatively new mode of hosting applications and services for users, both internal and external, on Infrastructure as a Service (IaaS), lends itself to additional security scrutiny. Inherently, this IaaS offering must be available via the public Internet for external consumers but also can be protected for internal consumers accessing hosted applications on the external service. The only difference in the consumption model will be that internal consumers will source their consumption from an on-premises subnet or location where a site-to-site type VPN can be offered. This site-to-site tunnel then terminates in the hosted cloud at some point sitting in front of the servers. Many organizations use a Network Address Translation (NAT) configuration as a security mechanism. The termination of this site-to-site VPN without the need to expose internally hosted services or subnets to the public for consumption can provide an overlay of security to the application or service in question.

Security solutions for remote or work-from-home users may also be delivered via the cloud. This concept may go by various names, such as Secure Access Service Edge (SASE) or Secure Services Edge (SSE), for limited controls meant to be combined with additional solutions to form a complete SASE solution. SASE is composed of cloud-delivered security controls, such as DNS security, anti-malware inspection, cloud-delivered firewall, intrusion detection and prevention systems, among others. The intent is to provide users with robust, enterprise-level security, even when they are remote and not connected to the enterprise network. By extending these enterprise-level controls via the cloud, organizations can choose to provide employees with greater flexibility by limiting or even eliminating the scenarios that require them to establish a user VPN connection. SASE provides the benefit of minimizing the footprint necessary for supporting these VPN connections and eliminating complexity for both engineering at scale as well as troubleshooting efforts.

The use of another service to host infrastructure does not exempt these workloads from being managed and accounted for in an asset management database. The asset management database will still need to identify the workload with contextual identity means. A governance policy must exist to define how workloads are classified, owners identified, life cycle validated, and purpose defined to ensure that the contextual identity can be used to validate access abilities. Metadata can be associated with the cloud-based workloads to ensure that they are "tagged" appropriately. The tagging process helps define any string of attributions that may be useful to operational and policy administrators, to determine who or what types of devices should have access to the server and from which locations.

An enforcement policy is possible based on the definitions of the metadata. In a cloud data center, a workload must have dynamic contextual metadata applied to enable enforcement. While static tagging is possible, as with any static configuration, it should be avoided where possible to ensure that the tag applied is most representative of the workload at a given time, which is best accomplished through dynamic means. This enforcement should have a consideration of what cloud enforcement layers of defense are supported to be applied to cloud workloads. Cloud enforcement policy should allow only required ports to be exposed to the appropriate identity consumer and should further extend the segmentation design and associated security concepts from an organization's other data centers.

Defining the current state or "baseline" of brown-field or existing cloud implementation should be a priority of organizations, prior to implementing a new segmentation architecture within the cloud environment. A configuration audit and validation of security best practices for the respective applications that reside on the cloud workload should be done. Security audits should ensure that each workload is clearly identified, and a valid security policy is applied to the workload based on communication needs of the solution. An audit of any consumer of the solution is authenticated and identified in their access, including access methods validated before being input into the workload. The audit of the cloud workload should ensure that the workload is properly configured in a secure manner. The current state in the industry is that we find that most cloud operations were not set up with a security mindset and should be understood and monitored well.

After the current state of the organization's use of a cloud service provider (CSP) environment has been "baselined," embedding the Zero Trust strategy within the cloud environment is required. Leveraging the available controls that the provider has deployed is foundational but should not be the end state or complete state, as organizations need to be able maintain visibility across the variation segments of the architecture into their centralized network operations center (NOC) and security operations center (SOC). The commonality of Zero Trust solutions deployed ensures a reduction of complexity for analysts, operators, and security incident responders. Organizations need to use policy orchestration solutions that connect to all layers of solutions and cross the boundary of each data center, segmentation solution, and cloud operation and enable the organizations to move more quickly through changes, mergers, and transformations.

Any traffic flowing to the application should be logged and analyzed through a centralization of logging and aggregation of identity events and security events to a SIEM. An audit of any changes made to the underlying virtual server should be logged and analyzed in an equivalent manner using change detection solutions like a file integrity monitoring or database monitoring solutions. Any events from these solutions should be aggregated and forwarded to the SIEM or other orchestration points. Any additional cloud defense in-depth measures would also include adding virtual appliances that can analyze and alert of potential intrusions or exploitation patterns when detected, flowing toward the servers or applications within the cloud infrastructure. See Figure 3-9 for a sample drawing.

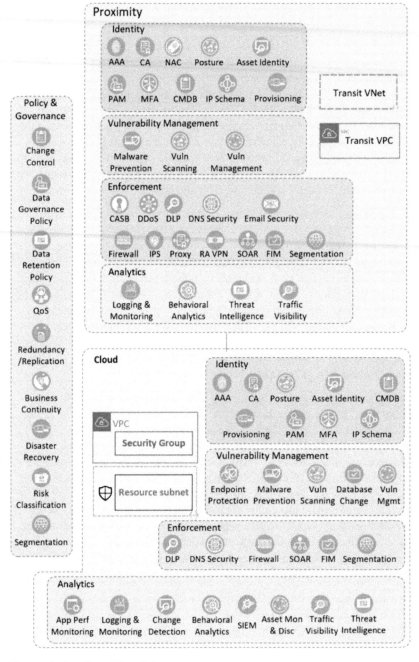

Figure 3-9   *Cloud Topology*

Summary

This chapter explored the Zero Trust Reference Architecture main service area locations. It discussed each area's Zero Trust architectural principles and presented examples in a smart building scenario. The service area locations in the reference architecture will typically include campus, branch, core network, WAN (wide area network), and cloud.

This practical reference architecture presented segmented enclaves based on an enterprise's application services, subsequent data access and process by these services, and the endpoints and users who are supported by these applications and data. Each of the previously mentioned service area locations may have unique or common enclaves, depending on associated application services and endpoints.

Finally, a Zero Trust Reference Architecture must include elements of protection and risk mitigation control capabilities identified in the five pillars discussed in the preceding chapter. Determination of specific capabilities to be used in enclave segmentation designs should be based on risk and impact mitigation, criticality, application functionality, and possible regulatory requirements for data that may reside or is processed within the enclave.

Reference in This Chapter

- Jill Aitoro, "IRS Servers Within Their Data Center Unauthorized," *Nextgov*, September 4, 2008, /www.nextgov.com/technology-news/2008/09/irs-finds-unauthorized-web-servers-connected-to-its-networks/42369/.

Chapter 4

Zero Trust Enclave Design

Chapter Key Points:

- This chapter describes the application of a Zero Trust model to an architecture between different layers of the network, including branch, campus, WAN, data center, and cloud.

- We address the unique challenges and nuances posed for each layer of the network and considerations when applying Zero Trust concepts.

- We also explain the impact of vertical industry and regulatory requirements on Zero Trust requirements, implementation specifics, and expected timelines.

The *enclaves*, as they apply to network and security architecture, come by numerous names and functions. Enclaves are commonly also referred to as *zones* or *segments*. Regardless of the terminology used, an enclave is a categorization of common functionality, common business impact, or common regulatory requirements. An enclave is used to provide common security policy to sets of assets where logical or physical grouping can be achieved. This grouping or categorization is used to define trust boundaries to other groupings or categorizations. Enclave design revolves around defining these categorizations that make common sense and business sense to an individual enterprise.

From a Zero Trust perspective, the enclave design is foundational to determining trust (what criteria need to be met for an asset to be placed in an enclave) and trustworthiness (what criteria need to be met to allow assets to communicate with other assets). As a practical matter, enclaves and trust criteria are expected to evolve as processes and technical capabilities evolve. Figure 4-1 illustrates a sample outline of various enclaves and their associated high-level logical groupings. This diagram can function as a basis for organizations to build upon and adapt to as a starting point for defining their enclaves as part of a segmentation strategy.

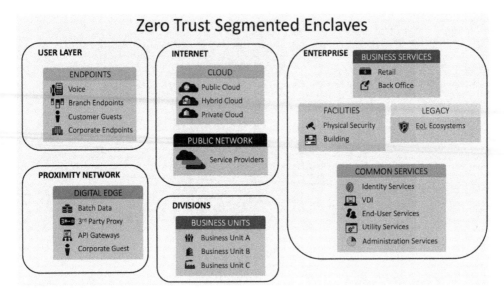

Figure 4-1 *Common Zero Trust Enclaves*

The following section presents several enclave designs as they relate to common categorizations found in most enterprises, along with unique functional or regulatory enclaves that are specific to an industry vertical or enterprise.

User Layer

In the realm of Zero Trust, authorized access starts at the network point of attachment. From a private or internal network point of view, organizations remain legally responsible for what originated from their networks. Thus, authorization and enforcement become increasingly important in a Zero Trust Architecture. Organizations need scalable ways to attribute an identity to an endpoint's session, including proving a certain user accessed the network on a certain device. Where nonuser devices exist, attribution remains just as important. It is paramount to authorize and enforce any identity accessing the network, regardless of connectivity means—remote access, wired, wireless, or otherwise.

Corporate Workstations

Corporate workstations will obviously be a key focus point for a Zero Trust Architecture. These systems tend to be some of the hardest to restrict in legacy architectures due to the wide-ranging nature of the work performed on them. Further complicating this conundrum, PCs are used for almost every role within an organization, providing for the expansive needs and capabilities of these devices. Zero Trust can help to simplify this through contextual identity. Ideally, these systems will have two separate identities that are considered, both independently and in concert, for decision-making purposes. The first of these is the identity of the device itself, referred to as the machine identity. This machine identity defines the device in respect to its unique identifier allocated to it in the provisioning process. It may also take into consideration the profile of the device, including attributes such as operating system and physical characteristics, such as a Microsoft Windows desktop or an Apple Mac laptop, but also its organizationally relevant attributes, such as its line of business or divisional use. This organizational attribute may be fixed in instances where the machine is assigned to a specific user or department. For organizations or business units that have shared PCs or kiosk PCs, this machine identity may be relevant to only certain use cases until the user is also identified. In either respect, the focus should be on the minimum required access, especially when no user is logged in to the device.

Common configurations for kiosk machines will be to limit the access of the device, using network enforcement mechanisms, to the basic requirements such as DNS, DHCP, and retrieval of certain program updates, like anti-malware definition updates or synchronization with Active Directory. It is important to consider that the minimum requirements will vary between organizations and that even these common protocols are common attack points due to their prevalence. As mentioned, these machines will need controls such as anti-malware but also an appropriate endpoint protection system to be able to track behavior and provide alerts. In combination with network visibility and behavior analysis systems, these risks that stem from having common ports and protocols open can be mitigated.

In addition to identity, it is critical to have a way to check posture of a device. The decision on what constitutes a positive posture result will vary by organization. It is also dependent on the approved configuration and build of the endpoint, as this basis will help to inform the required posture checks necessary. For example, if a configuration is standardized to utilize a particular anti-malware or extended detection and response (XDR) platform, then the posture checks would ascertain that the specified platform is installed, running, and has recent definition or update files. Commonly, a positive assessment will include checking to ensure that the security controls provisioned to the workstation, such as anti-malware and anti-spyware software, are running, and that the OS and controls on the machine are patched. These posture checks will tend to be tightly integrated with the network access control (NAC) system in use. NAC will be responsible for authenticating the workstation itself and then authorizing network access to the workstation based on the posture result and other attributes. Additional attributes that may be considered are Active Directory or other system integrations to confirm the organization's device ownership.

The second aspect of identity on these machines is the user logged in to the workstation. Combining user identity with the machine identity can provide for the ability to better control the access of data based on the contextual identity. The chosen NAC solution should incorporate the ability to combine both machine and user identity to allow for decision-making to occur based on both attributes. There are multiple ways to potentially achieve this decision-making, but common approaches include using service accounts for unmanned servers, interrogating machines for their logged-in user, and utilizing 802.1X leveraging the Extensible Authentication Protocol–Tunnel Extensible Authentication Protocol (EAP-TEAP). The decision for how to correlate user and machine data will depend on the chosen NAC solution and capabilities it provides, but the ability to do so should be a critical decision point for determining the appropriate NAC solution for a Zero Trust strategy. In the case of Cisco Identity Services Engine, the decision of which identity is provided is left up to the endpoint, while evaluation therein is able to be done on the combination of identities presented.

By combining both the user and workstation identities, a better decision can be made, such as confirming that the workstation is organizationally owned and managed and that the user is authorized for a certain level of data access. Missing either piece of this combined identity creates a blind spot that will inhibit the ability to properly vet and restrict data access in the organization.

Guests

Guest user and device access are quite common requirements for most organizations today. The requirements for how a guest can connect to the network can vary depending on the organization. For example, in the retail vertical, guest access may be seen as a convenience, but not a requirement by the users themselves. However, the amount of valuable information a retail organization might get relating to browsing, location, and shopping habits may benefit the organization's sale process. Therefore, a careful balance must be struck to ensure that the guest access barrier to entry is not too high.

In turn, a requirement such as creating a new account or requiring device registration will dissuade access. This requirement could harm business objectives that rely on the data from the guest network to better serve customers.

Alternatively, guest access in the energy vertical may be more of a benefit to the user than the organization. Especially in areas where cellular data may be limited in capacity or signal strength, user reliance on the guest network will result in an understanding of the higher barrier to entry. In these environments, approvals or extra steps may be seen as less of a burden, but rather a necessary requirement. The chosen methodology to be implemented for providing guest access must consider the environment in which guest users find themselves, the risk to the business, access the guest users might require, and the amount of time they will utilize the connection. Additionally, environmental factors should also be considered, such as whether surrounding homes or other businesses can attempt to access the guest network based on wireless signal strength. All these factors must be considered in approaching how a guest access policy is written. The organization may also need to have varying policies to manage various locations or guest user types.

Guest networks, even in legacy architectures, tend to be one of the few already-segmented pieces of a network. Guests tend to not need access to corporate resources, and these networks are primarily offered as a convenience to visitors to provide Internet access. However, guest devices may also be employee owned and/or managed. Commonly, organizations have begun offering employees access to the Internet by connecting through a guest network and authenticating with their corporate credentials. This is typically done when users have opted out of accessing enterprise resources and therefore have no need for the organization to manage their devices.

For guest users' noncorporate managed devices, both technical and legal limits prevent agent-based security solutions. Depending on the tool used for evaluating the guest device, there may be some limited ability to conduct a posture assessment on certain guest types. Typically, this ability is reserved for contractors who have written agreements with the organization or a passive means of evaluating the device.

Typical guest users are not able to interrogate their devices or determine whether they have security controls installed or enabled. Protection and visibility from the network perspective therefore become much more critical. Configuration of guest networks should be regularly audited and monitored for changes, and penetration testing through unauthorized access attempts executed upon. These attempts should include not only data access but also access and change auditing of routers, switches, firewalls, wireless controllers, and any other device passing guest traffic. Policies in place should ensure the configurations properly restrict against the ability to get to internal resources. A similar policy should be implemented for shared services if shared with guest users, such as those offered in the DMZ, such as DHCP or DNS. For many organizations, these shared services are isolated to guest usage only.

The need for visibility is also critical to ensure that attackers on a guest network are unable to move laterally among other guest devices. Similar to the need for visibility of corporate endpoints, utilizing methods such as NetFlow and network taps, these methods should be present in the guest network to evaluate access within the guest segment.

BYOD: Employee Personal Devices

Where users are willing to opt into management of their devices, it is recommended that a management platform be used to deploy a valid/trusted credential to devices, and the posture of the device be evaluated. This is typically done with an agent installed on the device that connects to a mobile device manager (MDM) periodically. This mobile device manager may be integrated with the network access control server to track contextual identity and exchange it with other integration points. This method of providing access, known as "bring your own device" (BYOD), then empowers users to access limited corporate resources on their own device in exchange for management, identity, and posture tracking, even if not owned by the organization.

IoT

The Internet of Things or IoT, is a recent but rapidly expanding class of devices on corporate networks. Though there may not be broad consensus for a formal definition of the term, a general description is any network-connected device that accesses Internet-based resources to provide data about systems or devices it is connected to or monitoring. Typically, these devices are managed, headless, and controlled via an Internet connection.

A commonly held example is a thermostat that provides the ability to control heating, ventilation, and air-conditioning (HVAC) systems and provide details on current temperature, humidity, and other environmental factors. The Internet portion, in *I* of the IoT acronym, is related to these thermostats and other devices sending this data back to a cloud service. This cloud service may be used for commands or programming made by an authorized user to alter its behavior or settings, as well as for storing data for reporting or analysis purposes, either for the user, manufacturer, or others.

The collection and storage of data within cloud services can cause unique challenges and concerns for organizations. Depending on the collection methodology and location, some IoT systems may either purposefully or inadvertently collect regulated or sensitive data. This data is then stored in the cloud but likely exists in a blind spot wherein the organization does not understand the exact scope of data collected or the protection measures applied. In some scenarios, the organization may not even be aware of these IoT devices. Take, for example, a remote user working from home providing customer support for a healthcare organization. An organization will likely provide either a dedicated workstation or virtual desktop infrastructure (VDI), as well as a voice over IP (VoIP) phone or softphone, to ensure that the data accessed on their systems is properly protected and has a sufficient audit trail. If this user is part of an insurance department interacting with patients and insurers to preauthorize claims, the user will regularly be disclosing HIPAA data over the phone as a regular and expected part of their duty. But, if this user also has smart assistant speakers, which are always listening for a trigger word, has the organization appropriately addressed this risk or even considered it? For those with experience using these devices, they quickly find they are not perfect, triggering inadvertently at inopportune times. There has also been some speculation that some assistants may collect data even when not initiated by their trigger word. This concern, if not already addressed, should be on the radar for any organization with remote workers, to ensure they have a strategy for educating their employees and mitigation strategies, such as advising that microphones be disabled or the device disconnected during working hours. Beyond this specific example, organizations should also perform auditing of existing or new IoT devices that are owned or controlled by the organization, with a focus on their physical location, proximity to areas where sensitive data may be contained or discussed, as well as the physical sensors available to the device. These details should be correlated with vendor-supplied details on when and how data is collected by these devices, where it is stored, for how long, and what cybersecurity principles are applied for data protection and disposal to define a risk rating and determine appropriate mitigations for each device.

These devices present unique challenges in that they are commonly headless, as the device itself does not have a user logged in and may not be regularly patched for vulnerabilities. In addition, they may be limited in onboard memory, error handling, and extensive functionality, as a trade-off for their small, portable size. Due to their headless nature, running agent-based controls like anti-malware or endpoint protection solutions is not normally viable. Potential lack of patching, either due to the vendor not releasing patches or the inability to centrally manage the devices in an operationally efficient manner, means that the IoT device is already at greater risk of compromise than a workstation. The upside is that these devices normally need minimal access internally, restricted to only needing to communicate with other devices in its ecosystem and externally to the Internet. As a result, network-based controls, such as segmentation and network behavior analytics, will be key components to providing protection for these devices and ensuring that their compromise can be detected and quickly resolved.

Methods to evaluate and prevent against known attacks against IoT must consider their limitations. IPS systems may be used to look for known attacks against IoT systems and prevent their ingress from the Internet. Regular vulnerability scans must be performed to understand what the level of risk is for each IoT device connected. Care should be taken with broad scanning techniques such as the utilization of Nmap due to the limited error handling and potential for causing the device to stop responding due to poor network stack implementation or programming. As with other areas, regular audits are critical to ensure that the network devices in path maintain proper segmentation and that these IoT devices, their Internet-based portals, and controls are properly configured. It is also imperative that devices be granularly profiled to ensure proper identification, such that the appropriate risk rating and mitigations can be applied. Where possible, control portals should be configured with multifactor authentication and logging to record access to data and changes of configuration.

Collaboration

Collaboration solutions can come in many forms or flavors. They must also be considered when considering a Zero Trust strategy. Examples of nontraditional collaboration endpoints, such as digital signage and audio/visual presentation equipment, are increasingly common to connect to the network. A benefit of this popularity has been the consumerization of collaboration solutions, forcing vendors to focus on ease of use. However, this ease of use also introduces potential exploits that can be used to bypass security controls. Access must therefore be governed, both to the device and for the device itself.

Collaboration solutions can be divided into managed and unmanaged. As an example, while some digital media players may only stream or receive video from a dedicated source, they may also employ the use of IP Multicast. This one-to-many way of communicating, based on subscription to a stream, creates access control challenges based on the size of the subnet to which the endpoint must always have access to. Additional challenges of data-plane encryption for sensitive content also introduce limitations of what security controls can be applied to communication sourced to or from these collaboration devices. Following are some of the common questions to consider when applying access control policies to collaboration devices:

- Who should the collaboration endpoint be accessible to? For traditional phones and video endpoints, anyone who enters the room may need access to the device to make calls. For digital signage, AV endpoints, and similar, access to the controlling node, or AV endpoint manager, should be secured to prevent unauthorized changes or access.

- Who should be able to use certain features on the endpoint? Traditional collaboration endpoints may allow for a user to log in to the endpoint and carry over personalized settings to it. With new technologies such as RFID and Bluetooth badging, users may be able to similarly authenticate and gain access to personalized information via digital signage or other collaboration devices. This capability should be restricted in the resources required to provide this service to minimize exploitation.

■ What access does the collaboration endpoint require to provide basic services? For many next-generation collaboration endpoints, local access can be set up to a file server residing in the same subnet or attached to the signage in a secure manner. Where possible, limited traversal of traffic should be preferred, ensuring that the potential for exploitation is minimized in its impact.

■ How do devices consume information for display, especially in wireless "screen-casting" type environments? Many devices receive streaming media via proprietary protocols, allowing mobile devices with integrated apps to display information. This capability is meant to minimize the footprint of the devices and allow for ease of use. However, exploitation can be a greater concern in environments where authenticated access to display the information is not required or is easily bypassed. Where capable, devices sending and receiving wireless streams should implement some sort of authentication, such as a shared secret, and validate authorization to display the information required.

■ How is the device configured or provisioned? Regardless of the strength of protections put into place to protect from unauthorized streaming, if a device can be booted into an unauthorized operating system or mode that bypasses these protections, the effort will be fruitless. Devices should be secured so that the underlying operating system or source of the video is protected from unauthorized access.

Lab and Demo

Another challenging environment to plan for Zero Trust Implementation is the lab and/or demonstration environment. Labs and demo environments are typically nonproduction networks used to test new endpoints, applications, or use cases and are inherently void of many of the same security features as production. The reason may be that these security features are being tested for impact within the lab environment itself. The nature of these environments becomes especially challenging when workloads or applications exist in a public cloud and are accessible only over an Internet connection. Based on this connectivity requirement and the change in which applications behave, some organizations have started to test workloads on their local area network before introducing them into the cloud, further blurring the lines between production and nonproduction. Regardless of location, the core principles of Zero Trust continue to apply.

Having a centralized policy and enforcement mechanism is key to ensuring a nonproduction network remains Zero Trust compliant. Limiting information flow outbound from and inbound to the environment is key to ensuring new technologies can be tested while minimizing risk to the broader organization. The ability to limit this flow comes in numerous forms but will typically be implemented as a firewall between multiple test segments within the lab environment, with each device to be tested registered with some central authority. To ease lab user experience, this registration can be akin to guest registration with a periodic registration or login portal where authentication must pass periodically. With this method, access remains rooted in a policy-based model governing resource access to conditions dictated by policy.

Proximity Networks

Proximity networks, such as the one in Figure 4-2, refer to the "Digital Edge" for most organizations. Typically, this segment is where an organization would segment API gateways, third-party proxies, externally reachable utility and administrative services, video networks, and software as a service (SaaS) platforms that have an on-premises and off-premises configuration. These services blend into the use cases served by Secure Access Service Edge (SASE) solutions, which provide for cloud-delivered security capabilities, such as firewalling, IPS/IDS, proxy, and other functions. The proxy function, being delivered in the cloud, further enhances the ability to provide protection to users accessing on-premises and SaaS resources without relying on VPN and traffic backhaul through corporate data centers.

It is protective to the overall design to have proximity network workloads and services available but not within primary enterprise segments. By separating these kinds of workloads and services, greater monitoring, tighter controls, and stronger policies can be enforced by the segmentation teams and organizational leadership.

Personal Area Network

Personal area networks and their associated technologies interact in increasingly unseen ways within an organization's existing network. Zero Trust strategies need to take these into consideration as attack vectors. PAN network communication methods usually restrict themselves to a small radius of communications. This creates a challenge for detection and remediation of these vectors. Wireless technologies including Bluetooth, IR, low-power radio, and other niche communication methods that may not be fully standardized are used between nodes within these PANs. These communications also include other forms of wired communication. These methods share a common theme of short-range, autonomous networks that may have access to sensitive network or environmental data.

Uses for these networks include file transfers, media sharing, environmental monitoring, health applications, and automation, among others. PAN technologies limit the number of devices intended to connect for a single purpose. Devices may limit the number of other devices they will pair or connect to. This limitation creates general-purpose segmentation within the use cases in these environments. However, these characteristics lead to a false sense of built-in security. One issue counter to this thought is visibility of activity and purpose. Another issue lies in the general lack of security standardization in the PAN. The general autonomy of PAN designs erodes at the perceived limits of the technologies involved. Detection and awareness of PAN implementations inside and around the organization introduce a resource-consuming effort to prevent malicious use.

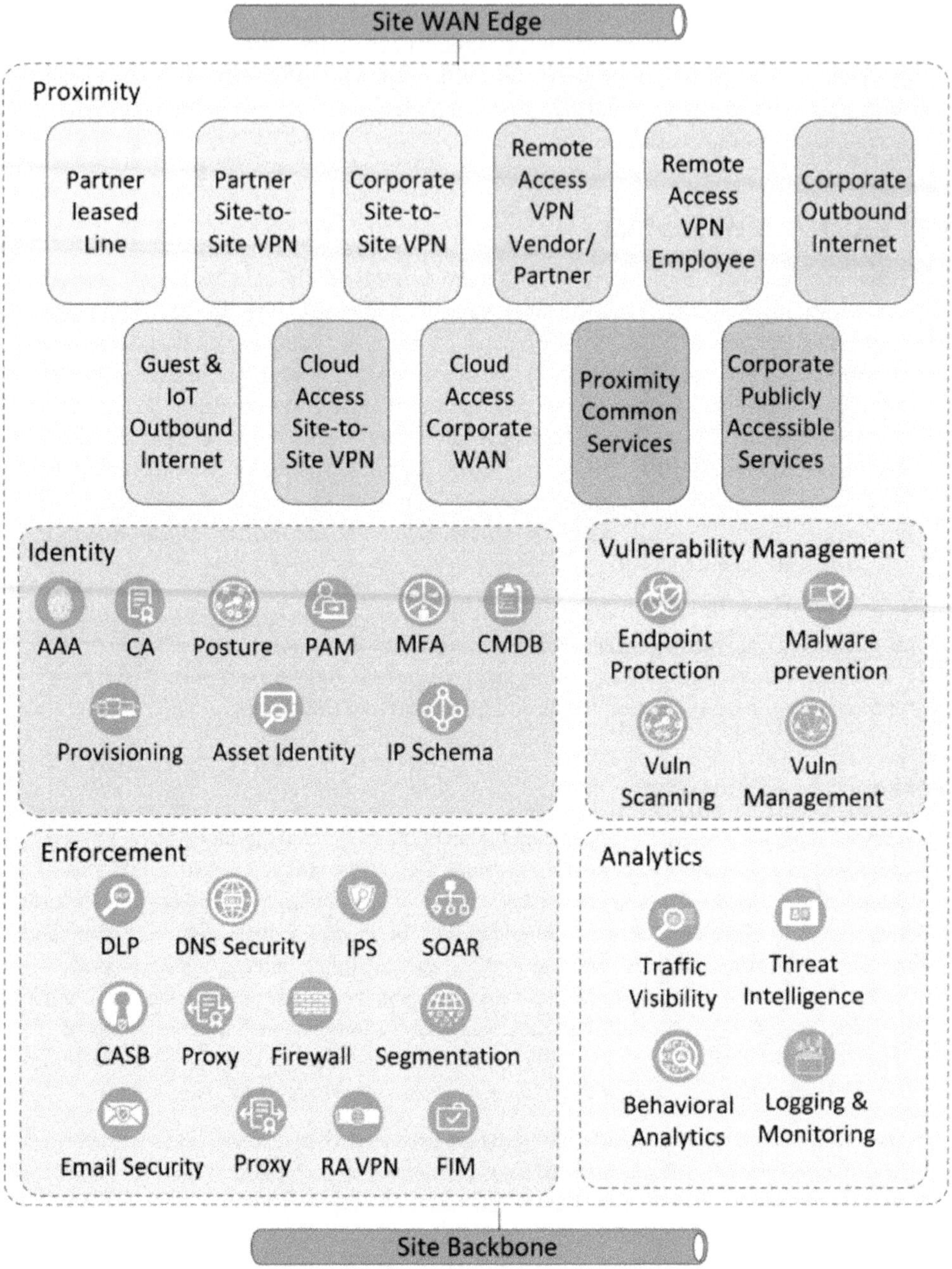

Figure 4-2   *Corporate Proximity Services*

Zero Trust assumes that any action not explicitly authorized is not trusted.
Implementations supported and controlled by the IT organization create structure and
rigor that provide the requisite context for authorization. End-user devices may have

capabilities that compromise the integrity or confidentiality of existing business systems. This situation creates a vector for unauthorized usage. PAN silently uses circumvent tools and capabilities implemented to enforce Zero Trust Architecture. Instances of organizationally controlled devices that have capabilities to connect at the PAN level also complicate the authorization of these connections. Compliance checks and machine controls introduce methods of authorizing device connections and usage. These capabilities provide tools to restrict access to mediums such as Bluetooth, USB, wireless tethering, and other PAN interfaces.

Security standards and strategies used in PAN technologies by manufacturers and users of PAN technologies lack the rigors of a Zero Trust Architecture. Bluetooth devices show a prime example of where a security feature, like requiring a PIN, provides a false sense of security. Devices may use all zeros, all nines, or widely known and published sequences that cannot be altered by the user in the name of user experience and friendliness. Devices marketed as low power omit security features or disable them to increase effectiveness. Lack of encryption of data at rest or in transit causes other concerns. Bluetooth or USB headsets approved for use in calls or even listening to music often lack the protections for filtering potential man-in-the-middle attacks used to intercept transmission.

Autonomy of the PAN creates the largest security concern to an organization trying to implement Zero Trust. PANs and technologies lend themselves to deployment strategies that circumvent security. Wireless borders extending through walls or floors provide extended attack surfaces that may not be controllable by network administrators. IoT devices complicate these scenarios, especially when they are connected to organizationally controlled resources or networks. Administrators also lack the capability of shutting down these networks when they are fully autonomous from the organizational controls available.

Administrators' and architects' use of Zero Trust strategies and policies of PAN technologies and communication methods provides the only defense to rogue networks creating risk. Defenses from these services rely on visibility of threats that exist outside of enforceable controls. Organizational policy on devices and uses of PANs also helps define what is considered allowed and what is not. Zero Trust encourages organizations to successfully converge policy, visibility, and controls prepared to identify the proper uses of technologies and networks that may threaten the security of the organization.

Cloud

The cloud is still a nascent capability that seeks to provide additional flexibility for organizations by enabling deployment options both inside and outside of the traditional data center. Commonly, organizations will have either a dedicated data center or a colocation—a reserved portion of a shared data center. In a colocation, equipment is purchased to be deployed with the purpose of running workloads and the network and security devices necessary to provide the connections to those workloads. A cloud provides a new opportunity to utilize another organization's capital to purchase not only this hardware but also the location and resources imperative to a data center to house it.

When utilized properly, the cloud enables organizations to achieve greater agility to perform actions such as standing up new workloads without costly capital expense. This use provides for greater flexibility by introducing the ability to dynamically scale up and down as workloads change, for highly variable system demand. The value of this scalability has not gone unnoticed. Cloud migrations, to varying extents, are being undertaken by organizations of all sizes as they look to leverage these capabilities to find cost savings and reallocations to run their businesses more efficiently.

Cloud computing, design, workload management, and alignment with business are massive topics well beyond the scope of this book. However, security therein, when substantial portions of a critical aspect of the network are not controlled directly by an organization, should be the focus when utilizing cloud providers. Cloud, being a relatively recent technology and increasing in its adoption, results in cloud technologies constantly being improved upon with regards to security. It's important to understand that while examples in the following sections of this book may not be valid in all scenarios, there is an intent to provide the foundational aspects that must be considered as a Zero Trust Architecture is applied to cloud resources.

Public Cloud

In a discussion of the cloud, it's important to define the key terms that describe the basics of cloud architectures. The first of these is what is commonly referred to as *public cloud*. Public cloud is the running of workloads or other services on a cloud provider platform only; it will have no connection to a private data center or other data source, in that everything for the operation of the application will be provided natively within the cloud provider platform. There are a multitude of public cloud providers, with the top three current providers being Amazon Web Services (AWS), Microsoft Azure, and Google Cloud Platform (GCP). Combined, these three providers are generally recognized as currently holding the majority share of the cloud market and will be the most familiar public cloud platforms to most professionals. Alternatives include Oracle Cloud, IBM Cloud, and VMware Public Cloud.

Within the cloud, services are offered fitting broadly within three models: Software as a Service (SaaS), Platform as a Service (PaaS), and Infrastructure as a Service (IaaS). Each model provides the demarcation of responsibilities between the cloud provider and the consumer. In the SaaS model, the cloud provider handles all aspects of the underlying infrastructure and application. With SaaS, the consumer is provided a running application that they may use without worrying about patching, storage, or other maintenance tasks. The downside to SaaS is a lack of control for when these maintenance tasks may occur; therefore, organizations may need to purchase a service-level agreement (SLA) for each SaaS application commensurate with the criticality of that application to the business's ability to function. In some instances, the SLA required may not be offered by the cloud provider; thus, the choice to utilize a SaaS solution over another cloud model or on-premises must be weighed appropriately. PaaS moves the demarcation point, where the consumer is now responsible for the application and data, while the cloud provider manages the remaining infrastructure and underlying systems such as the networking, storage, and operating system. In this model, the lack of control for patching or maintenance tasks on the application is once again transferred back to the consumer. It also enables the ability to run more customized or proprietary applications, which might not otherwise have an SaaS offering available, while also removing many of the requirements and capital expenses in comparison to an on-premises deployment. Finally, IaaS moves the demarcation again; now the consumer is responsible for the operating system and everything running on that virtualized system, including any middleware, runtime components, along with the application and data to support it. This model provides even more flexibility when requirements dictate a need for customizations to the OS or additional components such as middleware. Figure 4-3 illustrates the differences in responsibilities between the cloud models.

Data stored in a public cloud IaaS and PaaS should be assumed to be unprotected until the organization brings its security controls and processes to the platform it has chosen, most commonly through a combination of external tools with cloud native controls. Assuming that an environment is protected because it is in the "cloud" or assuming that because the applications and data have been moved to the "cloud" the environment is already segmented with a Zero Trust Strategy is a fallacy. This belief is common within organizations with vendors rushing to attempt to correct this belief.

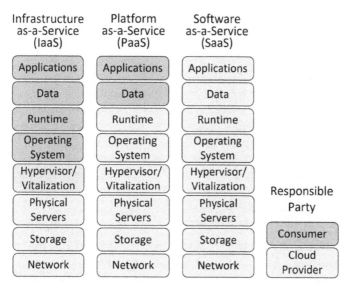

Figure 4-3 *Cloud Service Models*

The lifeblood of any organization is its data. When choosing where to house or store that data, many organizations will rely on a third party, or what many refer to as "the cloud." The term *cloud* is merely a colloquialism for someone else's data center or network of data centers. Cloud services such as identity services, file sharing, document exchange, email storage, and password storage have become increasingly popular with organizations over the last decade. Organizations should never assume that the custodian of data being housed—public cloud networks and their management in this case—will comply with organizational policies, regulations, or even laws. Organizations should carry out consistent and periodic audits of information stored in public networks, its accessibility, and controls, influenced by the type of cloud the organization chooses to use.

Private Cloud

With private cloud, this architecture focuses on providing the capabilities of the cloud from the point of automation and management systems but running these workloads using privately owned hardware within a traditional data center or colocation facility. Benefits of a private cloud platform include its ability to provide for easier scaling of workloads, faster and simpler deployment of services, and greater simplicity in providing redundancy for services. Private cloud offerings seek to provide these and other capabilities in a way that can be utilized with dedicated private hardware, which may be required by certain organizations due to regulatory factors or even organizational preference toward risk management. One of the most common examples of private cloud offerings is the open-source platform OpenStack, along with offerings from public cloud providers such as Azure Stack and AWS Outpost. Alternatives include VMware ESXi, VirtualBox, and Linux KVM.

Hybrid Cloud

For many organizations, not putting their proverbial eggs all in one basket is key. For those organizations, spreading workloads and applications among clouds in a hybrid cloud deployment is the preferred option. Hybrid cloud, as its name implies, is a combination of the other two architectures in which public cloud and private cloud are managed together. Workloads and data span both architectural offerings in collaboration via some secure traversal method. Azure offers this service through its Arc offering while Google Cloud calls its service Anthos. AWS is still building out this capability but has started to offer services such as ECS and EKS Anywhere. These systems do not necessarily provide the cloud services themselves but instead function as management and orchestration systems to allow organizations using one or more public and private cloud offerings to manage all their resources and assets within a unified system.

Hybrid cloud therefore involves having one or more public cloud platforms hosting services and one or more private cloud platforms also offering services, with a way to tie or integrate these platforms to meet organizational goals on managing services and data. Hybrid cloud introduces greater complexity due to this integration, both from a management perspective and a security perspective. Data may travel between public and private platforms, either out of necessity or inadvertently due to configuration complexity. In addition, most hybrid cloud offerings require the organization to configure a secure exchange method between the clouds and manage the secure traversal therein.

Hybrid cloud is likely to be one of the most adopted architectures for organizations that either have established data centers and owned assets or for organizations transitioning to the cloud. For most, assets and workloads that have minimal upkeep and maintenance costs continue to be utilized in concert with public cloud usage. Only once the upkeep and maintenance costs surpass the value that could be found in a public cloud do organizations migrate these workloads. Hybrid clouds assume that organizational policy and governance allows for workloads to be in a third-party hosted infrastructure.

Securing the Cloud

Public cloud platforms will offer several native tools available to provide security and visibility into the services and data on the platform. Though each platform will differ on functionality, major industry players such as Azure, AWS, and GCP will have similar capabilities. These capabilities will include controls such as identity, multifactor authentication, visibility and alerting, key and certificate management, data loss prevention, and encryption capabilities, to name a few.

Many of these native tools are helpful in adopting a Zero Trust strategy, especially for areas in which the administrator will have little to no access to underlying systems such as SaaS offerings. It is important to recognize though, especially if utilizing hybrid cloud strategy, that these tools are built to help secure data while it is primarily on the provider's platform. In some instances hybrid cloud offerings may help extend visibility or some level of security. In many cases, once data has left the platform, the security of that data will depend on other tools. Further, while the providers would make the best effort to ensure these tools are robust and dependable, it is critical that organizations do not forget a defense-in-depth strategy. Even if a native tool is working appropriately, there is no guarantee that issues with the underlying platform won't expose an organization to additional threats. There are multiple instances of security researchers exposing the ability to gain elevated privileges or access outside of the confines of a service and even starting to jump to other tenants on cloud platforms. These examples illustrate the need for additional visibility and controls to ensure that organizations understand where their data is going, who is accessing this data, and how it is being used.

No matter the architecture chosen, hybrid, public, or private, organizations must ensure they are building a robust Zero Trust Architecture that considers and mitigates the risks for each of these architectures. This goal is best accomplished by ensuring the native cloud controls match the capabilities for their control area with the capabilities defined as necessary within this book. If a gap in capability of the native control is identified, then organizations must search for an appropriate external control that is capable of filling that gap. Segmentation, visibility, and identity-based access are key factors that should be in place across all cloud architectures, but this will necessitate a combination of native tools, third-party solutions, and orchestration capabilities to ensure that access to data is tracked without gaps.

Zero Trust in the Cloud

Enforcement via segmentation is a key aspect to any Zero Trust strategy, and that does not change when considering cloud computing. Even though public cloud providers have segmentation between tenants, or stated differently, customers, there is still significant need for each organization to segment the access to the data they have stored or transiting the cloud.

Foundationally, the cloud is just a managed data center providing access to resources on demand. In this way, the thought process on data security will be as it is in an on-premises data center, which is to limit access to data as much as possible. This data access must also be controlled through contextually relevant identity data. Without knowing the identity of the data consumer, it is impossible to properly validate their right to access that data. Thus, the same identity and controls from that identity for a traditional data center or campus must be extended into the cloud. Further, this user identity must be continually evaluated to ensure that any substantial changes in context, such as access location, behavior, or granted rights, are evaluated whenever data access is requested. Finally, privileged access management must be in place to ensure that users are granted elevated permissions to cloud environments only when necessary and that this access is constantly audited to ensure compliance with governance and regulatory requirements as well as allowing for the identification of attacks or other threats.

Enterprise

As businesses perform their defined missions through engaging their customers and automating their internal processes, enterprise cybersecurity has become a critical component for success in today's world. Businesses have key imperatives to protect company data and resources from cyber threats and prevent security incidents that might interrupt business operation or disclose sensitive information. The scope of enterprise cybersecurity utilizing Zero Trust processes and technologies extends to all levels of a business's environments and includes more than just securing local systems' data and systems from common attacks. Securing business environments must include safeguarding information via additional mediums (that is, ERP service providers, wireless, and cloud).

Because security perimeters are getting harder to identify and protect, it becomes more important for a company to define and frequently review security boundaries and software environments. It is through these definitions that security zones, enclaves, and segments can be identified along with subsequently appropriate information security controls that will manage risk, support business advancement, and institutionalize these controls. Based on industry best practices and common regulatory guidance, the following are typical enterprise software and services environments.

Business Services

Enterprise business services can vary depending on a company's specific industry and subsequent applications needed to provide support and core mission services to its customers, employees, and partners. Typically, the following environments are always defined and segmented within an enterprise:

- **Development:** The development environment segment is intended to protect against malfunctioning applications and bugs. In development environments, applications and database developers deploy their code and test newly implemented services or features. Functional errors found in code or system changes are identified and remediated before re-deploying for further testing. Production and formal testing environments should be protected from this segment.

■ **Testing:** In the testing environment, developers validate application coding or systems changes and then deploy these changes to segmented testing environments. Deployment and successful results are a criterion of the continued testing. Testing developers and users will access the test servers and ensure that the application works as designs intended. Users will run use-case function and performance test plans. Test plans have been created to find applications or database functions that can be improved to provide intended results. Results from these test plans identify functional deficiencies (bugs) or additional requirements that are then used by developers to remediate issues. The development and testing processes are repeated until the code or process passes testing and quality assurance (QA) requirements. Testing environments can sometimes also serve for the purpose of nonlive user training. Finally, testing environments can be used to test vendor-supplied updates and patches.

■ **Production:** After evaluation, testing, and QA are completed and deployment of code, database updates, patching, or system changes have been thoroughly evaluated, they are then migrated to production systems for normal user and customer access.

■ **Customer and Partner Facing/Business Internal:** Production networks can often be further segmented based on purpose and source of access.

Fundamentally, business services can be broken down into two principal activity types:

■ Services obtained by outside customers or business partners.

■ Services that are undetectable and access is prohibited by unapproved users. Approved users will typically include only company internal or trusted partner employees.

DMZ

A demilitarized zone (DMZ) is a physical or logical perimeter network that segregates local area networks from untrusted networks. The DMZ can centralize internal traffic flow and simplifies monitoring and recording traffic. The DMZ provides a network segregated space for data communications to be controlled and public-facing services to be accessed separately from internal business systems. Common public-facing services include

■ **Remote access:** Systems providing authentication and authorization, VPN termination, Virtual Desktop Infrastructure (VDI) virtual machines, jump-servers, and web interface portals for gaining access to internal confidential data or systems

■ **Presentation:** Systems presenting approved controlled internal business services and data to external users

- **Utility/Gateway:** Systems providing proxy and intermediary externally based IT utility services

- **Cloud:** Services that can be managed as extensions of servers, data repositories, and networks. Fundamentally, the same requirements, principles, and mitigation should be applied to cloud systems and networks as if they were located on-premises.

Common Services

Common services are essential business operational services that are not directly related to producing products or services and are typically not accessed by customers. These services are often, in part or in whole, segmented from other business networks. Common services may include

- **Networking IT Services:** These services are crucial for the deployment of a business network. They encompass the building of network infrastructure, monitoring and response, cybersecurity, optimization and reliability, server and workstation administration, and operations support.

- **Backup and Restoration:** This service provides preservation of information by means of storage for business systems, applications, configurations, and customer and user data files. Once stored or backed up, these files can be used to restore damaged or corrupted systems or files. While this common business service is critical to reliable operations, it should be noted that these storage repositories become a sole source for all company data and could then be considered a target for threat actors. This business service is critical for business continuity and disaster recovery.

- **Mobile and Remote Networking Services:** These services support remote and mobile staff and partner access to the business's services. Systems providing access services may include authentication and authorization systems, data encryption/decryption systems, certification servers, jump services, VDIs, and thin client workstations. The systems that support these services are often targets for threat actors. Most commonly, these systems are targeted for accidental unauthorized access from misconfigurations.

- **Unified Communications and Management:** This service includes integrated software, hardware, and management for business communications platforms. Communications platforms include VoIP video conferencing, instant messaging, and email.

- **Software as a Service:** SaaS supports all software that is paid for on a subscription basis. This software is accessed over the Internet, and the ability to download and run it on the business's physical workstations is often optional. A typical SaaS example would be Office 365 and email.

- **Cloud Platform Services:** These services extend IT and business services to virtual cloud provider platforms, allowing dynamic flexibility and limiting financial costs that would be required to build the same platforms within a business's physical facilities.

Payment Card Industry Business Services

Payment Card Industry Data Security Standards (PCI-DSS) is a compliance requirement established by the major payment card issuers—American Express, Visa, Mastercard, Discover, and JCB International. These standards are enforced by issuers, and failure to meet them can incur heavy fines or even the loss of privileges of one or more of the issuer networks. Such consequences mean that organizations must be vigilant to ensure that standards are met to prevent a potential loss to the organization. While Zero Trust is not required to meet PCI-DSS standards, its focus on providing a more robust security posture means that in the process of deploying and maintaining a Zero Trust Architecture, many of the controls for PCI-DSS will be addressed. Further, it helps to ensure that future updates to the PCI-DSS standard that are likely to occur as time and threats progress will be either already accounted for or more easily met. Many of the current PCI-DSS requirements are met via disparate security controls that are brought together more clearly under a Zero Trust Architecture to ensure they interoperate effectively.

Facility Services

Facility services provide a business's facilities with services to support building automation, physical security, and emerging IoT networks. Traditionally, automation networks and systems have been deployed in isolated environments. However, new innovations and cybersecurity requirements related to these systems are driving the need for data convergence and automation control integration. Security segmentation becomes critical for the protection of these systems, as in worst-case scenarios, risk of human injury or environmental incidents could be possible. Principle services networks can include

- **Building Automation Systems (BAS):** These services control building functions such as HVAC, lighting, and people conveyances (elevators, escalators, moving walkways, and so on).

- **Physical Security and Safety:** These services provide physical security to protect people, buildings, and assets. Systems and services can include building door access, video surveillance, public address, physical intrusion detection, man traps, restricted law enforcement networks, emergency response networks, fire detection and response, on-premises radio, positive or negative room pressure control, and environmental hazard detection.

- **Internet of Things:** IoT services can support numerous specialized business-scale services. A few examples include campus traffic or parking management and smart buildings. IoT, in its simplest description, is a distributed transaction processing system in which the transactions result in monitoring input, automation control, and resulting status information output. Unfortunately, not all IoT systems that are being introduced to today's business networks are always deployed or managed by IT. Strategies for governance and management are still evolving. Due to IoT's functional requirements, cybersecurity control focus is primarily at the Internet edge. From a protection perspective, it should be noted that IoT systems have narrowly focused functions with limited memory and processing power and as such have limited capabilities for detecting and preventing an attack. Segmentation and microsegmentation to protect and monitor these systems are required. Special consideration within the application of segmentation needs to account for the endpoints' needs to communicate with management platforms and be deterministic based on needs to communicate between one another.

Mainframe Services

Mainframe services are often critical for large business's large volume transaction processing. Worldwide, mainframes are used for processing 80 percent of the world's data transaction processing and 90 percent of the world's financial processing. Mainframe cybersecurity is of critical importance, and several security elements in the execution of Zero Trust are used to ensure protection and risk mitigation for these systems' services. Of these security elements, the following are strongly recommended:

- Segmentation is essential for both practical communications and cybersecurity isolation. At a minimum, mainframe protocol communications network segmentation would include TCP/IP, including RDMA support required for

  - IP-based applications, including those using IPsec encryption

  - Web server connectivity

  - Internet connectivity

  - Management consoles using Unix-specific services such as rlogin, Unix telnet, rshd server, SSH, and TN3270

- SNA Protocols, with support required for

  - SNA-based applications, including those using SNA encryption

  - CICS middleware and high-volume transaction processing

  - IMS database and information management

  - Advanced Peer-to-Peer Network (APPN) communications between mainframes and related systems

- Privileged Access Management (PAM): Controls are inherently critical in mainframe environments. This element will often include logging of privileged user sessions down to every keystroke being recorded for these users' sessions.

- Session Behavior Monitoring: Also known as user activity monitoring (UAM), this element will monitor and track a user's behavior on systems and networks. This security element includes tools that can monitor system's use and network communications to look for anomalous activity and alert or automatically respond to threat events.

- Monitoring and Response (preferably automated): Due to the large transaction volume that mainframes can process, security threats and events need to be identified as quickly as possible. Systems and network-based logging, logging aggregation analysis, monitoring, event identification and alarming, and automated responses are all used to meet this security requirement.

Legacy Systems and Infrastructure Services

Legacy services often continue to be a critical part of business services. This can be particularly true for specific industries (such as healthcare, banking, and oil and gas). Legacy systems and infrastructure, from a cybersecurity perspective, are typically identified as systems that are limited in capability to employ up-to-date security control requirements. As a result, compensating security controls (such as segmentation, IDS/IPS, and firewalls) are employed to mitigate inherent risk of these limited legacy systems. System limitations may be encountered when either the device or operating systems cannot be patched, supported, hardened, or updated.

Summary

This chapter explored the different layers of the Zero Trust Architecture, including the branch, campus, WAN, data center, and cloud. Within these layers, we discussed use-case requirements in the context of the primary business application services supported across the network architecture. Based on these business service requirements, we can identify the Zero Trust enclave segmentation strategy as well as where and when to apply the Zero Trust principles.

Chapter 5

Enclave Exploration and Consideration

Chapter Key Points:

- All industries and verticals are affected by cyber threats and therefore benefit from the application of Zero Trust to their overall security infrastructure.

- We touch on applying strategies in applying Zero Trust concepts and view how different industry verticals have applied those specific considerations in their organization's Zero Trust journey.

Throughout this book, we have and will continue to discuss a model for implementing a Zero Trust design; however, it is inherent that the uniqueness of organizations will require variations within their respective architecture. In this chapter, we discuss and analyze some of the so-called gotchas or unique attributes for organizations and industry verticals, and call out considerations.

Addressing the Business

One of the key areas to start focusing on when implementing Zero Trust Segmentation is the segments that the business needs to function. Processes, regulations, rules, laws, and geographic boundaries create complex requirements and direct how an organization conducts its business. These requirements fundamentally cause corporate networks and all other environments to be fully segmented and segregated from all other solutions. The implementation of this segmentation has been a secondary concern when compared to the need for applications and users to conduct business. Zero Trust focuses more directly on the need to secure first; only then can we conduct business.

Segmentation is typically well understood in corporate networks. Service providers understand the need to be highly segmented for customers, shared services, and video networks all protected by access control lists (ACLs), Virtual Routing and Forwarding

(VRF) tables, private networks, software-defined wide area networks (SDWANs), Secure Access Service Edge (SASE), and other topologies, techniques, and technologies. A service provider's advantage is that it is given the requirements of each line of service and provides that segmentation in preconfigured offerings to the end customer. This strategy works well for other organizations outside the service provider, both from the perspective of familiarity of process and utility of service delineation.

To implement Zero Trust into a service provider footprint, a well-established security operations and network operations center is required. Combining these functions into a single focused operations unit is sometimes called a fusion center. Sensors for visibility solutions are required, with a robust threat mitigation team to manage regular distributed denial-of-service attacks. The security capabilities described in this book must be implemented with respect to each subscribing customer, because these customers will form separate business units. A standard set of required Zero Trust controls, including visibility, enforcement, and analytical tools and processes, should be created and will be applied to each subscribing customer. This set of controls may come in the form of a checklist or journey map. Risk mitigation must be a priority for these Zero Trust controls, focusing on the implementation and testing of business continuity plans. Engagement at a board or senior leadership level is key to achieving Zero Trust for service providers because many large companies may act as one enterprise.

Service providers' core business units comprise what the business offers as a service to its customers, which typically consists of delivering communication type services. Typical examples may include

- Video delivery services

- Video backhaul services

- Business communication services

- Microwave communication services

- Satellite communication services

- Content provider

- Network content provider

- Telecommunication services

- Mobile phone services

- Mobile device services

- Virtual private network (VPN) services

With some regularity, some service providers have branched out into cloud-based services. Their business models may have slowly shifted to offering cloud services such as

- Certificate authority services

- Cloud provider services

- Security solutions delivery services

- Infrastructure delivery services

- Platform as a Service

- Security as a Service

- Software as a Service

- Video conferencing services

- Back Office Services as a Service (as well as to themselves)

Identifying the "Crown Jewels"

Identifying what applications and services support the most critical business functions is essential for any organization to ensure that its key operations continue to function optimally. This knowledge helps a company prioritize and allocate resources in a way that maximizes its overall performance and profitability. It also allows a company to plan for potential disruptions or unexpected events that may impact its critical functions. By knowing what processes and systems support these functions, a company can take proactive steps to mitigate risks and develop contingency plans. Additionally, understanding the most critical business functions can help a company identify areas where it can improve its efficiency, reduce costs, and enhance security.

These "crown jewels" may very well be the initial focus in an organization's Zero Trust journey. Beware that the priorities and momentum behind them may change throughout the process of performing this identification. New services, technologies, threats, and people can influence this heavily. The energy sector is a prime example of where these shifting priorities can be seen in action.

Mergers in information technology (IT) and operational technology (OT) systems create new opportunities in the energy sector. These opportunities create a bridge between business operations and operational concerns, such as generation, transmission, and distribution. These opportunities present challenges to the security in both IT and OT systems and practices. Traditional methods effective at providing security in IT or OT systems separately are not effective at providing value and protection in the bridging of IT and OT.

Government actions are also urgently creating a push toward Zero Trust (ZT) strategies. Executive Order 14028 issued by the Biden administration in 2021 established agency responsibilities, findings, and actions that will develop into directives and regulations (see references at the end of this chapter). These items mention specific protections such as multifactor authentication (MFA), data encryption, and removal of implicit trusts, requiring continuous re-evaluation of explicit trust relationships, monitoring, containment of threats, and other methodologies in enforcing cybersecurity resiliency. In the European Union, the NIS2 Directive calls for similar improvements to the Network and Information

Security (NIS) framework creating directives focused toward the critical sectors of transport, energy, health, and finance.

Government and regulatory bodies clearly move the focus of security in the energy sector toward Zero Trust strategies. They will direct strategic legislative and regulatory activities in the direction of Zero Trust protections in critical infrastructure and utilities. Leadership in the energy sector must deliver effective strategies in meeting these demands. Cybersecurity administrators and network operation teams need to provide support in these efforts while avoiding working inside silos or small working groups. This section covers basic considerations when approaching strategies and applying protections.

One of the ways that the energy sector prioritizes which systems to focus on can be to assign priority by generation type. Securing energy generation relies on more than just the specific requirements found in any one generation method. Organizations must prioritize the implementation of strategies based on many factors that will vary by organizational, geographical, political, and regulatory considerations. Generation by volume can be an easy metric to start with. The United States Energy Information Administration (EIA) noted the following values of generation in the US in 2021, as seen in Table 5-1.

Table 5-1   *2021 US Generation by Type*

Generation Type	Percentage	Billions of kWh
Fossil Fuel	60.8%	2504
Renewables	20.1%	826
Nuclear	18.9%	778

Source: US Energy Information Administration, "Frequently Asked Questions (FAQs)," www.eia.gov/tools/faqs/faq.php?id=427&t=3.

Generation mixes vary by organization and a source of pressure to enact and implement strategies. Regulatory hurdles complicate this approach by introducing differences in maturity in existing facilities and groups. Aging controls cause increased prioritization for modernization due to lack of readiness in adapting to Zero Trust strategies. Generation type also adds to the complication of the process of defining priority. Plans for decreasing fossil reliance, environmental impacts to renewable sources, closing of nuclear plants, and innovations in each of these generation sectors will all drive individual organizations' desire and will to implement modern controls.

Network operators and cybersecurity experts prioritize addressing the balance of shrinking attack surfaces and vectors against providing availability of network resources. Introducing new techniques in sensitive environments often proves both challenging and stressful in production networks. Leadership will view these sensitive environments as a priority as ever-increasing pressure is directed at securing information systems from cyber attacks. Successful attacks or exploits executed against more sensitive and high-value targets create more risk to the business and provide prestigious or lucrative targets for attackers. Political, public, and security landscapes all collide in complicating the decisions in the implementation and execution of Zero Trust. These factors must all be used in the calculus of planning the roadmap of Zero Trust strategies in the energy sector.

Frameworks and regulatory bodies provide a rich source of valuable information when approaching strategy in architecture. The National Institute of Standards and Technology (NIST) 800-53 ("Security and Privacy Controls"), NIST 800-161 ("Supply Chain Risk Management"), NIST 800-171 ("Protecting Controlled Unclassified Information"), NIST 800-213A ("IoT Security"), and specific regulations provided by the Federal Energy Regulatory Commission (FERC) and the North American Electric Reliability Corporation (NERC) provide guidelines and regulations in the US energy sector that include cybersecurity considerations. Each country or region will have its own set of regulations, like the European Union and the European Union Agency for Cyber Security (ENISA). Grid security encompasses broad sections of societal stability and safety across the globe. The stakes are high for companies, governments, and consumers.

Identifying and Protecting Shared Enclaves

Business services rely heavily on multiple enclaves in most cases. There are many instances where even the services are shared between multiple entities. Approaching these enclaves with care is required to maintain the services and relationships with other partners. It is possible that a priority in one organization is not a priority in another. The principles of Zero Trust also apply to the organization the enclave is shared with. In many scenarios, the intersection between government organizations and private businesses embodies the complexities when a service or enclave is shared.

The public sector includes entities, organizations, and industries that are funded wholly or in part by municipality, county, parish, state, or national government economies, and are tied to public programs or services that are also controlled by the government. US public sector entities, organizations, and industries typically fall into one of three categories:

- **Core government agencies and departments:** Includes executive, legislative, and judicial branches at the national, state, or local levels.

- **Agencies providing public programs, goods, and services:** Primarily includes defense, law enforcement, public works, transportation, emergency services, public education, veteran's affairs, and social provisioning.

- **Public enterprises and nonprofits:** Includes government-independent goods and services agencies where the government is the primary shareholder but may have other sources of revenue and funding. An example would include the US Post Office.

Among all these entities and agencies, various arrays of information include public, private, personal, restricted, regulated, and classified data, along with the applications and systems that support public sector services. Reduction, interruption, or loss of services to these public sector entities and agencies, whether intentional or accidental, can directly result in the loss of shared public services. Depending on the criticality of these services, this loss may impact health, safety, security, social programs, and standards of living.

Concerning data security, these public sector entities are entrusted to protect valuable public data for all essential services. The required protections, classifications, and restrictions may not match or may even contradict a corporate policy. Adopting these requirements on shared enclaves is less of a choice and more of a requirement. There will also be instances where including these requirements and nonshared enclaves may be advantageous instead of starting from scratch.

Public sector threat actors may end up targeting nongovernment systems. Collateral damage caused by attacks from these actors also influences the controls used in each enclave. These factors necessarily affect the services and interactions within the organization as new surfaces and vectors are exposed. Organizations, including government entities, need to ensure they are protecting themselves from these attackers. Some limited examples of these are

- **Nation-states:** Sponsored actors will often target public sector–stored information with the intention to gain persistent access to public sector networks. Their intentions for attack can range from theft, compromise, or the destruction of information. These actors are either part of a foreign state agency or receive assistance and direction from a nation-state.

- **Cyber criminals:** Cyber criminals are most often considered more organized and emboldened to attack public sector entities. There is greater risk to the threat actors due to responses that could include government-level cyber responses to identify, pursue, and prosecute events. Their motivation is typically based on theft of data for monetary gain.

- **Cyber activists:** Cyber activists, also known as hacktivists, are usually groups of criminals who conduct attacks in perceived support of social or political causes. Whole industries or specific companies are typical targets. Cyber activists strive to drive change in outcomes through the theft or exposure of protected data or information.

Due to the elevated and organized capabilities and malicious intent from these threat actors, Zero Trust core principles stand to protect critical information and minimize impact should unauthorized access occur. Today's nontraditional access patterns— including expanding attack surfaces due to cloud and work-from-anywhere, emerging edge, and anywhere environments—make focusing on segmentation the highest priority. Driving this segmentation priority is a focus in visibility and identity-based access across the entire public sector attack surface.

International public sector entities, agencies, and organizations and the services they provide can differ, and as such have different regulatory and cybersecurity requirements. An example of another country's differences can be explained simply by understanding the distinctions between a national versus federal government structure. A national government's public sector services are completely centralized, and responsibility is not shared for providing services with lower government entities like states or municipalities. A federal government, like that in the US, has centralized government and yet shares some responsibilities with lower entities. Additionally, it is likely that each nation will have its own defined regulations that are like those previously described. Some may be more or less stringent.

Furthermore, some public sector entities operate at a multinational level. In this case some of a nation's defense or economic governing responsibilities have been ceded to a central multinational body. The European Union (EU), the North Atlantic Treaty Organization (NATO), and the International Criminal Police Organization (INTERPOL) are examples of multinational governing bodies. As such, there are corresponding regulations required about their public sector services information. Examples of these regulations include

- **NATO Comprehensive Cyber Defense Policy:** NATO Comprehensive Cyber Defense Policy defines a collective cyber defense based on international laws and member capabilities.

- **General Data Protection Regulation (GDPR) Compliance:** GDPR focuses on EU citizens' information and privacy protection.

Across all the previously mentioned public sector categories, there are many entities, agencies, organizations, and industries where Zero Trust protection methods and technologies can be applied. In this case, the same purposes, requirements, and regulations apply to all the previously mentioned public sector entities' categories.

Segmentation Policy Development

Once a design aggregates the potential tools for enforcement, and identity and vulnerability data has been collected, the largest amount of overhead goes into mapping out flows that would represent unique connections and defining how structures that group endpoints together into legacy entities interact. While individual tools can do this related to their collective format, organizations may use various solutions, such as Cisco Secure Network Analytics to group NetFlow data from various sources for tagging objects to be placed into the appropriate segmentation enclave and to enable policy enforcement.

It is recommended that an organization implement a solution that automates and orchestrates network security policy management on-premises and in the cloud. Being able to administer and orchestrate policy at all the various enforcement points within the organization—whether it be at the identity management system, data center, cloud provider, campus, remote office, affiliates, or service provider—is impactful to the organization and to teams by easing management and unifying policy between the stack of diverse solutions required to support any organization.

In addition to solutions used for the purposes of classifying objects into segments and unifying enforcement policy, it is helpful to have developers who can build solutions to process data from various disparate sources to understand which enforcement mechanisms may be required for implementation. It is an invaluable ability to correlate all aspects of what was collected.

The most effective logic for building out this segmentation policy looks like the following:

■ Use network access control systems to consume data and identify known identities within the flow logs: As mentioned throughout this text, utilizing identity to determine how entities interact with one another is the greatest asset that the proper network access control device lends to the data collection process. As opposed to dynamically allocated addresses, which sometimes cross mediums and are short-lived, identity can help determine how an entity traversed the network in an explicit manner.

■ Utilize Domain Name System (DNS) lookup, both against the local DNS servers and publicly accessible ones to look up the potential identity: Often for internal resources, and quite often for external resources, the entity interacted with was registered into the Domain Name System so that the identity can be provided and accessed easily, without having to remember the address of the endpoint. Where this exists and can be consumed into the data, additional context of what is being interacted with, especially within firewall logs and external to the network, is gained.

■ For entities in which a definitive identity cannot be allocated, solutions like an IP address management system can help determine whether the device has been allocated a static address. Assuming the device is not running a supplicant that would provide identity to the network to gain access, there may be a need to identify a device based on historical information or knowledge that is local to the organization, or even a single business unit. While additional processes must exist within the Zero Trust journey to account for this need to reach out to the owner and verify, as well as supplement the information to better identify the entity, doing so will reduce the number of unknown devices based on information that already exists within the organization.

■ Build a database of known endpoints, which can be dynamically updated as the new endpoint tribal knowledge is discovered. Using auto-discovery solutions and correlating the information with known information via a configuration management database, IPAM, asset management database, or an IP classification schema may be used to build the database of known endpoints. While not the most elegant solution, many organizations build a database in their tool of choice that serves as a similar resource to the IP address management system but is continually updated to document confirmed and suspected endpoints. In addition, this system may store details such as their IP address, static or dynamic address assignment method, MAC address, VRF table membership, detailed network ports and protocol requirements, location, owner, and network access device attributes such as network device name, address, interface, and physical medium.

The goal of processing the information from each of these sources is to build out the final one: build a database of known endpoints using automated and repeatable processes. This database of known endpoints and their communications, which includes the identity of each entity, is then used to classify entities into logical groupings based on defined policy enforcement models.

Within the Zero Trust journey, it should be noted that data used to create this enforcement policy should be augmented with continual trust updates provided by NAC, posture, XDR, and other behavioral systems that are constantly monitoring users, assets, and traffic patterns to understand normal data patterns and identify anomalies. When an anomaly is detected, the integrations are leveraged to allow that conclusion to pass from one system to the other so that policy can be applied to provide an alert, perform mitigation and enforcement on a particular user or asset, or in more extreme cases, restrict access to data for many users to mitigate a larger threat.

This data all works to inform the particulars to be configured within enforcement policy, and as continually analyzed and feedback provided from the analysis pillar. The NetFlow and baseline behavioral data as aligned with documented organizational policies combine to form the basis for the enforced segmentation policy. The conditions for allowing data access should incorporate both the current aspects of an identity, including the user or asset based on the data collected by the various discovery mechanisms used. Combining these two aspects ensures that only those who need access to the data and match the new requirements imposed by the enforced segmentation strategy can gain access. Importantly, because these new security controls are constantly monitoring and evaluating the Identity pillar, including user, assets, and data flows, any change deemed undesirable or too risky provides the capability to modify the level of access granted via the Enforcement pillar. This modification can be as minimal as requiring another factor of authentication or as extreme as complete network isolation and would be unique per organization and data type.

Modeling and Testing of Segmentation Policy

Once the enforcement policy is constructed, it is important to perform practical testing to ensure that no aspects were missed and that both normal access and restrictions due to changes in trust state are detected and performed appropriately. If a testing environment is available, this would be the recommended method to perform this modeling and testing. In many cases though, due to the size and complexity of a Zero Trust segmentation solution, it may be required to either route test data through the production environment, built with the enforced segmentation solution, or even use production data and workloads as part of the testing. In the latter scenario, it becomes critical to identify an appropriate test case. Doing so involves evaluating the selected workload, data set, and the identity's impact and gaining a complete understanding of the risk to the business.

It is critical to understand how data will be controlled when entering and exiting the enforced segmentation controls to ensure that only the required components of the test case are impacted and minimize the risk toward data inaccessibility or loss. When building out this test case, ensure stakeholders are identified and included from the start, including application owners, data owners, users, support teams, engineering teams, and key leadership. It will be leadership's responsibility to function as a moderator in this scenario and listen to any concerns and risks that are raised, help facilitate conversations, and ultimately either approve the test case or determine that another application or data set should be utilized for testing.

Once an application or data set has been selected, it is just a matter of documenting the expected outcomes based on constructed policy and developing a methodology to test each scenario. This step should include outcomes both for normal expected access, as well as changes in behavior, authentication status, and other variables that would negatively impact the level of trust of a user or asset to ensure that the various controls both detect and respond to those changes appropriately. For example, one test scenario may include a user having already authenticated and gained authorization to access a database when a critical process stops unexpectedly. This scenario should be detected within a defined period, based on configuration, by the posture system and notify the NAC solution to mitigate the risk or remove access to the data as appropriate. While it is not reasonable to test every single scenario, the outcomes are the most important, and the question to be answered in this phase is, Are changes in state recognized appropriately as a change in the level of trust, and is the overall solution performing the desired actions in response?

Bringing Blurred Borders Back into Focus

Defining enclaves and creating separation between functions, devices, and services are clearly defined in the beginning. These clear lines will blur as discovery and onboarding continue past those initial definitions. It is important to address any of these uncertainties as soon as they are found. Enclaves in the healthcare industry are particularly fluid in this way. Rapid evolution in the delivery of care, storage of records, interconnectedness of devices, and other changes in the landscape of care can challenge established definitions.

Medical IoT devices make up larger portions of all medical devices as time goes on. These devices' importance to the healthcare industry also represents one of the largest vulnerabilities to the industry. Infusion pumps have well-documented vulnerabilities, including exploits that would allow an attacker to remotely control the device. Medical devices and terminals are accessed by a wide variety of operators, which leaves little room for security hygiene in access practices. Access needs in many healthcare environments require fast and error-free access to be effective. This need creates issues when credentials may exist as physical tokens, like badges or smart cards, or as a known shared authentication method.

Hospitals contain most of these critical medical devices and the data they produce. Healthcare systems present themselves as large treasure troves of personal health and identity data. Proper authentication and authorization of users accessing the data go well beyond simple usernames and passwords. Validating the user's identity must also be weighed against the data requested and how it is being accessed. A holistic Zero Trust strategy must account for the many types of data, devices, users, applications, and locations that engage in any transaction. Network access control, profiling, multifactor authentication, and identity form the building blocks to forming a framework of controls to accomplishing Zero Trust.

Each of the preceding scenarios contains one or more transitions between otherwise well-defined enclaves. Enclaves need to be redefined, divided, combined, or eliminated when these lines become too blurred. Continuous improvement practices should be embedded in the initial creation and review of enclaves and service delivery inside the organization. Zero Trust requires not just the segmentation of the network but also the reconstruction of it after segmentation. This reconstruction also includes the smooth operation of business across entities.

Protecting patients and their data transcends the walls of the hospital and doctors' offices. Clinical roles demonstrate a primary focus when directly interacting with patients. Clinical responsibilities deal with patient treatment and care. Examples of clinical roles include doctors, nurses, technicians, therapists, pharmacists, and more. Zero Trust strategies should include interactions between these providers to only provide relevant data access. The spotlight of how security interacts with patient care shines brightly here but is not the only place in healthcare that needs to be considered.

Policies must adhere to relevant laws and regulations such as HIPAA in the US and GDPR in the EU. These laws extend beyond the clinical environment into the nonclinical interactions in the healthcare system. Areas where nonclinical interactions take place include billing, administration, marketing, and other roles. Pharmaceutical representatives present an example of where nonclinical relationships easily impact clinical decisions. Representatives may have access to prescription patterns and feedback that relate to patient data. Access to this data introduces both positive and negative consequences to the industry and patient care. Healthcare providers' and organizations' policies must consider how internal policy and public laws and regulations oversee clinical and nonclinical uses of patient data.

An organization is unlikely to know every single type of device connected in every crevice of the network. The same idea applies to data records and repositories as well. A successful approach to Zero Trust considers function over identity for its strategic approach, and for enforcement leverages identity to determine function as a tactical action. Architects face an impossible task if the dependency of knowing every device and every use case for those devices requires definition at the outset of strategy planning. Mapping macro segments of the environment along with function and policy direction illuminates a hierarchical structure of policy and design. Resultant deviations from that initial design either fall under a defined branch or merit the creation of a new branch. Administrators should consider defining no more than five to seven segments of the environment when approaching function definition. With this function definition will come the ability to define policies of enforcement and treatment of data based on functions mapped. Inherently, a hierarchy based on the combination of factors that include identity, use case, policy, and other criteria that hold relevance in the scenario will form with subsegments being created within the broader segments over time.

Monitoring Segment Definitions

If testing was completed within a test environment, then it is necessary at this step to migrate those configurations, upon successful testing, into the production environment and monitor to affirm that it operates as it did in the test environment. If running within the production environment already, it is still recommended to allow time for the monitoring of the first few use cases. The reason is that, even with full participation from all relevant stakeholders, modern business systems may still have use cases that are not well understood or known by their owners. This lack of knowledge could be due to users interacting with the system in unexpected ways, information silos between teams, or just the overall size and complexity of the workload may preclude the ability for one group to fully understand its complete function and intricacies. Therefore, it is recommended to allow the system to run for an extended period to collect more data and ensure users are not negatively impacted in completing their business functions.

During this time, it is also imperative that operations and support personnel be aware that a user's issues may be correlated to the segmentation solution testing and be reported to the appropriate teams for investigation and resolution. One of the most detrimental resolutions that operations teams can take, however, is the complete removal or bypass of enforcement from the port or session through which the entity connects. In many scenarios, this approach has been seen as a workaround to get the user or application quickly back onto the network and accessible. However, it precludes the ability to actively troubleshoot and determine which aspects of the enforcement policy are preventing access for the entity.

It is important to ensure that a defined monitoring period is agreed upon, after which the solution is accepted, and the next test case can be approached. With a change as major as enforcement for Zero Trust segmentation, it is highly recommended that multiple systems across diverse environments be evaluated. The more time invested in this testing phase, the better the outcome when full production rollout is performed. The testing and evaluation phase provides far greater flexibility because its impact can be constrained and quickly removed, something not as easily accomplished when in wide production use. Testing should encompass at least one application per segment and ideally more. Only after this testing has been completed to an acceptable degree should an organization look to move forward with production rollout of the solution.

Mitigating Security Holes to Overcome Operational Challenges

Accounting for the process and policy required when operational inflection points affect the organization presents architectural, procedural, and operational challenges. Any iteration through this process needs to trigger a reassessment of the process to apply any lessons learned. Iterative feedback and consumption of outputs from other pillars within the Zero Trust architecture ensures that the policy continues to adapt to changes in the environment. Feedback processes rely on the organization identifying and requiring any affected party to provide input on lessons learned. Feedback to the process should avoid absolute or draconian action that may limit the flexibility of the organization to respond.

Examples of places to look for feedback and improvement to existing policies include

- Communication channels missing or not used as identified via vulnerability management and traffic discovery processes

- Political and organizational power dynamics that disrupt normal operations with policies dictated in the Policy & Governance pillar

- New or modified controls or capabilities applied with the Enforcement pillar that have negative effects on business as usual

- Attack surfaces uncovered through operational and policy testing via the Analytics and Vulnerability Management pillars

- Deficiencies in provisioning and onboarding policies per the Policy & Governance pillar

Incorporating New Services and Enclaves

A blurred or evolving enclave presents numerous challenges, as we mentioned earlier. What happens when you need to consume entire segments, enclaves, networks, or new services? These actions happen in many forms at various times in the life and growth of the organization. Many organizations commonly approach a complete reworking of the new segment. This methodology usually proves imprudent or impractical. One common industry vertical that experiences this situation more commonly is financial services.

Financial services have many unique Zero Trust challenges. Most financial institutions have mergers and acquisitions on a routine basis. These activities lead to differentials in the organization's ability to implement new services and to respond to new business opportunities quickly. Legacy structures critical to the success of the business inhibit modern methods from being used with fear of disrupting the core business functionalities. The key focus area in the financial services is having a robust onboarding process for new businesses and a methodology for separating related traffic until the "new" business unit has had a thorough assessment, including pen testing and threat detection.

Each unique line of business (LOB) offers additional regulation requirements to a financial services organization's heavy load of regulation. Keeping the traffic of these LOBs separated reduces the attack and threat surfaces of the organization. Focusing on this requirement during mergers or business transitions will lead to a stronger security posture. The use of the strategies mentioned previously in the financial services industry can be adapted in more broadly purposed onboarding and analysis tools.

Onboarding: The Challenge of Merger Activity

Mergers and acquisitions happen with increasing frequency in today's landscape. Organizations face challenges from these activities that include legal, organizational, financial, technical, and ethical inflection points all throughout the process. Each of these challenges requires its own brand of due diligence before, during, and after a merger or acquisition takes place. Complications brought on by security concerns threaten the process as well as each of the individual organizations in the activity. Onboarding in particular takes on a new definition during the merger process as devices, users, networks, applications, processes, vendors, and almost any other aspect of the individual organizations become onboarded into the new one, where difficulties and complexities exponentially grow without easy answers. Mergers and acquisitions provide a unique opportunity for organizations to evaluate the current segmentation policy and modify it to fulfill the needs of both the originating and acquired organization on both a short-term and long-term basis. Even after an organization has moved into the enforcement pillar of a Zero Trust journey, it may need to start the journey from the baseline again, as new identities need to consume data by the thousands or even tens of thousands. However, the functional design and breakdown of how data is collected, which data is collected, and the integrations that are required to collect the data effectively can ease the potential vulnerabilities introduced by the merger. In addition, given an enforcement mechanism that is distributed effectively and protective of all segments of the network through which entities could attempt to access data, additional enforcement mechanisms could be applied surgically to the areas through which the acquired company would be accessing data from, while still allowing reasonable amounts of access that limit exposure of the acquiring company. Given the variety of enforcement mechanisms that could be used, this could result in further distribution of enforcement policy application or a consolidated area of enforcement.

Merger and acquisition activity comes with organizational restructuring. This restructuring brings with it substantial amounts of risk that will be experienced threefold. First, each party involved will undoubtedly lose key members of their teams. Second, the post-merger landscape will drive new innovations and ways of doing business that create new and unfamiliar processes, departments, and politics. Third, outside of restructuring and reorganization, natural waves of attrition will follow for years after the dust settles. Accounting for these risks, and the threats that come along with them, plays a key role in protecting every aspect of the organization and those it does business with.

Organizational debt increases when processes and culture lag the rapidly changing landscape across disciplines. As the gap widens, inefficiencies grow until they become risks and threats that can severely affect the organization in many ways. Mergers and acquisitions bring this debt from all the organizations involved into a concentrated form. Moving through the process, the organization makes sacrifices to get business done. These sacrifices compound organizational debt and increase risk across new frontiers of the organizational threat landscapes. Cybersecurity teams must prepare to protect the organization in these uncertain times, and as part of that preparation, they should build policies to minimize operational debt into the Policy & Governance and Analytics pillars of the organization's Zero Trust journey. Policies should be created and adhered to, and they should entail replacing equipment at the end of its useful life cycle. Useful life cycle typically relates to when the device is no longer under support and a failure of the device could not be resolved due to the vendor's policies relating to end of support. Alternatively, end of useful life cycle could mean that features that are critical to the business are not found in any software release of the equipment, therefore indicating a need to retire the equipment or cascade it into areas of the business where these features are neither used nor planned to be used.

Assuming the acquiring organization is the one further along with its Zero Trust journey than the acquisition, the acquiring organization has the responsibility, by utilizing the analysis tools and capabilities found within the respective pillar, to evaluate how organizational debt will be affected by the merger. The debt of legacy network devices, user equipment, connected endpoints, applications, and data will impact the Vulnerability Management pillar of the acquiring organization, potentially exposing it to far more risk than it was originally exposed to, solely based on the merger or acquisition. This policy, while potentially a politically influenced discussion, needs to be discussed and agreed to by both the acquiring and acquired company with relation to timelines for resolving organizational debt and minimizing exposure.

IT teams also experience increased technical debt as networks, applications, systems, and processes merge, appear, and disappear. Technical debt accrues in every organization when decisions to complete a task are made over the quality of the completed task. Unfortunately, even the Policy & Governance pillar of Zero Trust cannot prevent technical debt from being accrued where organizational culture allows projects to be ended prematurely or "fast-tracked" to hit a date, rather than a quality metric. In multiple places within this text, we have mentioned that the organization should take the time needed to complete each pillar to a defined capability measure as opposed to a time-based deadline. One aspect of the Zero Trust journey that can assist with buy-in from executives and business units is a milestones map outlining the goals of each pillar, cross-referenced with locations and other aspects of the business, to show small wins distributed over time and allowing for successes to be continual, as opposed to a singular big bang. This same methodology should apply to a merger or acquisition. While there is a need to bring the entirety of the merged company into the acquiring company, having small milestones indicating where the pillars of the Zero Trust journey are to be applied will get points on the board for key sponsors and demonstrate the Zero Trust program's success to leadership.

While an acquired organization is navigating the Zero Trust journey, the expectation is that new skill gaps throughout the IT organization will appear, and existing skill gaps will be widened without the proper attention. While the acquired organization may have a significant understanding of endpoints and entities on its network, to operationalize Zero Trust enforcement on the discovered and accounted-for entities will surely be a significant task for a newly acquired operations staff. Utilizing the functional design encompassed within this chapter to describe the processes an entity goes through to join the network can provide not only a starting point for troubleshooting with properly aligned skillsets but also a learning map for technologies that are new to the organization.

Technical and organizational debt brought on by the merger and acquisition activities demands payment in one way or another. The cost of this technical debt begins to increase as threats and risks to the business eventually become visible. Reduction of technical debt takes leadership and will require budgets that may be deemed too expensive to accept. Without reducing technical debt, the organization will pay in the form of threats that are easily exploited by attackers. The losses still show on the balance sheet whether they take the form of compromised data, reduced reputation, increased regulatory oversight, or compliancy costs.

No source contains a complete list of all the risks associated with merger and acquisition activity. It is therefore imperative that feedback be shared from each of the pillars into the others to assist with minimizing risk and exposing where each need exists. The judicious use of each pillar, in addition to due diligence, provides the best method of identifying and addressing threat surfaces and attack vectors. Additional considerations and questions to be asked of an organization throughout the merger activities include the following:

- Does the organization have well-defined policies and an understanding of their use cases, or are they "singing" the application of identity discovery, vulnerability management, and enforcement?

- Does either organization adhere to their policies from the Policy & Governance pillar, or do they use regulatory policies to make up for not adhering to their approved policy?

- What enforcement can be applied to systems and technologies, both based on what they can support and what regulatory requirements dictate?

- Do the network and cybersecurity components differ between organizations? Can policy and enforcement mechanisms be applied to both sets of components?

- What vendors and vendor requirements around policy, entity discovery, and enforcement of access exist in the end state of the process?

- Has either organization experienced recent security incidents?

- Do competing policies, processes, and procedures create unresolvable conflicts?

- Will existing and new certifications be needed to continue to do business? Do these certifications align with current policy and enforcement mechanisms?

- How will data be protected as it migrates across infrastructures?

Onboarding: The Challenge of Independent Purchasing Decisions

Zero Trust programs succeed or fail based on the ability of the organization to set and maintain policies via the Policy & Governance pillar. The foundational policies that protect the organization's strategy from change stem from the ability to identify, classify, but also optimize the ability to identify new devices and ensure that in their introduction to the network they abide by the policies of the organization. These policies include the provisioning of known devices before they are deployed throughout the network, detection and remediation of unknown endpoints, ability to operationalize network devices in an automated or minimal overhead method, and ability to identify components of the network that need to be investigated for not abiding by the known and established policies. Decisions to bring on new devices to the network happen both centrally and in a distributed manner. Processes and procedures that cover these actions need to plan for the existence of independent purchasing decisions made outside of normal channels.

As part of the Policy & Governance pillar policies that dictate purchasing, a focus should be put on central purchasing of endpoints and network components to ensure that identifiable models that abide by established policies are used. Independent purchasing decisions create two scenarios for onboarding and provisioning teams. The first, while not exciting, falls under policy. For organizations that employ a Zero Trust approach to the network, devices that do not allow for discovery or are part of a "shadow IT" operational process prevent the organization from understanding endpoints on the network and potential vulnerabilities posed to the network by their existence. Policies for both budgeting in alignment with business units that need to support advanced connectivity cases should be used to help offload this burden to the organization's network and ensure that all business units are supported related to their unique requirements and budgetary needs.

The second scenario is related to both technical and political implications. Organizations must prepare for the eventuality that when mass orders are made, the decision comes down to when and not if the network can be ready for them. The unfortunate truth is most organizations are founded to make a profit, and if that profit is interrupted by too much process—hence preventing the organization from doing business—the process will be changed. This change is rarely for the positive. There is the distinct possibility that discovery of devices may even happen well after the devices have already been purchased and deployed. A well-defined policy allowing for purchase of devices so long as they are onboarded in a consistent manner and in alignment with organizational standards is required to ensure that devices can be purchased preferably from a single portal or application with commonly available devices on the network and be more easily identified based on that common database. Regardless of the budgetary implications to purchasing outside of the common purchasing processes, this flexibility in purchasing can at least align required devices with minimal overhead to determine identity and evaluate vulnerabilities.

Planning for Onboarding New Devices

As new devices come onto the network, a process that is consistent and reasonable in its approach to get the device access is key to ensuring the ability to maintain the Zero Trust architecture. The first step in this process begins when the independent purchase has been identified. A policy exception process needs approval to allow the devices to continue to operate at a predetermined security level before onboarding can begin. The Zero Trust strategy for the organization defines what these levels are. Deviations from any level of security provided by the Zero Trust global policy require an architectural review before implementation. Visibility and enforcement mechanisms identified in the purchase also need to conform to the standards required by the organization. Controls and capabilities not present need remediation before moving on to any future steps.

Focus should turn to the second step, acquisition of the devices purchased matching the same configuration and build of any device proposed in the purchase. This step requires obtaining any bill of materials used by the party making the purchases to determine what testing needs to occur. Make note of any skill gaps, feature gaps, interactions, or changes to current standards that anything new to the network introduces. The test plan aims to document the operational modes and behaviors of any of the devices evaluated to allow proper policy creation. A proper test plan includes any of the needs that the team lacks to assess new devices successfully and fully. Acceptance of the finalized test plan becomes invalid if missing any of the identified prerequisites without an exception.

Policy creation and application comprise the last step in the process of onboarding new devices. The procedure for policy creation defines where each policy record exists along with any attribution of testing or documentation used in the making of that decision. Policy acceptance should happen only after it addresses all areas of visibility, identity, context, and enforcement. Operational testing of the policy must also occur in preproduction and production environments before final sign-off. The finalized policy also should include for any provisioning.

Using Automation in Enclaves

Automation is a key focus area for organizations as they attempt to reduce complexity and increase productivity. Automation helps to ease the burden on administrative staff and end users by providing low-touch solutions to common issues. Automation and integration points of Zero Trust help drive lower costs. The additional security provided by a Zero Trust architecture by constantly evaluating trust rather than the common implicit trust or single evaluation of trust at entry to the network helps to mitigate the risk from newer, more sophisticated attacks. These attacks, such as man-in-the-middle hardware attacks, as well as those used to bypass network access control systems, often attempt to reside in a retail environment. These attack types have been seen in the past and have shown difficulty in both identifying the cause and scope of the attack. With a Zero Trust architecture focus on visibility, the time to identify and resolve these attacks is shortened due to the use of things like network behavior analysis. Critically, automation assists an organization where detection within this network behavior platform can automatically cause the execution of changes to other security controls. This security control can take various forms, such as firewall rule changes to prevent data exfiltration or a DNS security update to block identified suspect domains from resolution.

One of the key components to a successful Zero Trust architecture and meeting these requirements in such a widely dispersed organization will be the policies and documentation that are built and maintained as part of the initiative. These policies and documentation sources will be the key sources to allow the organization to prove itself compliant with various standards and regulations. For PCI-DSS, as an example, this documentation is referred to as Report on Compliance (ROC) and must be prepared and submitted yearly to maintain good standing. For large organizations, this ROC discovery and documentation process can involve hundreds of employees and thousands of hours of labor to complete. Having this data readily available and maintained with high accuracy reduces this burden, providing cost savings for these types of reports. As a downstream effect, the expected cost savings due to the mitigation for the chance of a breach and the reduced time to resolution of any breach are also increased.

Considerations on the Physicality of an Enclave

The explosion of connected devices with the digitization of systems and services leads to new challenges for IT departments across all industries. Organizational control over user and device access created a false sense of security where movement toward mobilization and digitization has shifted the focus of control. Business objectives drive customers toward the demand of access for data and services when and where they demand it. Evolving security challenges created by these demands can create an immense task for the teams trying to implement Zero Trust strategies and frameworks that build the rungs of the ladder for scaling these challenges.

The logistics industry faces unique challenges for security, both in the physical and digital realms. The supply chain remains the easiest target for attackers to exploit for the largest amount of gain. Visibility is a key factor in securing the supply chain from both the physical and digital perspectives. The ability to detect and prevent attackers from unauthorized access marks the difference between a secure logistics system and a compromised one. Visibility that protects the supply chain varies with physical monitoring, digital tracking, transport planning, and even tracking provided to consumers. This double-edged sword also gives an attacker all the information they need to subvert the security provided by that visibility. The principle of least privilege effectively describes the best approach to secure access to this visibility.

Instruments serve multiple purposes in the supply chain. Drones can be used to survey a logistics center or deliver packages. Impact/shock sensors provide visibility in determining how an item is handled while also deterring improper handling by those who see it. Shipment and tracking notifications enable consumers to have confidence in the delivery of a package and the ability for that package to be retrieved before other parties can obtain it. Protecting the access granted to systems to only authorized personnel protects the supply chain. These examples provide just a small window into how physical security and the physicality of services play into enclaves. Facilities, building automation systems, security systems, and physical access controls may justify their own enclave(s) or be folded into another function.

Summary

Regardless of the industry vertical, considerations for mitigating security threats need to be implemented, aligning with the five core principles of Zero Trust. All industries and verticals are affected by cyber threats and therefore benefit from the application of Zero Trust to their overall security infrastructure. In this chapter we touched on applying strategies in applying Zero Trust concepts and viewed how different industry verticals have applied those specific considerations in their organization's Zero Trust journey.

References in This Chapter

■   The White House, "Executive Order on Improving the Nation's Cybersecurity," May 12, 2021, www.whitehouse.gov/briefing-room/presidential-actions/2021/05/12/executive-order-on-improving-the-nations-cybersecurity/

Chapter 6

Segmentation

Chapter Key Points:

- The OSI model is commonly used to describe application of discovery and enforcement mechanisms within the network stack. A brief summary of the OSI model is provided in this chapter.

- Segmentation can take many forms and is typically a layered enforcement model. Both upper layer segmentation models as well as network-centric segmentation models may lend themselves to the success of an organization's segmentation goals.

- Segmentation can be applied in a "north-south" or "east-west" manner. The determination of which is best for an organization is based on three key questions to be asked of the organization or business unit related to its segmentation journey.

- Segmentation can be applied throughout network functions and should be layered in a manner such that it can widely prevent attacks regardless of the attack vector.

- The chapter also briefly covers an ideal world "how to."

Segmentation is the process of defining and implementing boundaries around contextual identities, typically consisting of a combination of users, devices, and data. These boundaries may be physical or logical in their construction and utilize different means to achieve the goal of limiting the flow of traffic to only what is determined as necessary. Due to the proliferation of ransomware and other types of malware, segmentation has become a hot topic in the security marketplace over the last decade. While legacy networks have always had some segmentation built in by many accounts, either through VLANs, collision domain segmentation with switches, or even upstream firewalls, many of these solutions to the segmentation challenge have not yielded the expected results when it comes to preventing propagation of threats. In this chapter we explore the current forms of segmentation that are common in established environments, why change can be difficult, and the benefits of rethinking how segmentation is designed and applied.

A Brief Summary of the OSI Model

Throughout this chapter and the rest of the text, references to the Open Systems Interconnection (OSI) model help illustrate different segmentation models and the needs for each. For readers unfamiliar with the OSI model, we provide a brief explanation; however, you can find more in-depth exploration of networking concepts and foundational topics in the Cisco Certified Networking Associate official coursework.

The OSI model was developed as a standard approach to describing how interconnected devices communicate through a series of layers or steps. It is common to describe the concepts of networking, such as address, ports, protocols, applications, and mediums, by utilizing their respective layers of the OSI model. This has extended to referring to organizational challenges—politics and money required to accomplish an outcome, as extended layers of the OSI model in Layers 8 and 9. In all seriousness, the OSI model has seven layers, as can be seen in Figure 6-1, describing the interactions of devices, and can be described from a top-down or bottom-up methodology, depending on the direction of communication to or from a device. For the following example describing the model, we focus on the top-down approach and utilize various layers in the lower half of the model when illustrating segmentation techniques.

Figure 6-1   *The OSI Model*

When data is transmitted from a given endpoint, the transmission must be first triggered by an application of some sort. This application, represented by the topmost Layer 7 of the OSI model, initiates a need to send traffic outbound toward another endpoint. Applications such as web browsers do this regularly and by function.

There must be a standard formatting that applications can understand. Hypertext Transfer Protocol (HTTP), a human-readable, tag-based model of language, functions at Layer 6, or the presentation layer of the OSI model. The purpose of HTTP is to create a standard rendering of graphics, text, and models that can be interpreted by web browsers, can be exchanged, and can be rendered the same across any application capable of reading and displaying HTTP pages.

To exchange the HTTP information, there must be a standard approach, ensuring that the destination machine can receive and interpret the information sent by the source. The session must be set up, standards for exchanging the data agreed upon, and validation that the opposing side has started and finished sending or receiving the data. This all takes place at Layer 5, or the session layer.

When communicating between devices, the protocol or set of communication attributes, such as the source port of the communication and destination port, is encompassed within Layer 4, or the transport layer. Ports can be thought of as doors along a hallway into an office represented by an application. The application may receive messages from a series of sources, allowing for multiple messages to be sent to their respective applications simultaneously, but the door acts as a conduit to access the resources of the application contained within an office. These ports are therefore a potential for applying enforcement to, ensuring that only specific source ports, or doors within the same section of the hallway, are allowed to communicate to the application.

To communicate between endpoints, there must be an identifying attribute that can be used to reach the exact destination the source wants to communicate to. At Layer 3, or the network layer, attributes such as the IP address identify a device and allow this identity to be used in a pervasive fashion across the network when communicating between two endpoints. Whereas doors along a hallway contain applications, the same application may exist on multiple floors. The IP address identifies not only the floor to visit to access the door but also the building and the campus, to continue the preceding example. This is where the routing of packets exists on the OSI model, where IP addresses are used as an identifying mechanism to travel through the network to a destination via gateways and path selection mechanism.

Locally to a network, however, there is little need to use the IP address, because IP is meant to communicate across broad areas of the network and maintain the identity within the communication medium while doing so. The data link layer acts as both a local identity, sometimes carved out into virtual local area networks (VLANs) and identified by medium access control (MAC) addresses. These MAC addresses are used to communicate within the VLAN, similar to local knowledge within the hallway that office 1296 is Betty's office, but local office workers describe it as "the last one on the left." The data link layer also determines how two endpoints communicate across the physical medium, similar to a "rules of the road" within the preceding example that traversal should always be to the right side of the hallway to prevent collisions in traversal. Layer 2 is an interconnection between devices within the same routing domain, preventing the need for devices to traverse gateways or path selection devices to reach the destination, as it exists within the same domain.

Finally, the physical layer, or Layer 1, is the cables, lines, and wireless medium through which devices interact. This is the hallway itself; in the networking world this is the Ethernet, fiber, or wireless medium over which electrical signals are sent between devices to represent data in the form of binary signals.

For more information on each layer and their interaction within the OSI model, see Wendell Odom's *CCNA 200-301 Official Cert Guide Library* available through Cisco Press.

Upper Layer Segmentation Models

The application of segmentation is commonly aligned to the needs of an organization, but with a networking focus is more commonly described as the layer on which the segmentation model functions. This functionality can be defined as the layer that communications are limited to or enforced on, preventing communication in some way for the goal of the segmentation functionality. This chapter, while focusing on a networking approach to segmentation, acknowledges that segmentation needs to occur at each layer of the OSI model. It is common for many industries, such as defense and manufacturing, to break down segmentation utilizing even different physical cabling and cable colors to prevent devices from being able to ever interact. While the focus of this section is related to Layer 2-, 3-, and 4-based segmentation, an overview of segmentation models follows as aligned with the OSI model.

Application segmentation on a machine is a way of preventing applications from communicating with one another or allowing communication only in very specific ways when existing on the same machine. One example of this segmentation concept is the use of containers, common to platforms such as docker, to separate out application functionality and processing of data from the reliance upon a common set of resources to function. While most applications will require libraries and resources, such as memory and storage, from the host machine on which they are running, the processing of data that their functionality relies on can be separated into separate, nonoverlapping functions. The accessing, processing, and interacting with other containers or applications should be very specific in its functionality and behavior. This functionality and behavior cause the application layer to rely on other layers that have their own needs for segmentation design, but suffice to say, functionalities of applications that could cause other applications harm or prevent them from functioning altogether should be understood and prevented.

Presentation layer segmentation, like application layer segmentation, ensures that the common model for application consumption and interaction is separated from other resources that could inject or change the way that applications interact and interpret the data for presentation to the end user. In a similar text, Patrick Lloyd describes the ability for common attributes of interactions between voice over IP systems to be changed to embed information into the initiation of the session to relay information to the destination and receiver via man-in-the-middle type attacks. This modification can similarly be used to prevent communications or change the way in which an application consumes the exchange of information, diverging from a common way of interpreting the exchange. (See the reference at the end of this chapter.) To prevent against attacks at this layer, the organization can use checksums or validation of the entire message sent for consumption by the application, or dedicated exchange channels with encryption preventing exchange of data without validation utilized.

Similarly, the session layer ensures that the way in which the data is exchanged between source and destination endpoints, including the order of segments, retransmission mechanisms, and control channels for exchange of data, is structured. Therefore, segmentation related to these mechanisms would ensure that as applications interact, a dedicated control channel exists for that application and can be validated through some authentication method to ensure that the sender of the data and order in which they sent the data can be validated with a known pattern, protocol, or methodology. This segmentation mechanism would need to be implemented into the source code of the application or transmission mechanisms, ensuring that communications between applications were expected, accounted for, and validated in their communication methodology.

Common Network-Centric Segmentation Models

Regardless of the medium, whether cloud, wired, wireless, or VPN, Layer 4 segmentation is common and has been used in conjunction with Layer 3 segmentation methodologies throughout networking history. The transport layer of the OSI model is predominantly focused on how exchange occurs. In this case, the primary example is the protocol used—typically, Internet Protocol (IP), User Datagram Protocol (UDP), Transmission Control Protocol (TCP), or Internet Control Message Protocol (ICMP) for most enterprise networks. For most enforcement mechanisms and models, including segmentation utilizing firewalling, access control lists (ACLs), cloud security groups, or even security group tagging models, the protocol or Layer 4 transport mechanism can be cited in the control mechanism itself. Grouping together the use of access control lists, cloud security groups, and firewalls, because all can be seen as a set of access control lists with potential added processing functionality, one of the major arguments that either permits or denies traffic from source to destination is the protocol. Take, for example, the standard IP-based ACL or identity-based ACL seen in Example 6-1.

Example 6-1   *Various Access Control Lists*

```
! Standard Layer 3/4 Access Control List
access-list 100 permit tcp 192.168.1.0 0.0.0.255 host 10.10.64.1 eq 23

! Security Group Tag Layer 2/3/4 Access Control List
cts role-based access-list rbacl1
  permit udp src eq 1312
cts role-based access-list rbacl2
  deny ip log
cts role-based sgt 10 dgt 20 access-list rbacl1
cts role-based sgt 20 dgt 10
```

In Example 6-1, two formats of ACLs are displayed, showing the inclusion of Layers 2 through 4 attributes of the OSI model. For the standard access control list of 100, the Layer 4 protocol of TCP is used, from a Layer 3 (IP) source subnet of 192.168.1.0/24 going to host IP address of 10.10.64.1. This communication should be allowed only on the Layer 4 port of TCP port 23.

In the bottom example of Example 6-1, a host that has been assigned a Layer 2 source security group tag of 10, either statically or from Cisco ISE, should be able to communicate to another host allocated a destination security group tag of 20, which should be able to communicate via the Layer 4 UDP protocol, but only from a Layer 4 source port of UDP 1312. Similarly, communications established from a host allocated a Layer 2 source security group tag of 20 traveling to a destination host with security group tag of 10 should be denied any Layer 4 IP-based communication and the traversal logged.

This example shows the close-knit nature of OSI Layers 2, 3, and 4 when it comes to segmentation. Depending on the mechanism through which the segmentation is applied, whether via a Layer 3/4 access control list on a switch, router, firewall, or cloud security group, or whether via Layers 2 and 4 on a switch, segmentation can be achieved in various ways. The key to determining which method is best relies on the business need for segmentation, architecture, and level of segmentation required.

North-South Directional Segmentation

For any administrator who has pursued any architectural certification throughout their career—including but not limited to ISC[2] Certified Information System Security Professional, Cisco Certified Design Professional, or even college degrees in network design—segmentation has always been an underlying theme for designing a network. Many architectural conversations begin with a need to allocate IP addresses in an organized, contiguous manner with significant room to grow within the branch or campus, and typically with the ability to summarize allocated subnets at the edge of the branch or campus. These IP addresses are then typically broken down further into subnets allocated in alignment with VLAN structure and based on the number of current or future clients expected within the subnet. A design side effect of this VLAN alignment ensures that to traverse across subnets, a routing device in the past must make a path determination for the traversal packet. In this design, the only way two endpoints can communicate is via a gateway to traverse between VLANs. Figure 6-2 provides a sample architectural drawing of how this allocation of subnets and VLAN assignments may appear for a network with two large and two small sites.

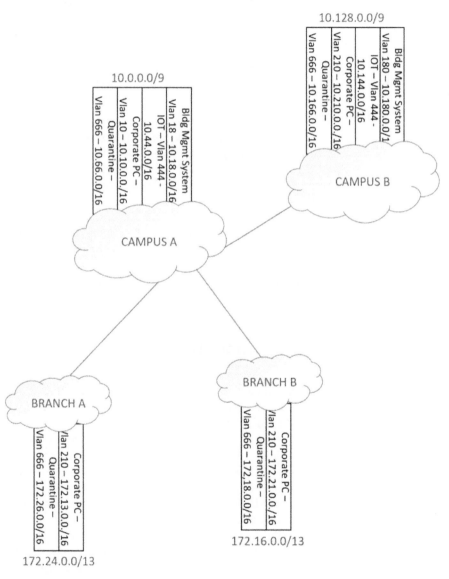

Figure 6-2   *VLAN-to-Subnet Mapping*

The concept of segmentation in a north-to/from-south direction is common to networks designed in this manner and has been implemented via firewalls throughout the history of networking. When the communication flow is traced in this type of segmentation, the source and destination of the communication typically are in different networking structures, or security "zones," and utilize an intermediary device to communicate with one another. This communication is typically routed at Layer 3 of the OSI model, because the devices will typically exist in separate subnets based on their positioning in the separate structures or zones. Therefore, the segmentation model related to this type of communication is based on the routing mechanism required for communication and is applied to restrict certain traffic from being transmitted. As the communication traverses the intermediary switch, router, firewall, or cloud transport mechanism, a Layer 3/4 access control list is applied to the communication to restrict it. This Layer 3/4 control mechanism denotes the Layer 4 protocol, source port and address, and destination port and address to allow or deny communication to and from.

For north-south directional segmentation, the reason segmentation is possible is that devices exist in separate security or routing segments of the network, with a need to traverse an intermediary device to reach the destination. This need to route across a device that performs Layer 3 actions, namely routing, provides an ability to easily apply policy to what can and cannot route between sources and destinations that traverse the intermediary device. However, this entails a need to also have a default policy or a nonexhaustive list of what can and cannot communicate across the device. In the example of a firewall that separates security zones from one another, a default policy of "deny all traffic" is typically utilized, and all exceptions traversing from one zone to another must be populated via a Layer 3/4 access control list. Common challenges with segmenting with this model are discussed in Chapter 7, "Zero Trust Common Challenges."

East-West Directional Segmentation

With modern attack vectors such as malware, referred to in the opening paragraph, deeper models of segmentation are required to prevent this spread, and limit the "blast zone," or impacted area, of the network should one client be compromised. Similar to worms found throughout the 1990s and 2000s, malware has adopted the ability to seek out open ports and protocols at Layer 4 of the OSI model and communicate to hosts via both IP addresses and MAC addresses at Layers 3 and 2 of the OSI model, respectively. In many of these cases, unlike the north-south direction of communication, the traffic traversal of the malicious software remains within the routing or security segment of the network. By doing so, restricting the communication becomes significantly more challenging, because devices may exist within the same virtual local area network (VLAN), routing segment, or security zone. Without the intermediary device doing path selection and routing between multiple segments, no enforcement point exists for a Layer 3/4 access control list to be applied to. This is what is referred to as a need for east-to/from-west segmentation.

A mechanism needs to be applied for segmentation in the east-west segmentation model that can prevent two devices from communicating between each other within the same VLAN. The most challenging aspect of this communication occurs without the use of their IP address, given a lack of path selection requirements. In this case, a security group tag can be applied based on the functionality it depends upon. A security group tag is a 16-bit identifier embedded into the frame, or Layer 2 construct, of the communication mechanism. As a device is joined to a switch or wireless LAN controller for wired or wireless access, respectively, a network access control server can associate the identifier with the contextual identity and the session of the identity. Because this identifier is embedded into the frame and associated with the session, even communication at Layer 2 of the OSI model could consider this identifier as the policy associated with the device. As the frame traverses from source identity to destination identity, the security group tag policy, as seen in Figure 6-2, can be dynamically written to the switch or wireless LAN controller and the policy applied to traffic communication between devices. Enforcement is done at the closest point to the destination that is aware of a policy for both the source and destination identities, ensuring that the destination network access device only needs to be knowledgeable of devices that are actively connected and their identifiers. Policies for what security group tags can communicate to connected devices are relayed via RADIUS to the destination network access device.

Determining the Best Model for Segmentation

Choosing which segmentation method an organization should employ beyond the currently implemented architecture is based on a handful of criteria. These criteria can be broken down into a number of common factors that can be considered when planning for segmentation.

A Charter for Segmentation

The first criterion is a determination of why segmentation is needed to start with. With multiple presidential executive orders that have established a requirement to segment the network, many organizations with defense contracts or working in partnership with the defense industry have been mandated to implement some level of segmentation between devices on the network. This mandate will commonly spread to the public sector after lessons learned are gathered and guidance can be written on the best and most efficient use of the technology outside of extraordinarily restricted environments. For other organizations, a need to protect critical assets either after a data breach or in preparation for one is a common reason to implement segmentation.

However, individual use cases for segmentation commonly drive a charter that focuses only on that singular use case and does not consider the impact on other areas of the business. Well before use cases are considered or individual departments are queried for how they are organized and what resources they rely on, three initial questions should be asked of the organization.

What is the impact of not segmenting the network?

After all, the network is currently up, running, and passing traffic to allow the business to run. When the organization implements additional restrictions and tools on top of the network to prevent traffic flow, there will be additional discovery, troubleshooting, planning, and onboarding for new users, devices, and applications. However, the trade-off of this additional effort may be that additional government contracts, increased market impact, shareholder confidence, positive repute of the brand, or attraction of workforce focused on such priorities may result. When companies are breached or exploited based on a lack of segmentation, they may suffer a negative impact on any of these aspects and could damage the business, in addition to losing data that may be crucial to competition in the market.

Is there a policy that allows us to enforce the need for segmentation of the network?

Well before any segmentation plan can be drafted and put into motion, the organization needs to consider the ability to enforce it, ensuring that users who are unable to maintain business as usual aren't given carte blanche access to the network. Commonly, in an exercise deemed "executive bling" by some, a user who escalates high enough or is high enough in an organization can force a help desk technician to remove the restrictions from the network access device just by claiming to need additional access to do their job. This behavior has been observed in many organizations that have executives with new devices they want to use on the network without any level of approval in place, leading to an inability for those charged with protecting the network to prevent this activity solely based on authoritative status. The only way to avoid this access is through firm policy on what procedures must be completed before allowing a device on the network. More on this use case can be found in the section "Challenge: New Endpoint Onboarding" in Chapter 7.

To what level do we need to segment the network while still maintaining business as usual?

Many organizations will classify all PCs as needing to be segmented from all other PCs to prevent the spread of malware throughout the organization. However, this policy does not consider many peer-to-peer communication use cases that must exist for aspects of the business to succeed. Across many industries, custom procedures and applications have been developed that require an exchange between devices for a multitude of business use cases. Exchange of financial reports to be generated or after generation, configuration exchange between Internet of Things devices to identify their management station, and ad-hoc backup of critical devices in case of failure are quite common across industries. Preventing any of these use cases may bring damage to the business or its customers. Therefore, a level of segmentation should be chosen based on how the business operates with stakeholders from all levels of the business involved to understand their business operational needs.

In addition to these business-as-usual requirements, attribution for the contextual identity of who or what is accessing data has become necessary in many industries. These requirements can drive the need for segmentation and potentially the level or model of segmentation. For organizations with a mandate to prevent devices on the same logical, or Layer 2, network from communicating with one another, two options exist: either breaking devices into their own individual logical segments to prevent communication without an intermediary (Layer 3) device or limiting access with a Layer 2 enforcement mechanism.

An Architectural Model for Success

As has been illustrated thus far, multiple models of segmentation exist, and the usage of each depends upon the architecture and the traffic traversal patterns observed within the network requiring segmentation. With regards to the architecture of the network, two design methodologies have predominantly been the focus of network architectures in recent years. The first has been Layer 2 to the access, as illustrated in Figure 6-3. In Layer 2 to the access, a switched virtual interface (SVI) exists for the VLAN, which contains the only IP address for path selection and is used only for communication outside of the switching domain. The SVI IP address typically exists only on the distribution or even core networking device, making for a need to traverse from the access switch up to the switch with the IP address before it can traverse between VLANs. Using this type of architectural model makes for a larger Layer 2 domain in which path selection is not required and MAC addresses are the main mechanism utilized for identification between endpoints, within what typically manifests itself as a larger Layer 2 domain. Furthermore, this type of architectural model can enable a model where a distribution layer switch is configured with the switched virtual interface and respective IP address, with multiple access layer switches connected to the distribution with no IP address allocation, on any of the access layer switches whatsoever. In the Layer 2 flat network model, there is an explicit need to use Layer 2 segmentation mechanisms to prevent spread of malware across multiple switches in the switching domain because no other mechanism would be able to control the traffic.

The second architectural model is Layer 3 to the access, as seen in Figure 6-4. Unlike Layer 2 to the access, Layer 3 breaks individual switches into multiple VLANs with the switched virtual interface existing on the access switch itself, rather than further north in the architecture. With modern switches, routing can even be enabled on the access layer switch to do full packet exchange between endpoints within different VLANs without the packet ever leaving the access layer switch. In these cases, standard RADIUS-applied downloadable access control lists can be applied to individual sessions on the switch for differentiated access and segmentation.

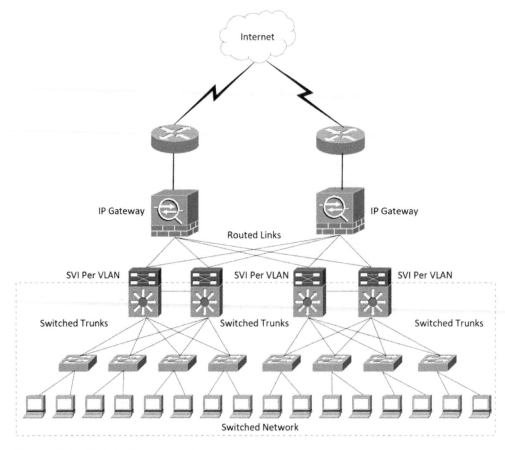

Figure 6-3 *Switched to Access Design*

When evaluating the best model for segmentation, the organization should consider the architectural model implemented. As a side effect of this currently implemented model, the organization also should consider whether that architectural model can change or be rearchitected based on the need for the goals of segmentation to be implemented. Layer 2 segmentation methods are very effective in preventing communication without changing a large, flat networking model. They can work in conjunction with a requirement to not change IP addresses within a site, common to manufacturing or medical environments where a third-party technician is required to change settings on older or less user-friendly devices.

For organizations that employ a managed services provider or in-house staff who are unable or unwilling to support the addition of Layer 2 segmentation methods to the network, redesign may be a consideration to utilize only Layer 3 segmentation methods. Some organizations find the effort to rearchitect the network offers a chance to improve on unforeseeable circumstances that have impacted the network design based on its growth, change in business need, and devices joined to it. This change will commonly result in a more efficient network that can have both Layer 2 and Layer 3 segmentation methods applied to it based on the specific needs of the organization at the current time.

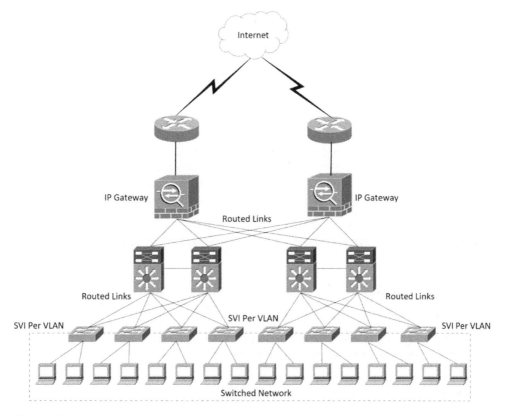

Figure 6-4 *Routed to Access*

Whether the Organization Understands Device Behavior

The third criterion is where organizations spend the most time and effort, and is often overlooked as a critical requirement. The typical goal of most organizations is to segment the network but to also have that segmentation and the enforcement therein be completely transparent to end users. Only when users attempt to access resources they are unauthorized to access should they be prevented. The only effective way to ensure that this goal is a success is to gather as much information related to the traversal of traffic on the network as possible, analyze that data, implement the policy, and cycle back through these steps. Therefore, a predominant criterion for this analysis is where, how, and for how long traffic can be collected to understand the traffic traversal. For organizations that have used a firewall to segment their network in the past, this aspect of segmentation is not unique. New devices as joined to the network would need to be allowed out to applications based on identifying characteristics of the source of the traversal. However, proper understanding of how the devices communicate or proper amounts of time to analyze what the devices are doing throughout their functional life cycle need to be considered. When an organization implements a segmentation model across the entirety of the access layer, this need to understand device communication is exponentially greater than traversal through the edge firewall.

For organizations that cannot commit to focusing on device traversal and the time it would take to understand all device communications, broader application of segmentation is typically a better approach. Broader segmentation typically will start with a simple "permit all traffic" or "deny all traffic" applied to the identity and get stricter in its application as more information is discovered relating to the device's behavior. It is common for this approach to require a much longer timeline with gradual implementation consisting of multiple segmentation methodologies as devices are better understood. This process can take years to perfect. One of the largest mistakes that many organizations make is assuming they understand the traffic traversal and blocking large swaths of users from accessing critical resources. More common mistakes are covered in Chapter 7.

Applying Segmentation Throughout Network Functions

To better understand the ideal-world application of segmentation, in this section we dive deeper into the application of each type of enforcement mechanism, its requirements for success, and the benefits it can provide to a segmentation strategy. As mentioned previously, the layering of enforcement mechanisms is always recommended to account for different use cases and potential misses in applications.

VLAN Segmentation

The use of VLANs is a common tried-and-true form of segmentation within any network architecture. VLANs break large domains of the network into individual, smaller domains to contain endpoints and therefore communication, with a need to communicate through a routing device to traverse between them. However, an overreliance on VLANs has manifested itself in the Zero Trust era, with networks broken into smaller and smaller segments, encroaching on the upper limits of both VLAN availability and policy to determine allowable traversal. This seeming overreliance brings organizations back to a consideration of the question "How many VLANs is too many VLANs?" The answer is solely dependent upon the organization, but questions that can be considered to make this determination could be of the following nature:

- Can the organization clearly describe why a device is part of the VLAN to which it is assigned as it relates to the risk the device poses to the network? In other words, when a device is grouped with similar devices into the VLAN as their logical segment, it should be assigned based on not only the device type but also the risk it poses to devices within the same segment versus those devices that fall outside of the segment. If this device were compromised and the compromise spread within the VLAN, are all devices within the VLAN sufficiently protected and do they have similar risk profiles when compared to devices that are not assigned to the segment?

■ Does the breakdown of logical segments make sense for operational personnel? If devices are split into VLANs based solely on risk and not accounting for additional protections that can be applied, devices may be put into larger numbers of VLANs that overlap in their function. This placement results in smaller numbers of devices within each VLAN of similar types. The question then comes back to how the organization decides which VLAN a device gets put into when multiple overlapping VLANS exist in a single geographical area.

■ Regarding the breakdown of VLANs, how will traversal between them be done, and at what scale? While routers or firewalls can be used to allow traversal between VLANs, policies need to be written relating to the traversal for environments that don't allow all VLANs to communicate between each other. Devices need to be able to handle the number of VLANs used, as well as the number of policies as an exponentially larger factor of the number of VLANs used.

This last bullet point raises another pertinent question when using VLANs as a primary segmentation method: "How many firewalls are too many firewalls?" The allocation of users to their respective VLANs eases the operational burden and design burden for administrators as users share the logical segment. However, network design hygiene does require that the VLANs exist on each access switch to which a user can connect and the infrastructure to allow that device to traverse to a default gateway where policy is applied. The default gateway is often a firewall to allow cross-segment transmission. When utilizing firewalls as the traversal gateway between VLANs, as an extension of the VLAN segmentation model, the organization should also consider additional aspects:

■ Placement of the firewall within the VLAN segmented network may have an impact on how many VLANs aggregate through the firewall, potentially approaching an upper limit. Firewalls, like any other network device, have upper limitations in the number of VLANs they can support in the form of subinterfaces. While firewalls can be localized to areas of the network to minimize the number of firewalls needed, this localization places an additional burden on firewall and rule management.

■ Firewall management must be done in a manner that can be scaled and planned for within the segmentation model. Centralized management systems for firewalls are becoming more common based on challenges in managing entire fleets of firewalls in legacy networks. However, attributes that indicate which rules are relevant to where those firewalls sit in a distributed model must be maintained and utilized in management. When VLANs may be local to one site or even one segment of the network, this information needs to be known to the management platform to ensure rules applied specifically to that VLAN and segment are only deployed to the firewall within its traversal.

■ The maintenance of rules, documenting why a rule or policy exists, for which endpoints, and the owning entity must be maintained within the firewalls rules or associated knowledge base. Far too common, as organizations scale out the number of firewalls they use within their network, they fail to scale out documentation on which rules exist for what reasons. When the time comes to audit rules, this information makes for a challenging justification for either keeping or cleaning up rules due to a lack of information related to them.

One potential ease in operational burden and cost associated with VLANs is the application of dynamic VLANs. While dynamic VLANs won't have an impact on firewall throughput and traversal, use of a dynamic VLAN to allocate an endpoint based on its contextual identity will ease the need for operations teams to statically assign VLANs. Given that dynamic VLANs can also be applied based on a name as opposed to number provides for the ability to use different numbers based on geographical location, minimizing impact of devices already contained within the VLAN.

Access Control List Segmentation

The concept of a standard or extended access control list allowing or preventing access to a resource is both common and familiar to most organizations and their network teams. ACLs are generally applied between logical segments and are commonly used on firewalls to allow or deny traversal at Layers 3 and 4 of the OSI model. Access control lists could be a layered control mechanism on top of the VLAN segmentation approach, mainly because they are used in the traversal of traffic between these VLANs. The ACL would be configured on the upstream firewall through which traffic is aggregated in the VLAN segmentation model. The advantage that the access control list provides is for both a stateful nature for traffic traversal when configured on a firewall and a range of limitations that can be applied to the traversal across multiple OSI layers. As was illustrated earlier in the section "Common Network-Centric Segmentation Models," when configured on a firewall, ACLs provide for a protocol, source and destination address, and source and destination port filtering ability when creating a policy for traversal.

However, unless an external management source is used, ACLs have three major flaws in their application in common use cases:

■ Error checking with ACLs is specific to only the syntax the ACL is configured with, as opposed to the functionality it is expected to have on the traversal of packets. When it comes to overlaps in addressing that could have an impact on whether a packet traverses when it should not or vice versa, there is little error checking to validate that a rule with a higher priority may not override one with lower priority.

■ Tracking of ACLs within a device's software is rare. Therefore, the life cycle of the ACL, owner, manager, and responsible party for maintaining the ACL are commonly placed in remarks preceding it, or not at all. The ACL life cycle typically used makes for evaluation of potential impact of the ACL extremely difficult, leading to unintended consequences related to packet traversal.

■ ACLs can control only traffic that is routed, or Layer 3 in nature. Devices within the same VLAN, as they will use their MAC address to communicate, will not be affected by applied ACLs.

When combined with VLAN segmentation, ACLs can lend themselves to a more robust segmentation model. With Cisco Identity Services Engine, ACLs can be written in a centralized engine and dynamically applied to contextual identities in a ubiquitous manner across wired, wireless, and VPN mediums.

TrustSec Segmentation

With either approach, allocation of endpoints into respective VLANs or application of ACLs even in a dynamic nature, the peer-to-peer concept of traffic communication is still present, with little ability to prevent communication within a VLAN due to its use of Layer 2 identities exclusively. Without the ability to prevent communication between devices within the same VLAN, threats can still spread in a peer-to-peer manner within the logical segment.

For many organizations, having IoT and risk-inherent devices present on the network is becoming a necessary reality. Use cases across industries exist for these devices, including the following:

- **IP cameras for physical security:** Physical security cameras are commonly used in most industries that utilize a network management station or network video recorder, either local to the network, in a remote data center, or even in the cloud. However, many IP camera models need to communicate between devices in either a broadcast or multicast fashion to determine where the management station is. Typically, this is done to allow zero-touch configuration of the IP camera, but there can also be a need to share video streams, meta data, or backups. Preventing this traffic would inhibit zero-touch functionality or, potentially, continuity between devices as they inform others of movement or other triggering actions within their view.

- **Temperature and humidity sensors for equipment cabinets:** Commonly, smart sensors that analyze the temperature and humidity in equipment cabinets and open racks are being introduced within data centers, with similar use cases in the oil and gas industry for pipeline operation. These devices, commonly installed in areas without reliable power sources or monitoring abilities, form a mesh network to minimize the amount of power and amount of data one sensor needs to store or transmit. By exchanging periodic updates with their neighbors, sensors can send significantly smaller amounts of data to save on battery, runtime, and storage needs to extend their usable lifetime.

- **Parking lot sensors:** Parking lot sensors are commonly used in retail environments where parking garages track whether a space is occupied, helping shoppers quickly find a spot to park in and increase their time in the retail establishment. Utilizing proximity sensors to determine where cars are parked in relation to the spot, these devices communicate between sensors, which then indicate whether the spot is occupied, as opposed to needing to communicate all the way back to a centralized management station. A centralized node that then stores this information can communicate back to the management station on the other sensors' behalf, populating a billboard at the entrance to the garage indicating current capacity.

■ **Door locks and sensors:** In an emergency, priority is typically given to occupants of a building, allowing them to escape the building. In many manufacturing environments, users must badge both into and out of a building, in an effort to control intellectual property and prevent data loss. For these types of environments, the loss of the controller that allows or disallows access could be catastrophic to human safety. In these cases, the loss of the management station needs to be overcome through peer-to-peer communication between locks and distributed control mechanisms to allow access without authorizing the action. A signal noting that the management station is down is sent between devices.

For these use cases and the organizations that utilize them, an approach to segmentation must be taken to allow both the securing of traversal between endpoints within the same VLAN or logical segment, as well as restrictions being applied to minimize threats to the required transmissions between devices.

TrustSec was invented to solve the need for granular segmentation within a VLAN or subnet due to the mechanisms within other protocols, such as ARP, allowing uninhibited communication between devices. In the ARP process, an endpoint first determines whether the device it seeks to communicate with exists within its broadcast domain. If not, the IP address is used as the communication address. When the destination device is in the same broadcast domain, the MAC address of the device is used, as discovered with a series of messages seeking to map the destination IP address to a MAC address. This "who is" message is sent within the VLAN or subnet, and if the destination device is present, it responds with its MAC address to allow communication.

There are limited ways to prevent this communication—limited to the previous references for allocating a new VLAN for one of the devices to connect to or creating an access control list based on the two MAC addresses. The operational overhead involved in maintaining this access control list is exorbitant, especially considering the need to create a potential matrix for every one of the ports that may exist on a single switch. To reduce complexity, dynamic application of policies based on the network device, is needed.

The inner workings of TrustSec rely on a field within the frame header referred to in the RFC as the Cisco Meta Data (CMD) field, which is 16 bits in length. These 16 bits allow an overlay grouping that can be dynamically applied in addition to networking aspects, such as VLAN, to classify the device and group it in with other devices with a similar contextual identity. For example, where PCs exist in the network, regardless of which IP space or VLAN they are part of, they all can be dynamically grouped to have the same policy. Policy can be further refined and made more granular by stating that PCs with a user from the finance department are all classified the same as opposed to PCs being used by an HR user or even all PCs being too broad of a classification. With this overlay identifier, classification becomes more easily applied, primarily when the identifier is allocated by way of a network access control appliance, such as Cisco Identity Services Engine. Policies are then created as part of the TrustSec matrix and are pushed to the network access device. The network access device installs only the policies it needs based on the tags it has recorded as assigned to directly connected devices. This matrix provides the control policy for each source and destination tag pair. The policies can be as granular as specifying the allowance of traffic for certain ports and protocols between the tags or as basic as a simple permit or deny any result. For example, two adjacent devices that exist in the same VLAN, sitting next to one another, can be prevented from communicating, regardless of whether they are assigned the same tag or different tags. Enforcement with TrustSec, in contrast to an approach using an ACL, is at the egress point of the network just prior to the destination endpoint. The network access device makes an enforcement decision based on the TrustSec matrix rules that it has downloaded.

Given that TrustSec relies on the frame and embedded information in the frame to function successfully, two considerations need to be made. The first is that applying segmentation to a device at Layer 2 could prevent it from communicating with most resources on the network, including its IP gateway if configured incorrectly. Applying segmentation to a device at Layer 2 yields a need to understand traversal and the required policy of all devices on the network to prevent service outage due to lack of communication abilities.

The second is the need to understand and classify devices into enclaves while avoiding going too granular without respective value in doing so. As we cover in Chapter 7, one of the largest challenges—after understanding traffic traversal that organizations have with TrustSec—is overcomplicating their tagging structure to be too granular. This manner of tag application hinders operations teams by overcomplicating troubleshooting due to huge policies that, in many cases, have identical policy rules or results.

Layering Segmentation Functions

Layered security mechanisms can allow networks to utilize the most relevant segmentation method for an endpoint in relation to the traffic traversal required by the endpoint. Utilizing a combination of VLANs, firewalls, ACLs, and TrustSec tags for the same contextual identity helps layer the enforcement mechanisms and minimize impact or re-architecture of these mechanisms based on attempting to apply them to a larger conceptual area than designed for. Overall, the following guidance can be used based on the previously discussed strengths and considerations in this section:

- VLAN segmentation is inherent to the network and should be used for broadly classifying devices into logical segments.

- Firewalls should be used in conjunction with VLAN segmentation to dictate the traversal across VLAN segments, or where additional firewall-focused functionality is required between segments.

- Dynamically applied ACLs should be used to offload based permit and deny statements at Layers 3 and 4 from the firewall and localize the application of those enforcement statements to the network access device through which the endpoint is connected.

■ TrustSec tags should be used to prevent access within a VLAN, where a singular subnet is used, or where a need to associate contextual identity to Layer 2 attributes of the endpoint exists. A common use for TrustSec tags is to differentiate between identities within the same VLAN to apply upstream firewall policy based on the Security Group Tag identifier.

Outside the Branch or Campus

Admittedly, most of this section has focused on segmentation in a branch or campus environment, which may cause some readers to take pause. While the data center and cloud have evolved in many ways, many of the same mechanisms exist to be layered for segmentation purposes, just in slightly different forms.

One major challenge to the data center is the common use of virtual machines within a hypervisor. The hypervisor commonly has a virtual switch used to exchange data between virtual machines, with this virtual switch commonly not supporting TrustSec as a protocol, but still having similar capabilities. Port groups containing ports similar to a VLAN or virtual private clouds (VPCs) are common across hypervisors and can have similar restrictions applied between members, similar to the L2 restrictions TrustSec provides for in the campus. Where this method of using the hypervisor to segment starts to fall short is the interaction of a device sourced from a branch or campus and communicating to the data center with a destination contained on a virtual server, within a VPC or port group. Commonly, a need to understand the contextual identity of the server more also exists, and its inability to connect to a medium that it can be authenticated and profiled on adds to this challenge. Products such as Cisco Secure Workload or Secure Endpoint client can be used as a client agent installed on the virtual machine to determine contextual identity and receive policy from a centralized policy engine to prevent or allow communication based on discovered communication pattern needs. These agents can lend themselves to a software defined, granular segmentation ability based on traffic communication discovery. These clients rely on the common IP tables feature or built-in firewall for server-focused operating systems and can write policies based on the expected communication patterns. By using IP tables or local firewall these solutions overcome limitations of the RADIUS protocol used in the branch and campus and, as a result, can also be used as a workaround for networks where RADIUS cannot be applied to network access devices as well.

How To: Methods and Considerations for Segmentation in an Ideal World

For many organizations, at this point the application of segmentation for Zero Trust may seem overwhelming. With a broad set of potential exploitations that vary by use case and business structure, teams need to focus on segmentation in the proverbial method of eating an elephant—in other words, one small step at a time. By maintaining a viewpoint of applying segmentation based on the five core pillars of Zero Trust—Policy & Governance, Identity, Enforcement, Vulnerability Management, and Analytics—organizations can apply enforcement mechanisms in a layered fashion.

The Bottom Line: Ideal World

The question comes down to "In an ideal world, which segmentation methodology works best?" The answer, simply put, is all of them. Segmentation should be layered throughout the network and used to protect resources in numerous ways from various types of potential exploitation.

- As the endpoint joins the network, it should be authenticated and authorized, with the authorization including a VLAN to allocate the endpoint into a logical segment onto the network. The VLAN plan should allow expansion of devices contained within it at the average growth rate over the past five years, or 20 percent, whichever is greater. This VLAN is aggregated on an upstream Layer 3 enforcement device that can filter traversal between VLANs as need be.

- Along with the VLAN, the endpoint should be allocated a security group tag that assigns the enclave within the logical segment to which the endpoint belongs. These enclaves, as discussed in Chapter 4, "Zero Trust Enclave Design," should be aligned with the business purpose and trust boundaries of endpoints on the network, while breaking devices into groups small enough to contain a potential attack.

- In the theme of distributing the enforcement mechanisms across the network as opposed to continuing to use a firewall as a centralized policy enforcement point, downloadable ACLs should also be part of the authorization policy and limit access between internal segments, well before the transmission reaches the Layer 3 routing point. The application to the specific session can minimize the number of restrictions that need to be applied locally to the device, thus minimizing the length of ACLs found at the router or firewall upstream.

- As alluded to in the preceding bullet points, the need for a firewall still exists within the segmentation architecture, mostly based on advanced features that can be implemented and utilized within a segmented topology. Advanced malware detection, intrusion prevention, TCP normalization, VPN termination, and a myriad of other features present on firewalls still make them a valuable addition to the segmentation architecture, even while attempting to minimize their burden by distributing enforcement across other devices closer to the endpoint.

To accomplish the necessary tasks to fulfill these guiding principles, we go through focus areas and practical methodologies in the following sections, as also illustrated in Figure 6-5.

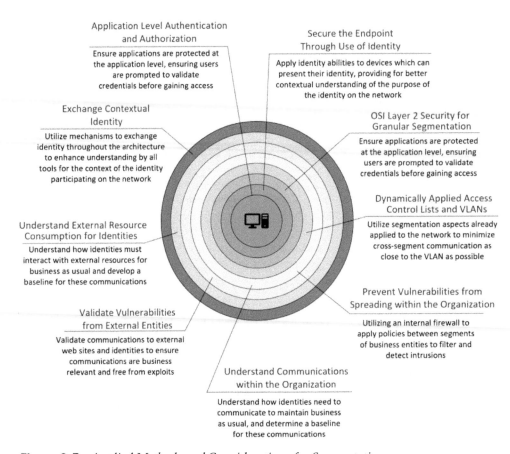

Figure 6-5   *Applied Methods and Considerations for Segmentation*

Understanding the Contextual Identity

For any organization to start down its segmentation journey, we have focused on the idea of contextual identity throughout. Contextual identity, or the questions of, is the basis behind segmentation:

- Who is on a device?

- What type of device is being used?

- Where is the device located?

- When did the device connect to the network?

- Over which medium did the device connect?

- What vulnerabilities does the device pose to the network?

This basis is enabled by a combination of tribal knowledge and the use of RADIUS being sent from network access devices to Cisco Identity Services Engine. RADIUS provides the ability to understand whether the device supports authentication, and whether it is configured to present the user, machine, or both sets of credentials because a device should always respond with credentials if it has an enabled supplicant. These credentials serve to authenticate the device, but additional functionality inherent to the device, which can be used to further identify it, can also be consumed by ISE to gain better understanding of what the device is. Interception of information such as DHCP and HTTP headers can be used to determine the type of device based on known patterns and expected contents.

Understanding External Resource Consumption of the Device

Once an organization understands the contextual identity, it serves two purposes. The first is in understanding how identities present themselves on a network. For example, are the devices capable of identifying themselves, or was significant historical knowledge required to identify the devices? Defining the method that the segmentation team will use to understand the environment can provide valuable information for how to classify devices when segmentation policies are aligned with—for example, preventing access to certain resources that are unable to actively authenticate to the network and rely on their built-in MAC address to do so. The second is it serves as a mapping of how the network is currently laid out, more specifically which contextual identities are currently members of which VLAN through a static configuration on the network access device. For organizations that are either interested in deploying VLANs to devices dynamically and then filtering at the gateway or are interested in breaking the flat network into business aligned segments, this identification is the cornerstone of that ability. Contextual identity of identities will feed internal consumption aspects described in the next section.

Next, classifying resources to which the endpoints communicate needs to be a priority. The identity already gained through contextual identity helps the team understand how that specific identity interacts with the rest of the network. This is done, more specifically, by exchanging the identity into a traffic collection mechanism via the Platform Exchange Grid (PXGrid) protocol or similar abilities to integrate this information with the traffic collection platform of choice. For Cisco technologies, Identity Services Engine being used at the access layer for devices in the campus and branch allows the identities found through RADIUS to be exchanged into Secure Network Analytics for injection into NetFlow. This NetFlow collection can be done on the ingress to the edge device at the campus or branch to avoid erroneous conversations inbound to the external interface of the same device. In addition, where firewalls exist in the campus or branch, collection may be done by inserting identity information into firewall logs, or into other data center logging information. The Cisco Secure Workload solution, being both the collection and enforcement mechanism (when an endpoint agent is used), simplifies corelating contextual identity, log information with CMDB information by enabling operating system level software defined segmentation control.

These methods can all be key to creating a more restrictive policy that ensures the endpoint behaves within its baseline. This baseline, as covered in the Vulnerability Management pillar of Zero Trust, provides both an understanding of the device's required behavior but also its expected behavior, which can be monitored and alerted upon when the device deviates from this baseline. While multiple examples could be referenced to the point, it has not been uncommon for sites to be compromised somehow, serving data or malware to devices that the manufacturer did not intend. Streaming devices such as Android OS-based microcomputers, for example, have built-in web browsers, unique app stores, and even torrent download capabilities. For organizations that utilize these micro-computers for streaming, analysis of baseline traffic can help uncover threats to the organization and block them well before exploitation. While some may argue that threats are commonly blocked by a firewall, layered security should still ensure threats are blocked in each respective threat domain.

Validating Vulnerabilities to External Sites

A key to understanding aspects of the risk that devices on the network pose to the organization is the traffic traversing to external sites. The organization can use intrusion prevention systems (IPSs) on all firewalls within the organization and use Layer 7 security mechanisms such as TCP intercept, TCP randomization, application discovery and mapping, anti-malware analysis within packet headers, and similar features to gauge the vulnerability posed when associated with identities on the network. One potential way to accomplish this is to use a Layer 7 firewall, such as Cisco Secure Firewall, which can discover applications based on observed traffic flows. Policies can then be applied as close as possible to the endpoint through other mechanisms, allowing the blocking of specific ports even within the organization to ensure that known vulnerabilities can be minimized. A firewall with IPS as an alerting mechanism or endpoint posture agents or vulnerability scanners all offer the ability to consume identity and report on observed versus expected behaviors.

Understanding Communication Within the Organization

In a similar fashion to collecting and identifying common communication patterns external to the network and within the organization helps the organization understand business-required communications for peer-to-peer use cases described previously. For organizations that have no restrictions on traffic traversal between internal networks, this will be a net-new addition. Luckily, the same tools used for discovery of external communications—NetFlow collection via Cisco Secure Network Analytics, for example—are used to determine this traversal. However, while DNS may be used to resolve external identities when mapping traffic traversal, traffic internal to the organization relies on contextual identity and, therefore, the integration of this contextual identity into the traffic collection tool. This same prioritization of contextual identity carries over to organizations that have cross-segment firewalls for internal communications, such as those that segment the network with Virtual Routing and Forwarding instances already.

This firewall, responsible for controlling data between VRFs, can also serve as a second layer in the security spectrum, with known traffic from any given VRF being allowed only in as granular a manner as needed. The externally facing firewall serves as an alerting mechanism once again. This use of a VRF-focused firewall also offloads much of the processing load from the edge firewall. Similar to the use of downloadable ACLs within VRFs and between VLANs, the internal firewall filters out packets that are intraorganizational instead of relying on a single "do-all" firewall.

Validating Vulnerabilities Within the Organization

While intrusion prevention systems are typically a focus for externally facing traffic traversal due to the potential threat of allowing malware or similar exploits into the organization, an IPS in the organization where firewalls exist for cross-VRF traffic can provide for additional controls between business units. This intrusion scanning and detection ability to understand how business units interact can also prevent malware from spreading based on business unit–specific security policies. For large organizations that have many acquisition companies or divestiture companies, it is expected that security policies may differ between business units or the acquired/divested company. The need to onboard or offboard these companies is a relatively high-risk period because a single administrator may not be able to tell what vulnerabilities are present in the company's network. Additionally, large, flat networks from legacy connectivity-minded companies can serve as a much larger attack surface. In these areas, collecting contextual identity, analyzing the flows, and understanding potential vulnerabilities are key to securing the business.

Understanding Communication Within the Broadcast Domain or VLAN

One challenging aspect of the segmentation methodologies is understanding communication within the broadcast domain or VLAN. As mentioned throughout this chapter, much of the challenge relating to this approach is around a lack of documentation or understanding of how devices interact on the network. Understanding these communications requires already having a contextual identity deployed to endpoints. Only with an understanding of the contextual identity and understanding of the flow between identities within the VLAN or broadcast domain can enforcement be applied as close to the endpoint as possible. There also must be an understanding of how to identify devices that cannot provide an active identity. Collection of this information about communication patterns may rely not only on tools to gather the contextual identity but also historical knowledge. This process must start with observing what is on the network and which contextual identity it may align with. It can then be honed and narrowed down based on collection aspects and both passive interrogation and data collection.

Armed with this information, it is then much easier to apply policy to endpoints as granular as required. For many organizations, policy application will be a very general permit- or deny-based policy, with devices that could potentially affect each other in significant manners being denied and the devices that must interact being permitted. These policies can then be refined to ports and protocols required for communication. It is highly recommended that an organization evaluates what it can not only design based on endpoints but also operationalize. Far too many organizations start with too many segments based on contextual identity, attempting to replace primarily authentication-based mechanisms, such as Active Directory, with TrustSec tags. Mechanisms that provide for more robust identity, including having multiple groups that can be used to validate a user's role, are better used to identify the device and then be added to a collection of groups within a single tag. More on the challenges of segmenting large networks can be found in Chapter 7.

Restricting Peer-to-Peer or Jump-Off Points

Key to the success of a segmentation plan is preventing jump-off points and potential attack vectors while maintaining business as usual. The policies used within, across, and external to the network will depend on the traffic collection and analysis used to determine what traffic communications are required for business to continue to operate as usual. This is because of the typical attack vector observed in most attacks: find a weak device able to be used as an entry point, and jump to additional devices until the target is exploited. Therefore, the organization needs to consider the risk of devices currently joined to the network, the destinations to which they communicate, and what level of restriction might be able to be applied to those communications. In many cases, other security restrictions already applied to devices will minimize the need to restrict communications heavily or allow increased restrictions over time. It is highly recommended to treat the analysis and eventual enforcement of restrictions as a long-term goal and a journey over time as opposed to a "big bang" approach to segmentation.

Part of this journey over time is creating an "endpoint segmentation plan" to illustrate what types of devices exist where in the network, in a business alignment view. Classifying devices into their respective business units, or segments, can help plan where restrictions must be applied, in what order, and to what extent over time. This segmentation plan typically includes some level of detail relating to how devices will authenticate, need to be authorized, and what restrictions need to apply between business units or device types. This segmentation plan may also be referred to as an enclave plan. An example of this endpoint segmentation plan can be seen in Figure 6-6.

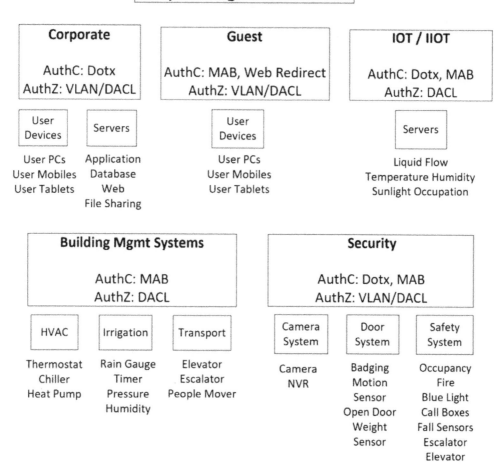

Figure 6-6 *Endpoint Segmentation Plan*

Summary

Segmentation is key to the Enforcement tenet of Zero Trust. However, it is also the most challenging aspect of Zero Trust due to the business's reliance on devices traversing in unknown traffic patterns. In this chapter, we covered an in-depth approach to understanding how devices interact with each other and with external resources. Once an understanding of traffic traversal is present, enforcement mechanisms aligned to the specific risk needs of the business or individual business units can be applied in a layered manner. These layers range from dynamic allocation of VLANs, security group tag application, downloadable ACL application, firewall enforcement, and DNS policy enforcement. Knowing that many organizations have limited enforcement mechanisms applied in legacy connectivity-based environments, we cover common challenges and approaches to overcome these challenges in Chapter 7 when working through this data collection, analysis, and enforcement.

References in This Chapter

- Patrick Lloyd, "An Exploration of Covert Channels Within Voice over IP," Thesis, *Rochester Institute of Technology*, 2010, https://scholarworks.rit.edu/theses/814/.

Zero Trust Common Challenges

Chapter Key Points:

- Organizations with a goal of segmentation will encounter many challenges throughout their data collection and focus on contextual identity and traffic traversal.

- A connection-focused mindset for legacy networks has created a slew of challenges that must be overcome in a Zero Trust Architecture. These challenges can be overcome with proper focus and discovery, while keeping in mind the goal that an organization's Zero Trust journey is driven by.

- Identifying and understanding the identity of devices and using that identity to determine the expected behavior both internally and externally are key to securing devices throughout the network.

- Many other, seemingly unrelated processes contribute to segmentation. Consistent onboarding processes, determination of whether the organization needs micro or macro segmentation, and determination of the best application of an enforcement mechanism can ease an organization's Zero Trust journey.

Across all industries, the evolution of endpoint connectivity to the network has changed in a significant manner. In designs used even 5 to 10 years ago, focus was put on connecting endpoints to the network, as opposed to securing their connectivity. However, challenges related to malware, ransomware, and potential compromise of endpoints leading to unrestricted access due to a connectivity mindset have led to a need to authenticate and authorize entities to only the resources they require access to. In alignment with the NIST tenets of Zero Trust, endpoints should be considered untrusted and compromised until proven otherwise. Specifically, NIST states, "All resource authentication and authorization are dynamic and strictly enforced before access is allowed." The enforcement core principle of this text's model aligns closely with this tenet.

However, many organizations that attempt to move toward a strictly security-based mindset quickly find that the problem, especially on wired networks, seems insurmountable. The security-based mindset was forced upon architects and designers with wireless networks from their inception and is considered commonplace. Wired networks, on the other hand, have been seen as the "safe" option—both because of their proximity to administrators but also because of their fallback role to the secured wireless network. Taking away this "safe" option means addressing challenges that are years or decades in the making. Namely, these challenges align to the five core principles, and begin with understanding the contextual identity of endpoints, understanding their behavior to manage potential vulnerabilities, and only then implementing an enforcement mechanism that can secure connectivity while providing required access.

To resolve outdated past practices means a change in policy, a change in process, and the need to overcome challenges related to both. These challenges are discussed throughout this chapter.

Challenge: Gaining Visibility into the Unknown (Endpoints)

It is not easy charting the legacy of those who have built and pioneered the network into what it is today. Many organizations encounter a lack of documentation as the first hurdle in answering this question. Others find resistance from owners of applications and architectures due to perceived invasion into their domain. Sponsors and leadership may see these efforts as unnecessary and an impediment to an acceleration of the implementation. The team responsible for this task may react adversely if the task seems overwhelming in the scope of this exercise.

These roadblocks and inhibitors begin to dissolve when the team frames the ask with the simple terms of looking at where the organization is today. Access to a subset of the answers to these questions will already exist if exercises like the workshop mentioned previously were completed. The level of thoroughness of the workshop, or similar exercises, directly reduces the effort of this task. Teams inside the organization with excellent documentation and rigor in their work also ease the task's difficulty. Teams to target begin with those eager to showcase their work.

The introduction of a new endpoint onto the network, regardless of the medium through which it accesses the network, should immediately kick off a similar process of understanding what that endpoint is and what its expected behavior is. Unfortunately, distributed purchasing ability within most organizations—allowing anyone with a corporate credit card to purchase new devices and connect them at will—makes this process of understanding endpoint contextual identity a significant challenge.

Continuing along the lines of a need to authenticate and authorize all devices that are introduced to the network, policy and governance must be used to ensure all endpoints introduced onto the network are properly vetted, onboarded, and configured for access based on their contextual identity.

Overcoming the Challenge: The Use of Contextual Identity

To revisit the concept from Chapter 1, "Overview of Zero Trust (ZT)," contextual identity takes into consideration the identification aspects of who, what, where, and how, but adds additional concepts, such as how the device interacts with the network. This contextual identity seeks to move identification of devices away from an IP address and provide more contextual clues for the need to have the device on the network. To break down further:

- **Who:** There needs to be an understanding of who the user is who owns, uses, or manages the device. This distinct identity of the user attempting to use the device can be acquired in a multitude of ways. The most common way to determine this identity is through directory services integration for devices joined to the domain; however, there are many use cases that prevent joining a device to the domain. The greatest challenge to understanding who owns, uses, or manages a device comes with these use cases. For devices that have no ability to join directory services, this lack of identity can be a contextual clue in and of itself. In these cases, the challenge can be overcome through the use of an asset management database to track devices and associate them with an owner, user, or manager of the device.

  The second greatest challenge to tracking the user is having a consistent and well-executed onboarding process for these devices without a user. Many organizations will purchase devices, assuming an ability to join them to the network without impedance, only to find out an existing process prevents connectivity without service tickets, testing, approvals, or additional overhead. In these cases, organizational management must adhere to the policy of onboarding the device as a strict rule. For many organizations, one-offs are created to bypass the process due to an arbitrarily chosen timeline or loudly complaining consumer of the device. In doing so, even with the best initial intentions, it is all but guaranteed that the device will never go through proper onboarding processes, and the owner, user, or manager may never be assigned.

- **What:** In addition to understanding who is attempting to use the device to perform a business-relevant action on the network, it should also be understood what the device is. The challenge of cheap, feature-rich, user-friendly IoT-based devices available on the market and to the average consumer is fueling a need for understanding whether the device has actual business relevance in its operation. Increasingly, many devices presenting themselves as having legitimate business purposes are being used to spoof identities, look like devices that they are not, or take unsanctioned actions on the network. Determining what a device is can be a challenge in and of itself. Thankfully, as with identity, a multitude of both passive and active means to identify a device can be implemented as part of an onboarding policy.

  The best approach to determining device identity is through active probing, testing, and evaluation of the device and its behavior on the network within an isolated onboarding area of the network. This onboarding process should evaluate the business need for the device, its branding, identifying characteristics such as MAC, organizational unique identifier (OUI), serial number, part number, or other unique identifying characteristics, which can then be logged in to an asset management database and associated back to a user.

The greatest challenge to the organization in which these devices are connected is a lack of onboarding policy or operational staffing to onboard tens of thousands of new devices joined to the network regularly. In these cases, the most common methodology to determine what a device is can be accomplished through active and passive means of identifying the device. Active profiling techniques derive information from the device in question by interacting and gathering data from the interaction with the device. Profiling a device by querying data from a secondary system is not active profiling. Requesting a secondary system to initiate a process of gathering data directly from a device does constitute an active profiling technique. Execute active profiling with care because use cases may prohibit specific interactions with active techniques. One example would be actively profiling a low-level network-connected printed circuit board (PCB) or building control system with an intensive NMAP scan. Due to the limited network stack and processing abilities of the PCB, the device may crash or stop responding when interrogated with the NMAP scan. Determine at least partial device identity before initiating active profiling. Common active profiling is covered later in the chapter.

NMAP

Network Mapper (NMAP) was originally created as an open-source and free-to-use utility for network discovery and security auditing. NMAP is commonly built into network access control products because of its ability to be triggered and pointed at a given device or IP address and scan the address for open ports. Information from these open ports, which is sent back to the NMAP server, contains a description of the port usage should a service be configured on the device. This identification technique overcomes the challenge of unknown devices that also cannot be identified due to a far-too-common or not-common-at-all OUI. Combinations of ports may be open on certain operating systems, or responses to queries to certain operating systems may indicate their use and be able to better identify what a device is, solely based on its ability to run the operating system. Apple devices, when queried by NMAP for their operating system, will typically respond back with a string containing "Apple iOS," whereas Windows devices will typically respond back with "Windows" and the version of the operating system, such as "Windows NT 11," "Windows 10," "Windows XP," or "Windows Vista."

One limitation to NMAP is with regards to devices that have a limited ability to be scanned, such as legacy medical devices and manufacturing devices. These devices, due to their limited implementation of a network stack and error detection, may crash if a scan is performed on them. Therefore, caution is advised when utilizing NMAP for identification purposes.

Operating System (OS) Detection

An operating system detection scan uses multiple TCP and UDP packets and the responses of those packets to determine the device's operating system based on fingerprinting techniques.

- **Host Discovery:** This scan utilizes ICMP, TCP, UDP, and other probes to determine the existence of an active host located on the network.

- **SNMP (Simple Network Management Protocol) scan:** This scan evaluates whether SNMP ports are open and attempts to query data about a device if it is using SNMP queries.

Vulnerability Management Integration Systems

Vulnerability management systems can return information based on scans and data retrieved while monitoring a system. Profiling takes advantage of this active monitoring by requesting active scans or inventory information to identify the system and its state. Contextual identity can change if a device is vulnerable or introduces an expanded attack surface to the environment. The advantage of integrating vulnerability management systems into the identification process is that it allows administrators to remediate a device to allow assignment to the initially intended identity.

Sneakernet

Sneakernet provides an inefficient, inconsistent, but time-tested method of identifying a device. If the network cannot identify the device, manual intervention may be needed. Sneakernet involves a person moving to the device's location to use their senses and experiences to identify the device physically. There are many reasons for validating a device in person. The device may be malfunctioning. Other automated and manual identification systems may return unsatisfactory results. A rogue device that bypassed onboarding connects to the network and needs to be manually verified. This process should be a last resort because it can be time-consuming and costly to perform.

Profiling

Profiling is a method of associating a device type and operating system information to act on the asset using Policy & Governance controls. The expression of practical profiling is accomplished through the inspection of packets as they are communicated on the network. The inspection of the network traffic enables policy to be applied to classes of assets or control asset features or functions.

One aspect of identity that is a common challenge for most organizations as they start to evolve their Zero Trust journey toward security is what happens when a device is unable to identify itself through an active means. IoT manufacturers use controls such as

Manufacturer Usage Description (MUD) or with legacy capabilities built into the authentication method, this is becoming easier. However, in these situations, some other method of identifying the device needs to be utilized to determine its unique identity.

Passive identification is a less preferred fallback, utilizing unique identifiers such as a MAC address or the embedded serial number provided to it. An additional consideration is that these means of identifying the device can be spoofed if exchanged in plain text or with simple forms of encryption. When plain text means of identity are used, the organization should employ, through passive methods, an additional overlay of verification that the device presenting the plain text identification information is what it claims to be.

Profiling is the ability to observe how the endpoint behaves without influencing the device in any way. This observation is utilized to determine behavior, thus validating the identification aspects of the endpoint. This identity is then utilized to determine the potential vulnerabilities that this device poses to the network. The methods of this passive observation and collection of information regarding the device's behaviors can take many forms but will typically consider the natural need for most devices to interact with the network in some way to perform their business purposes. Utilizing headers and known format patterns for protocols such as DHCP, CDP, LLDP, DNS, HTTP, and performing active NMAP scans on an endpoint can provide additional factors and considerations to be address when evaluating whether an endpoint is what it presents itself as.

For example, knowing that a corporate PC is running a standard provisioned package of Windows 10 with Firefox browser, the PC should dynamically request an IP address through DHCP that gives no fewer than four aspects that can be checked:

■ The endpoint should dynamically request its IP address, as opposed to presenting a statically assigned address as provisioned by the user.

■ The DHCP options presented to the network when requesting an address conform with the standard options presented from a Windows 10 device, or any custom options forced through company provisioning.

■ The HTTP header IP User Agent Option identifies the device as a Windows NT 10 operating system utilizing a Firefox family browser.

■ The NMAP scan of the device should indicate that ports 445 (SMB), 135 (Domain Services), 3268 (Global Catalog), 3269 (Global Catalog), and 53 (DNS) should all be open for communication, with the ability to query these ports for potential operating system information on top of just the open status of the ports.

The profiling process can also lend significant information into the Vulnerability pillar of Zero Trust by determining whether SMB version 1 or version 2 is enabled. We highly recommend against version 1 because it increases the potential risk score.

■ **Radius:** Within the radius probe, information such as the MAC address, OUI, originating authentication device, port on the device, username or hostname, and IP address can be used to determine what a device is. The OUI being registered to a company and hard-coded, or "burned in," to a network interface card allows an easily identified characteristic of the endpoint to be matched against a centralized registration database. That said, while the MAC address is considered to be hard-coded, some existing software utilities do force the device's network interface card to present a chosen identifier. This process is known as MAC spoofing. While MAC spoofing can be overcome with active identification methods, such as interrogating the device in person, this passive profiling mechanism can be augmented with policies to connect such categories of devices to specific network access devices and ports, adding to their contextual identity. The nature of the radius lends itself to understanding presented characteristics of devices very well but is limited to attributes a network access device can send while complying with the open standard.

- **SNMP:** Simple Network Management Protocol can be used to query or receive unsolicited information from a network access device. Overcoming the lack of visibility into when a device connects or disconnects to/from the network, unsolicited messages called traps can indicate the presence of a new device. This indication of a new device being present can help determine when to interrogate the device for its contextual identity. To further add color to the contextual identity, SNMP information can include various attributes and can be triggered based on electrical signal being provided to the endpoint from the connecting port. This included information may consist of the device's MAC address, VLAN to which a device belongs, Cisco Discovery Protocol (CDP) or Link Layer Discovery Protocol (LLDP) information such as platform or capabilities, interface description as configured on the network access device, and can even be the trigger for an NMAP scan. Other aspects that can be queried from the switch are based on the SNMP Management Information Base (MIB) table present on the switch. These aspects can be custom configured in network access control products, such as Cisco ISE, to be queried in accordance with the MIB schema and expected information presented from the network access device.

- **DHCP:** For a device to connect to modern networks, an IP or IPv6 address is assigned, either statically, or more commonly dynamically via Dynamic Host Configuration Protocol. Within the request for an address, information is also included in the packet that could assist in overcoming challenges in identifying the device. The hostname of the device, MAC address requesting the address for binding purposes, device class, and vendor attributes or custom administrator-assigned attributes can all be included in the DHCP request, among a wide variety of other options. This information can be replicated to a network access control server and be used to uniquely identify the endpoint as it joins to the network. This information can be used on its own or can be combined and compared with other probe information.

Revisiting the note in previous paragraphs that the combination of factors identifying the device would need to be changed to prevent successful identification, DHCP is one of the more challenging protocols to change due to its integration with a device's operating system. For example, the MAC address, also found in the RADIUS

probe, is included in the DHCP packet and can be compared across the two protocols. This validation can ensure a second layer of security is added to the endpoint's
join request. For more network access control systems, a certainty factor, or weight,
is utilized when passively identifying a device. Protocols such as DHCP should
therefore be weighted higher than more easily spoofed attributes such as the MAC
address, and the combination of the two matching in their contents also should be
weighted accordingly.

- **HTTP:** Hypertext Transfer Protocol isn't just for browsing the web; it can also be
used as part of the identification process and overcome challenges in determining
what a device is. Included in a standard HTTP header is the user agent that the endpoint is utilizing, which can indicate the web browser, operating system, and versions
of both to help identify what the device may be. Within the specifications for HTTP,
these attributes are used to render the page correctly so that the receiving browser
can present it to the user correctly. However, these attributes can be used to "profile" the device, and better lend information to the network access control server to
identify the device passively.

- **MUD:** Manufacturer Usage Description is a relatively new attribute that IoT vendors
are introducing into their products to present in an open format how the device is
expected to communicate on the network and operate for administrative validation
purposes. For organizations that are starting down the path of understanding device
behavior or, better yet, introducing modern IoT devices, expected ports and protocols for devices can be consumed if the devices support MUD. MUD works by
sending out a URL to which a network access control server, or MUD Manager, can
retrieve information and utilize that information to indicate the expected behavior
of the device on the network. Network access control devices such as Cisco ISE can
query the MUD usage information from the device if available and use this information to validate the device's type based on identification therein.

- **DNS:** Domain Name System servers contain mappings for devices and users' FQDNs.
Services, applications, and other network devices rely on accurate DNS information
to allow network services to function. This functionality also provides a valuable
source of information to the contextual identity of a device and the user. DNS information can be gathered by

  - Querying an organizational DNS server through DNS requests or via API

  - Utilizing SNMP to query data collected by a network device

  - Querying a service that maintains and updates DNS information to the DNS
    server

- **CDP and LLDP:** Cisco Discovery Protocol and Link Layer Discovery Protocol provide discovery data at Layer 2 of the protocol stack. CDP is Cisco proprietary and
provides a wealth of knowledge on Cisco devices. These protocols allow devices
to advertise attributes that are important to the operation of that device. Device
power requirements sent by a device to request a power level are one example. Voice

devices commonly utilize LLDP or CDP to function efficiently on the network. CDP/ LLDP information can be obtained from access switches on the network. One use of CDP/LLDP involves validating the identity of a phone to provide QoS or PoE functionality.

System Integrations

Systems performing identity-based operations should communicate where necessary. More information available to a system allows for better accuracy when determining contextual identity. Profiling happens on the network, with multiple brokers relying on their processes. Difficulty increases for an attacker posing as something or someone else as the number of systems they need to fool increases. Integration, automation, orchestration, and validation across systems increase the ability for policy to be applied accurately to a device. Implementation plans should document all system integrations possible when creating the implementation plans for Zero Trust. Architects should also include available integrations in their calculus when selecting platforms.

- **Where:** Quite often, the challenge of identifying a device within a massive set of known assets within an organization can be narrowed down if the location where that device is connected is known. The location, especially when combined with the details of the who and what characteristics of the device, can also be extremely valuable in organizations that use a robust asset management database. Many organizations, despite having a centralized purchasing system, and therefore having consistent types, brands, and models of devices, deploy these specific endpoints only to a limited subset of sites or geographic locations. Knowing these geographic locations means being able to narrow down devices based on that location. With this information, policies can be created within a network access control server to help both identify and enforce policies for these types of devices that may not be required in other locations.

- **When:** For many organizations, a challenge exists in knowing whether a device is being used in a legitimate purpose at a given time of day. While work-life balance is a goal that many organizations strive for, patterns can typically be drawn from the average workday, even for around-the-clock operations. For organizations in which the majority of staff utilize the network during a typical 8:00 a.m. to 5:00 p.m. workday within a given geographic area, deviation from this norm should be considered in the contextual identity. The act of a device or set of devices coming onto the network with a newly established session at a late-night hour or early morning hour may be indicative of compromise or remote control of that device. In these scenarios, policies can be established to determine how much access should be provided to a device outside of standard working hours, especially in highly sensitive environments with mission-critical data access.

- **How:** In combination with other aspects of contextual identity, how a device came onto the network can provide valuable insight into whether the request is a valid request or spoofed device type. In most cases, an Apple iPad, for example, will rarely connect to a wired network. If seen to access the network via a wired port, additional scrutiny can be applied, and investigation as to how, why, and whether the device is what it presents itself as can be undertaken to ensure that the medium through which a device accesses the network makes sense in context of its identity.

Utilizing the contextual identity of devices can help overcome a visibility challenge commonly seen on most networks. The who, what, where, when, and how, combined with passive probes to identify what a device is in a relatively accurate manner, can help understand a device and then be combined with behavioral aspects of the device. In the next section, we explore how expected behavior can be gathered and how it can utilize contextual identity to validate this behavior and make an additional vulnerability assessment of the device.

In addition to focusing solely on contextual identity, an overwhelming concept in and of itself, techniques that also reduce the complexity of this task include

- Breaking down the network into functional elements

- Using agile methodologies to show consistent and timely value of the work both inside and outside of Zero Trust efforts

- Creating or reusing a common system of documentation and mappings for controls and capabilities

- Convincing architecture teams to update logical documentation on their systems with benefits that directly apply to them

- Inviting integrators, contractors, consultants, application owners, and vendors to validate their dependencies and designs

- Initiating reviews of the CMDB and other sources of truth based on a comprehensive asset management program

- Soliciting buy-in and sponsorship from leaders by advertising the intrinsic value, even outside of Zero Trust, in participating in these efforts

Defining one functional area of the network map is all it takes to move on to help overcome this challenge. Agile methodologies provide a fluid movement of workstreams. Organizations should expect to receive incomplete and in-progress maps of the network and its inner workings. Delays begin when teams get caught up in trying to provide perfection. The steps laid out here transform imperfect and incomplete data into usable elements in implementation planning. Minimum viable products provide value in accelerating implementation planning. The effort in mapping the existing network starts with these tiny bits of information. The process uses this data to pinpoint deeper meaning and draws out the next steps in mapping how the existing network can be transformed to start the implementation of Zero Trust.

Challenge: Understanding the Expected Behavior of Endpoints

Part of the contextual identity that has not yet been defined in the previous section is the threat or risk that the device poses to the network. As aligned with the Vulnerability Management core principle, understanding a device and how it interacts within, between, and external to an organization's network can be an indicator of whether the device is what it presents itself as. This risk can be mitigated and challenge overcome through a series of building blocks related to understanding the expected behavior of endpoints.

Overcoming the Challenge: Focusing on the Endpoint

Devices define the smallest building blocks of the network and make up a large subset of the initial data sets delivered to the implementation team. The next step in creating a holistic view of the existing network is assigning context to a device. This context creates new meaning for these devices. Treatment of network traffic from a Zero Trust framework relies on the identities of devices and those using them. Combining the factors that define this contextual identity results in a functional mapping to act upon in a network transaction. No magic combination of factors exists to create a reusable cheat sheet between any two organizations. Implementation teams bear the responsibility to define these functional characteristics. Utilizing workshops, as previously mentioned, to define a framework that fits the organization is necessary for contextual mapping identity to a device. A contextual identity decision tree provides a framework that leads to adjustment as the discovery continues.

Creating this tree allows any device on the network to be profiled based on existing network controls. This is a manual policy decision process and should begin with all stakeholders. Automation can be used in later cycles as the process becomes refined and well documented. Controls answer the questions about a device needed to place the device in a functional grouping. Figure 7-1 shows an example of top-level identity mapping that provides identity groupings based on top-level organizational functions. These top-level groupings should not extend more than two more levels. One example of a device that may exist in multiple branches of the tree is a phone. Contextual identity of the phone, determined using the questions who, what, where, when, and how, is possible. This exercise will use this example to show how different answers to these questions result in a separate contextual identity.

- Who is using the device?
    - No specific user is associated with the phone, and the identity is a guest phone. The phone belongs to Customer Services.
    - A service account is used to register a VoIP line to an intercom device. This phone (line) belongs to Facilities.

- A network engineer is using a hardware phone at their desk registered to them. This phone belongs in Campus/Branch.

- What type of phone is it?

  - The phone is a softphone on a desktop used for customer support. The phone belongs to Business Services.

  - The phone is integrated into a telepresence system used for conferencing. The phone belongs to the Campus/Branch.

  - The phone is a displayless hardware phone in a lobby for guest use. The phone belongs to Customer Services.

- When is the phone being used?

  - The displayless hardware phone is used after hours. The phone belongs to Facilities.

  - A director's hardware phone at home is being used during business hours. The phone belongs to User Services.

  - A director's hardware phone at home is being used after business hours. The phone belongs to User Services.

Did determining these identities seem arbitrary? Is it possible for each of these scenarios to have different answers? Both questions have the same answer: yes. This example demonstrates why all the questions around contextual identity need to be answered in a decision tree such as that seen in Figure 7-1. True contextual identity is never just "phone," "printer," "laptop," or "camera." Does it matter when a director uses their hardware phone at home? Does it matter if a call is business related or not? Does it matter if the director's friend uses the phone? This example shows how complex contextual identity contributes to decision-making in a Zero Trust environment. Remember, every transaction on the network must be explicitly allowed and accounted for. Continual reevaluation is required because this is a constant process including when events or incidents reveal a device or identity is compromised.

Other areas to focus on in this drive toward allowing each transaction to occur include

- **Protection mechanisms on the endpoint's operating system or firmware:** It is thankfully becoming less common for devices to not have the ability to authenticate a user before providing access to the underlying operating system. While many devices use a standard username and password that are easily found with a simple search, some mechanism to provide authentication-based access is significantly better than open access. While we do not advocate for maintaining default credentials of devices, as a method to prevent the inexperienced network scanner, they are better than open access.

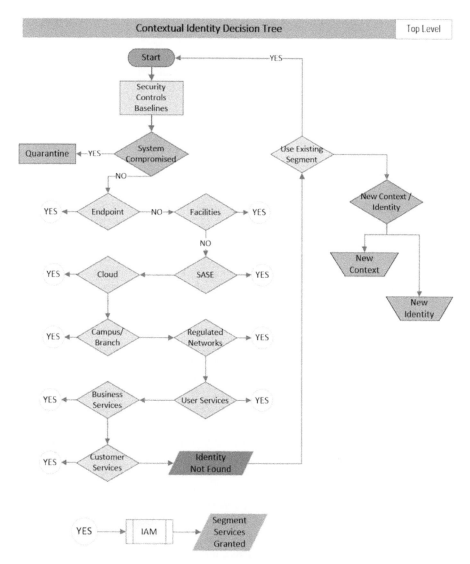

Figure 7-1 *Determining Contextual Identity*

Signed software images are also becoming significantly more common for devices that transport packets across the network. A combination of validating the device has a signed image when queried, attempting to log in to the device with default credentials, and requiring configuration information from administrators can be used to evaluate the operating system or firmware of the device. Additionally, access to the underlying operating system or firmware, utilizing system accounts or configured credentials, can help indicate the expected behavior of an endpoint while on a network. On Linux devices, for example, it is expected that connections should be present and accounted for using a **netstat** command, or processes available via the **ps** command. In addition, some operating systems have an automated tracking operation, such as logging configured, to indicate when credentials are escalated. These aspects of the operating system should be investigated and will show unknown processes, behaviors, or connections in relation to device operation.

■ **Protection mechanisms installed on the endpoint's operating system in the form of software:** In addition to mechanisms used to secure the operating system itself from unauthorized access or modification, software in the form of anti-malware, anti-spyware, or anti-virus (anti-X) is commonly used to protect from software being installed on the device to deviate from its expected behavior. The mere presence of this software may be able to be used as both a protection mechanism to overcome potential risks associated with software interaction on the network, but also a consideration for evaluating the risk an endpoint poses to the network. Centralized management of these anti-X software agents can help to determine whether software, files, or behaviors of the endpoint are in line with baselines void of infection. Secure endpoint software, such as Cisco's Secure Endpoint including Advanced Malware Protection for Endpoints, provides the ability to detect both virus infection and malware based on crowdsourced data of observed malware behavior in the wild.

■ **Posture evaluation agents and validation software:** Speaking to the mere presence of software on an endpoint (as indicated in the preceding bullet), evaluating an endpoint for installed applications, services, keys, and definitions is referred to as evaluation of the "posture" of an endpoint. In addition, while an operating system may have anti-X software installed, should that software be out of date on the scale of months or even years, the protection it provides is significantly lower, and the risk that the endpoint poses to the network is significantly larger. A third-party agent can evaluate the presence of the software on the endpoint, as well as provide details like when the last policy definition was applied. This information can be compared against a point in time or the most recent definition version provided by the vendor and then trigger remediation if the appropriate conditions for these are not met. With proper definition of the baseline of software that must be installed on a device, the organization can overcome the challenge of what a device's acceptable level of vulnerability to the network is. Software such as Cisco AnyConnect with the Posture and Compliance Module snap-in, as well as Duo for endpoints, can help minimize the risk and actively use that risk factor for subsequent enforcement action.

■ **Understanding the expected communication of the endpoint to fulfill its operational need within the network:** The set of resources that a device requires to fulfill its purposes on a network can range in complexity, but a baseline understanding should be built to understand the ports and protocols used to access destinations internal to the network. Without this baseline, the significant challenge of understanding whether a device is behaving as expected certainly could be considered insurmountable. Tools such as Cisco Secure Network Analytics utilize NetFlow, sFlow, and OpenFlow to capture device communications and map the device-to-device communications observed. This information can be integrated with contextual identity to better map identity-to-identity communication, as opposed to the less valuable IP address.

Many IP cameras, for example, require access to a centralized network video recorder (NVR) to send video to, either periodically or in a real-time streaming manner. However, many of the same IP cameras require an administrator to either configure each individual camera with the address of the NVR or will need to query its peers for that address. In many cases, this individual configuration has proven to be administratively complex and time-consuming. Therefore, many IP cameras use peer-to-peer communication to determine the location of the NVR on the network and dynamically configure themselves. This communication can be seen in some environments as a potential botnet or worm-like behavior, with configurations from one device being relayed and consumed by another device, potentially many times over. While this does ease management of the devices, the risk posed by not understanding the communication patterns of the devices, validating that the communications are occurring in accordance with expected behaviors documented by the software manufacturer, and understanding the risk of ports used for communication between devices of the same type can be significant.

- **Understanding the expected communication of the endpoint external to the network to fulfill its operational needs:** The expansion of IoT devices using cloud controllers, management consoles, or databases has led to a unique operational challenge where administrators may not understand the upgrade timeframes, processes, or destinations that endpoints rely on. While an expectation is generally present that a device will be patched and remediated for the majority of security-related vulnerabilities present in the software, it is rarely known where these devices communicate to and from to receive these fixes. Geographically distributed points, typically used for redundancy, add to this challenge that must be overcome. Finally, the nature of cloud resources, and their ability to be quickly and dynamically created or removed based on scale experienced by the software provider, adds to the significant risk incurred by organizations that don't use some mechanism to track such information. With the potential for many of these devices to have their firmware changed to "jailbreak" them from their centralized management, it becomes significantly more important for administrators to understand the expected patterns of behavior of these types of devices. This challenge is further explored in the next section.

- **Understanding the change in expected baseline behavior:** With the feature-rich devices that are available on the market for relatively low cost-to-feature ratio, understanding what a device can do versus what it is currently doing when connected to the network becomes paramount. Devices that can be customized to perform several finite responsibilities on the network should be documented in a manner that defines what features are currently being taken advantage of and the ports and protocols required to support those features. However, potential features and abilities of the endpoint should also be documented, with a complete listing of ports and protocols that a given device can use, coming from the documentation or testing of the device in a granular method. Ensuring that there is a repository that can be consulted to better utilize the devices already present on the network, should new business requirements be uncovered, should be a focus of organizations as part of the vulnerability management evaluation. By doing so, not only can the security posture easily be updated for documenting the expected communication of the endpoint on the network, but this can also lead to capex savings and a better security posture, maintaining consistent and predictable behavior of devices utilized in the most efficient way possible.

Challenge: Understanding External Access Requirements

The largest challenge that network security administrators have regarding endpoints is determining when they should expect the endpoints to contact an external resource, as well as which resources the device requires for updating or researching inquiries. In industries that utilize IoT-enabled devices, such as smart assistants, room scheduling panels, temperature sensors, humidity sensors, and human safety devices, increasing utilization of these devices has created a need to understand what resources are being consumed to evaluate their risk posed to the network. Increasing interest by many employees and business units to utilize smart devices to automate workloads not only at home in common tasks but also while in the office has increased adoption in even the most unlikely environments. The conveniences of having smart speakers present in the office are numerous: to automate tasks through voice inquiry, to consume large amounts of information and respond back with the most relevant answer to the user. Even tasks that used to be synonymous with remote working environments, such as playing music to concentrate, answering quick inquiries while multitasking, or allowing communication back home without the need to interrupt other workflows, are finding commonality in the workplace. As an author's note, this chapter would not have been completed without a smart assistant's ability to play music to help focus.

Overcoming the Challenge: Mapping External Communication Requirements

Convenience, as with anything Zero Trust, must be balanced with the "as a service" offering encompassed by such endpoints. Understanding the communications needs for an endpoint to external sites and services is undoubtedly a daunting task. The mixture of corporate, industrial, and consumer grade devices utilized within organizations of varying verticals makes for reliance on product vendors to provide documentation of network interactions a recipe for disappointment. Additionally, due to the nature of device manufacturers, it is quite common for IoT vendors to use elastic cloud-based infrastructure, associated with dynamically updated DNS names within the cloud of their choosing. Therefore, the overwhelming decision of either allowing these services to access anything for their respective vendor domains or taking the time to track patterns for when these devices are typically used and in what way is further compounded with validating these usage patterns to add to the challenging Zero Trust or security-focused architecture.

In practical implementations of these sorts of devices, the only way to overcome these challenges is to spend the time and effort to map out patterns of commonly accessed external resources with tools that are typically common to the network. In most organizations, the use of either a firewall at the edge that maps all communications into and out of the network or an Internet proxy is a common control that provides a treasure trove of data related to the connections. The most value related to understanding these connections comes with integration of either an IP address management (IPAM) system, or the integration of contextual identity into the flow logs themselves. By consuming context, value is realized when communication patterns are able to be mapped in a human-consumable manner. This human-readable format is how contextual identity has been described throughout this text: a user on a device, in a location, over a medium, at a specific time to another such identity. This communication pattern can then be used to create a baseline to evaluate observed device communications against.

Similar to the mapping of communications internal to the network, as discussed in the section "Overcoming the Challenge: Focusing on the Endpoint," additional tools that observe the source, destination, port, protocol, and header information can also be used to overcome this challenge. NetFlow connection and processing tools such as Cisco Secure Network Analytics, organizational firewalls internal to the network, and endpoint network analytics agents such as the Network Traffic Analysis module for Cisco Secure Endpoint can be used to develop baselines for comparative analysis and should include machine learning abilities, where possible, to minimize administrative overhead. Further out from the endpoint, Internet proxies, edge firewalls, and intrusion prevention systems can be used to consume identity and find a centralized point of traversal for all internally sourced endpoints. Finally, the use of a centralized, managed DNS services such as Cisco Umbrella can be used to map and baseline where similar devices communicate externally to the network via analysis of their naming system inquiries. With most cloud providers, there is the expectation that resources to run the business and facilitate functionality of endpoints will be longer lived and more commonly accessed than malware-infected resources, which will need to change servers, hosting providers, or cloud services on a regular basis to avoid detection.

What this example does not consider is what happens when an industrial IoT device, humidity sensor, or smart speaker, having no concept of a supplicant or interactive identification ability, is not actually what it presents itself as, but rather a device that is spoofing how the target device appears to the network. So long as the only identifying mechanism used is an IP address, and baseline nonexistent, as would be the case in a connectivity-focused architecture, the device can interact with broad swaths of resources without detection. A baseline of communication for that device, as associated with its contextual identity, should be required before connectivity and tracked as part of the Zero Trust Architecture. This example is meant to demonstrate the need, but already common practice, for understanding external access requirements of endpoints but reinforce a need to monitor this behavior as associated with contextual identity as part of the vulnerability management process. This concept, specifically understanding traffic flows to allow access, has existed for much longer than the Zero Trust concept. However, with Zero Trust and the constant churn of IoT devices on a network, this vulnerability management technique becomes much more important.

The tracking of behavior is still largely in need of significant investment. Going back to the concept of the movement from connectivity-focused network architecture to security-focused network architecture, even when connectivity was the primary goal, resources had to traverse a zone-based security protection mechanism, typically a firewall, to be allowed out to the public Internet. In many cases, this firewall allowed for a state-based traversal back into the network, allowing traversal inbound only when there was already a connection first established outbound. This outbound rule was explicitly configured. However, the life cycle of these rules rarely included review or retirement, or even evaluation of overlap. In addition to tracking this behavior and understanding a device's traffic baseline, a change management system to be able to determine the requestor, owner, device, and life cycle of the rule must also be utilized. In environments where rules are never audited, it's common to have hundreds of thousands of rules, with large percentages representing overlaps in address and purpose. Now defunct rules also commonly exist and are never removed due to the risk they could pose to affecting business as usual, a risk directly related to rule management. A need to track these aspects of a rule should exist to overcome a challenge of stale rule sets that allow unintended communication patterns, or inhibit changes to rules for progress toward Zero Trust.

Zero Trust moves toward bringing the same level of enforcement found at externally facing devices as close to the endpoint as possible and applying policy based on the contextual identity of the endpoint. With the contextual identity, a specific communication can be allowed for that identity and assigned at its entry point to the network. This is often made possible by using NAC products such as Cisco Identity Services Engine and combining multiple protection mechanisms as found in Chapter 6, "Segmentation."

To summarize, overcoming the challenge of external access requirements is best done by first understanding the contextual identity of the endpoint and then creating a baseline of required communications. Much of this required communication will need to occur at an externally aligned firewall, which may contain quite a bit of information related to the device's external communication needs already, if well maintained. In the case of most organizations, the explosion of firewall rules lends little to this effort, and a need to map the communications of the device may be less labor intensive to start from scratch. These communications can be discovered utilizing multiple tools, a firewall continuing to be one of them. Working under the assumption that most exit points of the network will have a firewall as a protection mechanism, the firewall logs can be integrated into the identity of endpoints that traverse through it, utilizing the contextual identity aspect of the device to match up with a known IP address previously contained within a firewall rule. Enforcement can then be applied via policy to the endpoint session via access control list or other controls close to the network ingress point. This approach not only serves the purpose of distributing policy to the access layer closest to the endpoint but, as a side effect, allows cleanup of poorly managed firewall rules relied upon in a connectivity-focused architecture.

Potential means of mapping external communications are further covered in the following sections.

Taps

Network taps commonly exist across organizational boundaries but not commonly inside single segments. Taps provide a 1:1 view of network traffic too complex to consume in any raw fashion. Tools that aggregate these flows to security devices gain the ability to illuminate insights into the traffic without the burden of direct interaction. Taps exist inside and across data centers as troubleshooting and visibility tools.

NetFlow

NetFlow provides varying levels of detail based on the device's source collecting the data. NetFlow reporting from clients, like the Network Visibility Module in Cisco AnyConnect Client, not only provides detailed NetFlow data but also contributes to visibility via Security Information and Event Management (SIEM) dashboards, such as Splunk. Note that some NetFlow sources only send sampled NetFlow, typically indicative of a high-throughput backplane present on the device in question. Organizations may need to consider aspects of flow collection devices, such as Cisco's Secure Network Analytics Flow Collector, as part of implementation and visibility into these areas. NetFlow and analytic tools empowered by NetFlow data provide excellent visibility into inter- and intra-segment flows.

Encapsulated Remote Switch Port Analyzer (ERSPAN)

SPAN and Enhanced Remote SPAN (ERSPAN) send copies of traffic from devices through alternate interfaces sent to devices like a tap. Network taps rely on hardware specifically designed for the task and may not be feasible in all scenarios. SPAN configuration adds load to existing network infrastructure and operations teams. SPANs can also collect data on the wire that may be useful in troubleshooting. Aggregate networks with bulkier traffic flow may benefit from SPAN sessions but should also consider the planning, configuration, and resources needed for implementation.

Proxied Data

Data provided by resources that are positioned as distributed points of the network provided aggregate data. This data enables teams to gain insight that would not be seen in singular points. Like Cisco Secure Workloads, these controls provide mappings of flows and behaviors that are integral to Zero Trust and microsegmentation. Planning teams' use of these tools also expands to identifying workloads to migrate to the cloud. The valuable data interpreted from these systems leads directly to policy creation used in implementation planning. Tools in this arena exist in various forms and areas of the network but provide the most valuable and detailed data for both inter- and intra-segment communications.

Source of Truth

Teams encounter systems containing data from multiple sources when exploring contextual identity, traffic flows, business requirements, and policies. These systems may have provenance over an individual area of the business but not as a single source of truth. Organizations should strive to create and maintain a single source of truth. Difficulties abound with maintaining the accuracy of individual sources of truth. Implementation teams need to highlight opportunities to update or create documentation to improve the existence and accuracy of these systems.

CMDBs

Configuration management databases provide an inventory of IT assets and data about them. These assets are recorded as configuration items (CIs), which contain valuable information in framing identity. The CMDB enables implementation teams to identify devices active on the network, but it also acts as a check to ensure that decommissioned devices are inactive. Proper ownership and attribution of CIs will help implementation teams identify components of environments used in Zero Trust implementation phases. This data also improves auditing and reporting capabilities to ensure that accurate assignment records report if an application or team ownership of a specified asset moves or changes.

APMs

Application performance management solutions help organizations track the existence and impact of applications. An APM allows the value of an application to be logged against the purpose of that application. The ability to compare applications with similar functions instills intrinsic cost savings. From a Zero Trust perspective, APM provides ample opportunities to protect applications as segments and measure meaningful value from the implementation. Zero Trust protects applications from attack surfaces and fosters optimization by allowing applications to communicate only as needed. An example of this savings comes from cloud enablement by restricting applications from utilizing resources when unnecessary.

Challenge: Macrosegmentation vs. Microsegmentation for the Network

The ability to distribute policy to sessions or ports to which endpoints are connected does beg the question "What level of segmentation does an organization need?" While many organizations go to such an extent of claiming they already have segmentation based on their firewalls, others would claim that there is never enough segmentation so long as any two devices within a geographical area can communicate with one another without restriction. For some, this includes ports adjacent to one another on the same switch, same VLAN, and consecutive switchports.

Legacy network design would typically define segmentation as "any unique area of the network that can be separated through routing and policy application, to prevent unauthorized segments from communicating with one another." To boil this down for clearer understanding, this definition essentially meant that the network was broken down either into VLAN-based logical structures, IP subnet logical structures, or Virtual Routing and Forwarding (VRF) instance logical structures, which were all aggregated through a firewall or similar device. This firewall then had a traversal policy applied between the logical segments, or potentially the outside world, which dictated how endpoints within that segment could communicate when traversing the security boundary. This did, however, consider the security boundary existing multiple hops away from an endpoint, and neglected the idea that multiple endpoints would exist within a given logical segment, enclave, or structure. This was mainly due to a lack of easily implemented microsegmentation methodologies applicable to the area in question.

These endpoints would then be able to communicate with one another unrestricted unless every endpoint was put into its own logical structure and policy applied across those logical structures for each combination of endpoints. When using one of the more commonly used logical segments, VLANs, this would imply that in a flat network with multiple switches that aggregate through a firewall, the greatest number of segments, based on the use of Multiple Spanning Tree, would be 4094. This further implied that if every endpoint were put into its own segment to create policy between them, and preventing peer-to-peer communication, no network could expand beyond 4094 endpoints, a number that pales in comparison with modern network needs.

Overcoming the Challenge: Deciding Which Segmentation Methodology Is Right for an Organization

An organization has to ask what the acceptable "blast zones," or affected areas of the network, should be in the scenario of a compromise. In other words, how many devices, and more importantly what contextual identities, can exist within a control point (where the applied control mechanism sits through where devices are connected) for acceptable risk tolerance? As documented in the challenge, the design theory of segmenting devices manually with VLANs would have significant overhead operationally and minimize the possible number of endpoints in a geographic area. What is needed is a dynamic engine with the capability to assign endpoints to segments, deterministically, regardless of medium. In addition, as illustrated in the challenge, VLANs are restrictive in their scalability and must rely on another upstream device for enforcement between any respective pair. With this restriction in mind, the organization becomes reliant upon the hardware of the upstream device and must upgrade based on its processing capabilities.

While the firewall and other security aggregation devices have not diminished in value to a layered enforcement model and ability to segment the overall network, their role in segmenting endpoints has been determined to be less valuable than a distributed segmentation model. Organizations are realizing that mechanisms allowing an endpoint to have its contextual identity determine what access it receives lower overhead and provides for required access applied closest to the endpoint. For an endpoint that has a user present on it, the ability to analyze the user's groupings from a mechanism such as LDAP or Microsoft Active Directory provides an additional mechanism to determine what risk level that user poses to the network or other users. The use of enforcement mechanisms—such as Cisco TrustSec to determine access within the VLAN or local segment, a dynamic VLAN assignment to assign the local segment, with downloadable access control lists to control access outside of the segment, and firewalls to control external access—creates a combination of enforcement mechanisms that makes up a layered model of segmentation.

With distributed policy application also comes the common question "How granular is too granular?" This decision has to take into account various factors but commonly consists of

■ Risk being mitigated as it related to endpoints within a "blast zone"

■ Data gathered to show how contextual identities interact within, across, and outside of a given segment

■ Operational overhead of the proposed implementation of segmentation

■ Capabilities of the access device to support the scale of the segmentation mechanism

In most cases, organizations will start with a proposed level of segmentation that is far too granular or far too broad. For those that start far too granular, there is typically a motivation of minimizing blast zones to be as small as possible, without evaluating the true risk contained within the analyzed traffic patterns. These organizations typically focus on each contextual identity and their unique port and protocol communications without considering whether the contextual identity would even respond to an exploit sent to a port not included in the control policy. For example, if a device operates on 80, 443, and 10666 but will never acknowledge a packet sent to 10669, blocking this nonresponsive port may not have much value. Grouping other devices that communicate on 80, 443, and 10669 into this blast zone carries little to no risk and expands the size while lowering operational overhead of an additional policy assignment.

In other cases, organizations group together devices that have overlapping ports and protocols based on not considering the risk of device exploitation. Grouping mission-critical servers or grouping a three-tiered web, application, and database set can be disastrous should one become compromised, leading to multiple endpoints being crippled and significantly hampering business as usual.

That said, the most successful approach has been seen to start by grouping devices together in a broad fashion and getting progressively granular over time. In their analysis, Cisco Security Services and Cisco Security Business Group have found that customers who use dynamic application of enforcement policy have the best likelihood of success when they start with no more than five to seven groups or enclaves while applying granular enforcement for segmentation. This segmentation must be built upon a firm understanding and application of contextual identity and mapping of traffic traversal within, across, and external to the local network. These enclaves, or segments, serve as a base structure for expanding the dynamic application of granular segmentation, however. The approach to doing so is by classifying devices into broad swaths based on contextual identity and traffic analysis (both of what is sent and what the device will respond to) as best found in an onboarding process. While classifying devices, where significant deviations occur between groups of devices, or where additional risk is observed but has limited exposure, an additional child grouping can be made for future application. Once a segmentation methodology is implemented and operationalized effectively, including operational teams able to troubleshoot and apply mitigation, additional granularity is added into the segmentation design.

Challenge: New Endpoint Onboarding

Commonly, organizations will place the majority of their focus for segmentation on what is currently in the network and what it already has access to. After all, the teams that are most involved in the segmentation of a network will be the same teams that administer it on a daily basis, including network teams, network security teams, network operations teams, and application administrators. But where many organizations find they have the biggest challenge is in "day 2" operation of segmentation as the business continues to evolve and decisions need to be made on where newly purchased or introduced devices belong in the segmentation model. Before segmentation is introduced, it is common for network security teams, and specifically firewall administrators, to receive a ticket or call from departments within the organization asking for their IP ranges to be given access to external resources in the form of DNS names or IP addresses. Associated with this request may or may not be an explanation of what is accessing the resources or why. As teams move to a security-focused architecture that requires validation of the contextual identity and traversal patterns before providing access, processes must be put into place for new devices to be identified and provided access via distributed enforcement mechanisms described throughout this chapter.

Overcoming the Challenge: Consistent Onboarding Processes

Provisioning as a service has become popular in corporate environments. A manufacturer and its respective business partners in the provisioning as a service model will take a customized image from the organization, install it on the device in question, and ship it directly to the user. This approach saves time for corporate devices and can be used to ease the largest pain point that organizations have in their segmentation strategy, namely the corporate endpoint. The second largest challenge to overcome for organizations is the use of IoT and nonstandard imaged devices on the network. These devices are typically shipped directly to the organization or the purchaser within the organization. For ease of access, a policy should be implemented that if a new device is ordered for use on the network, the device is shipped to a centralized receiving area for network devices. Of course, this policy will need to consider identification of the owner, purchaser, and manager of the device to be successful. When the device is shipped to a centralized receiving area, network teams are the first to unpack, observe, and connect the device to the network.

Once connected, the device should be onboarded to create a contextual identity and evaluation of the risk it poses to the network. One common way of doing so is by having a secured network access device local to the receiving location that has a more lenient network access control policy applied to it. This lenient policy allows the device to be dynamically added into an authentication group, provides for full authorization, but is secured by being on its own network, typically with a firewall upstream. In some environments, this is a separate direct Internet access line to prevent any potential for the device to compromise corporate networks. The network access device to which the endpoint is connected is configured with NetFlow collection, and an onboarding checklist notes the IP address of the endpoint, what it reaches out to externally, and what it attempts to reach out to internally. For onboarding to be successful, an understanding of the architecture should be provided with the device. The combination of creating the contextual identity, gathering traffic from the local network access device, collecting any logs from the upstream firewall, and observing the behavior of the device will not only provide a secure connectivity for the device but can also contribute to documentation about the device and its architecture due to the need for this information at onboarding. The combination of controls can ease troubleshooting and mean time to resolution significantly.

After a contextual identity is formed and traffic traversal collected, capabilities of the device should be documented, including whether the device has the ability to authenticate to the network with 802.1x, evaluated for posture where applicable, enrolled in any management systems where applicable, and grouped with other devices that have a similar capability. These groups are typically static in nature, where a device is assigned to the group within the network access control server. This group will result in an authorization result that provides the device its required access, which is centrally managed on the controller and distributed to network access devices.

Challenge: Policies Applied to Edge Networks

Due to world events, 2020 will be known as the year that sent workers home, and the year that began the capitalization of work from home tendencies. The exclusive work from home environment, which has persisted for many, presents a new challenge. The need for users to connect to the network while away from the centralized network became of the utmost importance, while maintaining standard security practices. A secondary concern, sometimes a perception rather than the reality, voiced by many was that the connection of a VPN slowed applications and workloads in a measurable manner. This led to VPN-less architectures consisting of identity gateways through which endpoints can connect, validating their identification session to the network resources they wished to consume. This identification session still utilizes contextual identity as a security mechanism. While many would argue that requiring a VPN client is a small inconvenience for the value provided, such as the ability to assist in identifying the endpoint via hooks into the operating system, VPN has received additional scrutiny on the network and as a key part of the remote edge network.

For administrators, users connecting from remote networks present the challenge of needing to apply the same restrictions to remote access sessions as users connecting in an office. Many technologies focus on one aspect of connectivity exclusively, either on campus wired and wireless connectivity or on remote access connectivity.

Overcoming the Challenge: Ubiquitous Policy Application

With a properly architected Zero Trust network, where users connect from should matter very little to the access they receive. The use of contextual identity remains the same, with the exception of the location from which the endpoint has connected; previously, it was the network access device and now it's a remote network. This aspect of the contextual identity can be utilized to provide policy based on risk evaluation of the endpoint. This is especially true in scenarios where broad access is given to remote access devices. In these cases, additional restrictions should apply based on the resource risk of being accessed from outside of the company's visual oversight.

VPNs come in many forms. A client-based VPN, or software that encapsulates data and delivers it over an unsecured medium to a secure gateway for de-encapsulation and routing to its destination, is the most common use of the VPN for corporate edge remote access networks. This software-based VPN is very low in cost and can provide information such as the operating system and can even be integrated with additional products. For example, it can ensure that the client is using a consistent DNS server or redirect packets to inspection mechanisms for vulnerability or packet analysis, or even redirect users to validate the posture of their devices. The overhead due to requiring users to connect via VPN is small relative to the benefits that it provides.

An alternative to the software VPN is a clientless VPN. This type forms an encrypted tunnel through the VPN termination point and routes traffic coming from the application in question through the tunnel termination point as part of the encrypted session that was established. The challenge with this type of VPN is that only traffic opened in the specific application that formed the tunnel, typically a web browser, can be redirected through the tunnel and be encrypted within the currently established session. Although this alternative method offers a lower overhead for time to establish the tunnel, while still providing an identity-based solution to ensure packets are encrypted and sent through a centralized termination point, the minimal overhead can result in minimal use cases with modern devices that are working outside of the web browser for many of their business operational needs.

Where client- and clientless-based VPNs are not in line with requirements for protected traffic access, or in scenarios where an organization desires a true office feel, a distributed VPN termination architecture can be implemented; it tends to be the most in line with a Zero Trust Architecture. The distributed VPN architecture can also be referred to as "branch in a box" because it deploys a small router to the home Internet connection of an employee, typically with a larger number of ports available on the router as compared to a standard corporate router in the core or data center areas of the network. This router then establishes a VPN connection to a VPN head end, securing the tunnel over the public Internet, utilizing DMVPN, GETVPN, or IPsec VPN, depending on the design use case for the organization. This connection gives the user a true office experience with the ability not only to plug in a PC but also have a hardware-based phone or video unit, test units, servers, and other hardware required for the role that the employee plays as part of the organization.

Another option previously mentioned is the use of an identity gateway-based platform, such as Cisco Duo Access Gateway, which allows connections to be made across the Internet without the need for a full VPN tunnel. In this setup the user will connect to an application, usually web based, as if they were in the office or on VPN. The user's web request is redirected to the application gateway, which, in turn, queries a user agent installed on the device. This user agent is responsible for interrogating the machine to ensure that it is appropriately managed and meets any defined posture requirements. After the necessary conditions have been satisfied, the user is either granted access to the application or given an error message as to why access was denied.

With the hardware-based VPN as part of the Zero Trust Architecture, it not only allows a larger number of devices to be connected to the network within the home of the employee, but consistent application of policy becomes much easier because the same configurations from the in-office switches and hardware can be applied, with minimal changes, to the hardware deployed at the home of the employee. As opposed to configuring a centralized head end with a larger number of sessions and attempting to sort through large quantities of logs being produced by all endpoints terminating there, additional contextual identity can be factored into logs and information coming from the hardware, including the hostname of the device that can identify where or to whom it has been allocated and is located. Devices connecting through the hardware do not require the ability to establish a web connection or utilize a VPN application themselves, but rather can be connected to the hardware via a direct connection and allow the hardware to use any presented identity to authenticate and authorize them as if the device were present in the office. Vulnerability management also becomes easier with the ability to scan a device that connects over the hardware based on it being connected to a corporate overlay network at this point, with routing built to communicate back to the device, as opposed to having to allow the traffic to be tunneled back to wherever the endpoint is located and encrypting connections from. While higher in cost than the software VPN client, when the use of hardware is compared with the cost of software licensing, this solution may save money over the longer term if fully adopted and preferred over the software-based implementation.

Regardless of the model of connectivity provided to the user, centralized management tools should be used to consume a policy from a network access control server and apply that policy to connecting endpoints. For client-based VPN connections, this includes the configuration under the tunnel group through which the endpoint connects to authorize the endpoint dynamically against the network access device. Where clientless or identity-based gateways are used, they should similarly consume the contextual identity from the network access control system and apply a standardized authorization result as centrally configured. While the contextual identity may change related to the connection location, a centralized policy taking into account the other four aspects of contextual identity should continue to hold.

In the spirit of revisiting the previous sections, the administrative overhead must also be overcome as part of the application of ubiquitous policy. One consideration in relation to this administrative overhead is the provisioning of the remote access client or endpoint configuration, where applicable. While application of Zero Trust configurations to allow visibility, vulnerability management, and enforcement on the head end may be relatively straightforward and able to be done quite easily, application of clients to the endpoint may not be nearly as easy. To gain the contextual identity, for example, a VPN termination point can be pointed at the policy server, and a consistent policy can be applied to the endpoint's session. This application of policy will still be session based and unique to that endpoint; however, it will require that the endpoint connect with a software client, implying the need to assist users in their connectivity and a deployment mechanism that provisions or provides clear instructions on how to provision the configurations required for the client to be connected successfully. A process that is becoming significantly more common is the use of a software provisioning tool, such as a mobile device manager like Meraki Systems Manager. In this process, the user merely downloads the client from their app store of choice, is provided a registration code, and logs in to their network with authorized credentials to provision the management agent. This provisioning can even include the addition of two-factor authentication during the authentication and authorization process, post registration code verification.

For hardware-based implementations, such as Cisco's Virtual Office product set, providing a router (with built-in firewall and wireless capabilities) and a hardware-based phone to be more streamlined in its ability to be set up and configured, preprovisioning the hardware in an office or by a technologist is typically the most efficient. For clientless-based implementations, browser isolation may require settings pushed down to the endpoint, which can be done from a centralized management console. For either solution, the goal should always be to minimize the number of steps the user must take to gain connectivity after the solution is chosen and provisioned for the user.

Challenge: Organizational Belief That a Firewall Is Enough

As discussed throughout this chapter, in most organizations, firewalls have been used as the first line of defense for years, acting as a secured gateway between the external world and the internal network. Many organizations may decide that firewalls are enough security for their use case and to protect their networks. Typically, these organizations are focused on a more connectivity-focused mindset or have a large firewall estate already. As discussed previously, firewalls can protect a network that is properly broken into segments, by forcing all segments to route through the firewall and have explicit rules on how segments interact. However, using the "firewall only" segmentation methodology presents the challenge of being reliant upon the throughput and number of firewalls needed to pass data as expected. The implication of this challenge is when any sort of significant growth in users or throughput needs presents itself, there is a need to not only increase the number of access layer connection abilities but also the number of firewalls when link speed or number of segments must grow. Where firewalls are also used for remote access termination, this is a much more common need.

Where this challenge has been most commonly resolved, and where lessons can be learned from past experience, is in university and research networks. Two unique aspects of universities lend themselves to lessons learned in Zero Trust. The first is the unique aspect of university networks, where few of the devices that sit on the network are ever trusted. Universities run very large demilitarized zones (DMZs) consisting of all research endpoints in one, and typically all dorm-based endpoints in another. On these networks there may be ongoing needs for research to work with potentially hazardous technology, such as actively deployed malware and honeypots. Instead of requiring specific ports and protocols to be allowed through the firewall or trying to route all traffic through a firewall and create a large number of segments in which endpoints exist, the application of defense in depth is a significantly lower-cost alternative.

The second major challenge universities and research networks have that can provide for significant lessons learned is the distributed nature of campuses under a single administrative domain, such as state university systems. In these cases, placing a set of firewalls at every campus may be cost prohibitive and duplicative in their configuration for accessing the same resources from each campus or university site. Instead, direct Internet access may be protected by a proxy- or cloud-based security filtering solution, while a separate tunnel for business critical traffic is also present, providing for secure transport to a centralized data center, and over which identifying characteristics can be carried and identities validated before flowing through a large, centralized firewall at the data center edge.

Overcoming the Challenge: Defense in Depth and Access-Focused Security

It can be argued that university and research networks are the model for implementation that most organizations are now attempting or should be attempting to implement based on their treatment of the endpoint. This model, to break it down into a series of bullet points, consists of the following:

- Treat every endpoint as if it were a threat to the rest of the network.

- Segment endpoints from the rest of the network with the exception of critical services and interactions.

- Require users of those endpoints to agree to policy and governance stating the explicit requirements to get this level of access.

- Within access policies, require the level of contextual identity that the organization can facilitate. This facilitation is directly related to which tools the organization has currently deployed.

- Apply enforcement and vulnerability management techniques at the ingress to the network, which requires active registration for headless devices or credentials for devices capable of presenting them.

Revisiting the challenge of the belief that firewalls are enough to overcome the Zero Trust requirements of an environment, in addition to points already made about reliance upon firewalls for throughput needs, the administrative overhead to maintain firewall policies for pure segmentation application is extraordinary. Because most firewalls are designed to act as edge devices and control inbound and outbound traffic, to attempt to utilize the commonly implemented concept of subinterfaces associated with VLANs has the same limitations as covered earlier in the chapter: a maximum of 4092 usable VLANs, inability to apply control mechanisms within VLANs to prevent peer-to-peer communication, and a need to implement what is commonly seen as hundreds of thousands of rules for inter-VLAN traversal. The largest overhead for these traversal rules is commonly with shared services that need to be allowed from every subinterface. This equates to no fewer than six rules for every subinterface:

- UDP DNS outbound/inbound for name resolution

- TCP DNS outbound/inbound for large packet name resolution (greater than 1024 bytes)

- DHCP outbound/inbound for address assignment unless static addresses are used with all devices in each subinterface

- UDP authentication outbound/inbound for active authentications and contextual identity

- Remote access protocols for remote administration of devices during troubleshooting processes

- Domain controller or management system traffic for each endpoint

This basic set of requirements of endpoints flowing through a firewall segmented to even half of its capacity, 2046 used VLANs, would create an initial rule set of over 12,000 initial rules. Alternatively, distributed policies and rules could be layered in a defense-in-depth approach to allow standard rules to be applied in addition to identity-based rules to provide a similar layer of protection while also validating endpoint behavior.

When Zero Trust is aligned to this design, all principles can be implemented to overcome the reliance on a firewall. Before a user ever connects their device to the network, they must agree to a policy stating what would be required of them and their device to connect. It can take the form of a signed policy or a terms and conditions page presented before endpoint registration. This terms and conditions page would then transition to a registration page for automated onboarding of nonuser devices via their authentication mechanism, which is typically the MAC address. When an endpoint connects to the network, it authenticates to a policy server and is evaluated for its contextual identity. As part of the contextual identity of the endpoint, the endpoint would have a policy that would force it to undergo interrogation into its posture, where applicable and supported by the operating system. After these aspects are fulfilled and associated with the contextual identity including location, a policy is applied based on the contextual identity.

The applied policy should be dynamically applied based on the contextual identity, meaning that each device no longer has to be governed by a centralized policy present on a firewall multiple hops away. The policy should be centrally administered to be applied to the contextual identity, which means that while a repetition of the preceding six lines will be present in each device's applied policy, different sets of resources will be available to be applied based on identity. For example, for devices needing a department-specific DNS server, this access can be facilitated based on group information associated with the user or the device's profile. Where inbound traffic is required, this access can be applied via policy as well. In addition to this policy applied for Layer 3 (inter-segment) access, additional policies for its local segment based on Layer 2 (intra-segment) access can also be layered on top. This is the main differentiator between using a firewall and enforcing on network access devices.

Even while policy is applied at the access device for both intra- and inter-segment access, additional aspects are enabled, such as the ability to monitor behavior of the device via NetFlow and dynamically change policies applied to the device based on its behavior. The same goes for DNS filtering and access, with access to nonbusiness-relevant sites or potentially malicious sites being able to change the device's access to the network. This change in access may force a redirection of the endpoint until the user agrees and acknowledges the behavior that they were forbidden from undertaking. Logging of this action, the applied policies, and the change in policies would all be centralized for later inspection and to build lessons learned.

Finally, this migration away from a centralized firewall can also facilitate the split in how an endpoint accesses the different networks. For example, for external access to the Internet, a firewall may still be put in place, and services such as TCP normalization, intrusion protection, malware scanning, data loss prevention (DLP), and a multitude of others also may be put into place. This firewall, because of the subset of traffic required, can typically be a smaller model with lower throughput than one that governs all traffic traversing from the campus, branch, or site. Other possible alternative designs could also include a cloud proxy or gateway, content-caching engines, centralized tunnels sending all traffic back to a data center or point of presence firewall, or just a singular router with outbound traffic allowed with access control lists, similar to a firewall.

To determine whether endpoints are aligning with policies, various means exist to scan, analyze, and manage endpoints. The following sections cover the potential means to do so.

Vulnerability Scanners

Vulnerability scanners are one of the key platforms that should have a full feed of intelligence data. These scanners rely on this threat intelligence data to understand what threats exist and how to identify them when running network scans. The value provided by vulnerability scanners is therefore closely tied to the quality of the threat intelligence data available to it. When an organization is evaluating current or new vulnerability scanners, it is essential to consider the threat intelligence feeds and ensure that the platform allows ingestion of various feeds or that the feed provided to the platform gains its source data from disparate sources to provide the best possible coverage. It is also vital to ensure that the deployment of the chosen vulnerability scanning platform is correctly configured to allow authenticated scans. Even with the best possible threat intelligence data, the value provided will still depend on the vulnerability scanner's level of access to the network. As discussed in other sections of this book, authenticated scans and their value prevent loss of visibility and result in security posture reduction.

Device Management Systems

Device management systems may take on multiple names depending on their focus and scope of capabilities, such as mobile device management (MDM), enterprise mobility management (EMM), unified endpoint management (UEM), among others. For threat intelligence, though, the differences between these platforms are not as significant as the messaging on why each will be critically dependent on threat intelligence data. These management platforms provide a few key features that are commonly available regardless of their specific classification, particularly device posture validation. This posture validation is configurable based on organizational requirements and device function and capability. However, it can include current patch status, vulnerability to known exploits, anti-malware definition dates, and other feed-dependent items. To correctly classify a device's posture, these management systems need to have the most current threat intelligence data to ensure that the compliance determination is made on the most recent and complete data possible. The quality of this determination will rely on the quality and frequency of the threat intelligence feeds that provide this data to the platform.

Malware Prevention and Inspection

Malware prevention platforms act to identify malware and attempt to prevent its ability to enter or at least stymie its progress through a network. These tools can utilize various techniques to identify malware, including heuristics, signatures, sandboxing, and static analysis. Signature-based detection—while older and can be avoided based on techniques such as polymorphic code—requires threat intelligence feeds to update known signatures regularly. Other techniques, though, will require regular updates to be fed into the system. Heuristics, for example, may need updates made not for a specific piece of malware but to update the system on new techniques that families of malware may utilize to infect a system, disguise themselves, or propagate between devices. Sandboxing, in the same vein, is effective only if the system can detect anomalous behavior, and like heuristics, this behavior can evolve as threat actors come up with new techniques to exploit device vulnerabilities to allow malware to gain a foothold within the system; therefore, it must be able to adapt and be fed updates to understand how to look for this new behavior. Even emerging concepts for detection, such as using artificial intelligence or machine-learning trained code to identify malicious behavior, will require updates based on improvements to the underlying code and models. All this still falls into the domain of threat intelligence. The capability to rapidly update these detection mechanisms must be present in an organization's malware prevention and inspection tool sets.

Endpoint-Based Analysis Policies

Whether anti-malware or more advanced detection and response systems, endpoint protection systems will all require regular threat intelligence feed updates to provide their total value. For the context of this section, these systems each provide the ability to detect and respond to threats, either via automated remediation or alerting for human analysis and intervention. The ability to detect these threats is directly correlated to the completeness and timeliness of the threat intelligence feeds being provided to them. The same basic principles that require the need for quality threat intelligence data in other systems also apply to endpoint-based systems. Endpoints are the most common target for malware because they are far more prevalent than network infrastructure or servers and may have general access levels due to the lack of current segmentation and the diverse requirements for users employed in separate roles within an organization.

In many cases, the endpoint is also the initial introduction vector into a network, made possible by actions such as a user downloading an unknown file, plugging in found USB drives, clicking a risky link, or performing other numerous actions to expose a device. The platforms present on the endpoint then have a critical role in detecting threats as soon as possible and doing their utmost to prevent or limit their impact. Much of this capability will be provided by the threat intelligence data provided to these platforms to give them the necessary knowledge to identify these threats, especially as the threat landscape continues to evolve and malware or other threats become more discrete and complex in their actions taken to propagate and avoid detection. Thus, having consistent, quality threat intelligence feeds is critical for these platforms to limit an organization's exposure to threats.

Overcoming the Challenge: The Case for Securing the Application, Not the Network

Even after securing internal resources with a distributed application of security, an organization should also carry out additional security related to the application, further layering security throughout the network. Within the preceding scenarios, most of the exploration has considered contextual identity, network access controls, and hardware controls to be the primarily applied controls. While we have thus far not stated the need for these controls to also apply to the application and software being served outward for consumption by clients, it has not been forgotten and is part of the defense-in-depth strategy.

That said, many of the same principles still apply throughout the consideration of the five core Zero Trust principles. When it comes to the access of any application on the network, identity has become a must-have in recent times, as opposed to allowing for anonymous access. The identity accessing an application can be gained through a direct login to the application, with accounts stored on a local system. However, a better alternative would be to have some sort of identity provider that allows external validation of identity, without the need to store identity in a potentially risky manner on the network. Identity providers such as Facebook, Apple, Google, and Twitter have started to allow social media login—that is, verifying the identity of a user to an application using their publicly available identity as created on one of these platforms. As an alternative, and typically for internal applications that exist within an organization, an identity broker can be integrated with single sign-on (SSO) providers, which can be further integrated into two-factor authentication applications. These two-factor authentication applications typically consist of the ability to send an email, call, or text the user at an identifying and previously stored address or phone number when the account was first created. This identity is then stored as a "token," which is referenceable throughout the applications on the network, and can be used to validate the user having a valid session, cutting down on the number of times the user needs to log in.

In relation to the application, vulnerability management is more related to the validation of information passed to and from the application than it is an inspection of the endpoint in some way. Validating the headers of a packet as the application is accessed, ensuring that the schema or format of the request is one that the application can handle and is willing to handle based on configured security features of the application, is extremely important. Without this validation, cross-site scripting, SQL injection attacks, and many other exploits can be executed. The same goes for the information passed to and from the application after successfully logging in. Validation of the information received in the header and body of the packet ensures that the data and requests of the application are within the bounds of the application's ability to deliver. This validation also needs to consider the source of the request, utilizing DNS-based lookup services. The ability for DNS-based lookup services to check where an IP originated and determine patterns around the application's access by certain geographical regions and even the ability to look up hostnames from requestors to determine whether they are potentially hosted in a risky cloud segment are both advantages when exposing applications to broader audiences.

Enforcement for the application is typically role-based in nature and defines what pieces of the application or containing data the identity can access. Each access should then result in an accounting mechanism for later analysis, whether through syslog, debug messages, or other mechanisms built into the application for this explicit purpose. These logs should detail the identity, what it accessed, how and for how long, like network-based logging. These logs should be sent to a centralized logging authority for analysis if or when needed, such as a Security Information and Event Management (SIEM) or similar event management server.

This exploration of application security and validation of the five core pillars of Zero Trust has a larger implication, however, in the cloud-based age of technology. Many vendors have argued that security is no longer a responsibility of the network, but rather of the application, especially considering the move of applications from on-premises into the cloud and an increasing exposure of these applications to the Internet. The availability of these applications across the Internet is typically a result of integration into an identity provider, extensive backend integration into logging mechanisms, an ability for the application to determine whether a request is legitimate or that of an automated script or bot, and then applying specific permissions to the session. This enforcement mechanism becomes the largest focus of the application of a Zero Trust strategy, as the application being exposed to worldwide audiences could spell disaster should a malicious third party gain unauthorized access and consume data not meant for them. Without a hardware firewall, intrusion prevention system, data loss prevention system, and additional automated checks, as was done with applications that exist internal to the organization, significant risk is assumed. This can also explain why cloud vendors and application owners are utilizing "as a service" (aaS) models more heavily, given their interest in offloading most of the security of an application to the service's vendor. While most application vendors do have some sort of vulnerability management service, they run on applications deployed within their premises, looking for vulnerabilities or misconfigurations in the application; these should not be relied upon solely for security of the application but merely a health check of the application and its ability to fend off attacks.

Summary

The journey an organization takes to change the architecture of its network and be more aligned with Zero Trust principles will undoubtedly seem insurmountable on first glance. The most common challenge that many organizations ask is "Where do we start?" This chapter attempted to provide for a blueprint of the inevitable challenges an organization will encounter as it starts into its Zero Trust journey and how to overcome them, combined with the technologies used to enforce policies found in Chapter 6. This blueprint starts with gaining visibility and understanding the endpoints and assets on the network, utilizing the concept of contextual identity. Contextual identity provides more than just a username and endpoint, but provides information on where, when, and through which medium the device joined the network to assist with determining what levels of restrictions will be required for it. This determination is done via active and passive means.

The journey then continues into understanding the endpoint, its operating system or firmware, and its expected communication within, across, and outside of the organization's network. While the bulk of threats may be considered outside of the network, this chapter covered how lateral traversal of threats can endanger the network and how baselines can minimize this risk. Only after this traversal and risk are understood can a segmentation plan for both existing and net-new endpoints be created and enforced in a ubiquitous manner on the network.

Finally, the chapter covered defense in depth as a methodology to protect the network and secure the network from the application layer all the way out to the perimeter edge. The next chapter covers a model for how to sort through and plan with the immense amount of data and application of segmentation within the network.

References in This Chapter

- Amazon Web Services, "Shared Responsibility Model," https://aws.amazon.com/compliance/shared-responsibility-model/.

- Scott Rose, "Planning for a Zero Trust Architecture: A Planning Guide for Federal Administrators," NIST Cybersecurity Whitepaper, May 6, 2022, https://nvlpubs.nist.gov/nistpubs/CSWP/NIST.CSWP.20.pdf.

- Network Mapper (NMAP), https://nmap.org/.

Chapter 8

Developing a Successful Segmentation Plan

Chapter Key Points:

- After an organization collects contextual identities, examines traffic traversal, and understands what technologies can be used in the current environment for segmentation, the organization must create a segmentation plan and deployment structure to continue to guide it down the segmentation path.

- When an organization is planning to deploy segmentation and pursue the Zero Trust journey, the first step in the journey should be to ask what the drivers are for pursuing Zero Trust in the first place. The only way to guarantee success is to have clear problem statements for why Zero Trust is important.

- The Zero Trust problem statement and the need to change the way the organization does business must have wide-reaching buy-in across teams in the organization. Without buy-in from all levels and teams involved, political inhibitions will prevent the program from getting off the ground or lead to analysis paralysis.

- Understanding the capabilities already present within the organization and how these capabilities are capitalized on already will prevent the organization from reworking solutions already explored or help prioritize the need to revisit these problem statements.

- The exploration of the Zero Trust journey should encompass a plan for what the future of Zero Trust looks like within an organization. This exploration includes the potential ways that segmentation will be deployed, additions in control measures, and where enforcement mechanisms will be applied over time.

Chapter 6, "Segmentation," presented a definition of *segmentation* and methodologies for implementing segmentation; it also included a discussion on how to gather information to understand traffic flows for business as usual. Chapter 7, "Zero Trust Common Challenges," presented common challenges encountered when developing a segmentation architecture, along with solutions to overcome these common challenges. This chapter assumes that readers have an understanding of how devices interact, and their flows within a VLAN, across the internal network, and to external resources. Here, the organization now strives to develop a plan to classify and segment endpoints while maintaining business as usual.

It is fully expected that when exploring and analyzing data for the segmentation aspect of Zero Trust, most organizations will become overwhelmed quickly. The application of a Zero Trust Architecture may occur over time and in phases. In the initial phases, organizations work toward building the foundations of the architecture as it applies to their physical infrastructure, their users, their services, and most importantly their business objectives. This foundation includes a need to consider all the Zero Trust principles, ranging from

- Validating policies that enable the organization and users to conduct business

- Establishing identity to determine which entities exist on the network

- Employing vulnerability management to determine what access each of the entities needs and what their potential risk profile looks like in relation to the network

- Preventing access for those entities that do not conform with policies related to risk or fail their authentication mechanism

- Analyzing the outcomes of each phase related to both business and technical objectives

The role that network segmentation has as it relates to Zero Trust is foundational. However, to achieve segmentation, an organization must be able to identify and classify the users, endpoints, and workloads that it is responsible for. With the segmentation plan, found at the conclusion of Chapter 6, a plan is developed for how interactions must occur for segmentation to be successful in its enforcement.

The key to success in achieving segmentation is an initial effort focused on defining what segmentation means to the organization, either based on data it finds during analysis, or based on the objectives the organization has related to segmentation. This analysis must also consider to what extent the business can continue to operate while absorbing the segmentation method. Often, there is an initiative driven by regulatory requirements, risk assessments, or penetration test results, or a general initiative to protect critical assets. All these drivers recommend segmentation as a means of mitigating risk, containing threats, or reducing the attack surface. What these drivers may not do is give any direction as to what level of segmentation is required for reducing this attack surface and how to accomplish this goal. Therefore, when an inevitable discussion needs to occur on why one business unit or another cannot have unrestricted network access or endpoint types, organizations must have artifacts from planning for the enforcement methodologies showing that not only was a significant amount of due diligence applied to align with regulations but that business considerations were considered.

From a Zero Trust Architecture perspective, planning is a crucial component. The following sections focus on what should be involved in a plan that sets the foundation for success of an organization to accomplish its Zero Trust goals.

Planning: Defining Goals and Objectives

As a first step, it is essential to have a clear understanding of the business drivers of the organization that lead to a need for segmentation. These business drivers will typically provide a charter for the need for segmentation, either by helping determine the level of segmentation required or helping break devices into groups that need more or less segmentation within and across them. This section covers many typical drivers for segmentation from a business and technical perspective.

Risk Assessments and Compliance

Risk assessments can come in many forms. Various regulatory standards provide templates for using risk assessments to evaluate a network; they range from self-administered risk assessments through a thorough audit of controls and the application of security via these controls. Some of these regulatory standards have both aspects, including the Cybersecurity Maturity Model Certification (CMMC), PCI (Payment Card Industry), and ISO (see references at the end of the chapter). Depending on the focus of the risk assessment, it may indicate a need for improvement in the policy for what is allowed onto the network, may find a need for visibility or enforcement of access for endpoints when they're already on the network, or may reveal a gap in the historical analysis of endpoints that had previously been on the network. Typically, the higher an organization wants or needs to align with a regulatory requirement, the more stringent and focused the audit related to the requirement becomes. Regardless of the findings, the risk assessment provides a gap analysis that should be resolved and should be the focus of the ultimate goals for the Zero Trust Architecture.

As an example of a risk assessment, the Department of Defense publishes assessment guides for Cybersecurity Maturity Model Certification, which include excerpts that directly correlate to the structure of Zero Trust built within this text. The following passages evidence many of the aspects of the five Zero Trust principles illustrated here:

Policy and Governance (from page 16 of CMMC Level 1 Final Draft 20211210_508):

> *Determine if:*
>
> *[a] the types of transactions and functions that authorized users are permitted to execute*
>
> *are defined; and*
>
> *[b] system access is limited to the defined types of transactions and functions for*
>
> *authorized users.*

Identity (from page 13 of CMMC Level 1 Final Draft 20211210_508):

Determine if:

[a] authorized users are identified;

[b] processes acting on behalf of authorized users are identified;

[c] devices (and other systems) authorized to connect to the system are identified;

[d] system access is limited to authorized users;

[e] system access is limited to processes acting on behalf of authorized users; and

[f] system access is limited to authorized devices (including other systems).

Vulnerability Management (from page 18 of CMMC Level 1 Final Draft 20211210_508):

Determine if:

[a] connections to external systems are identified;

[b] the use of external systems is identified;

[c] connections to external systems are verified;

[d] the use of external systems is verified;

[e] connections to external systems are controlled/limited; and

[f] the use of external systems is controlled/limited.

Enforcement (from page 38 of CMMC Level 1 Final Draft 20211210_508):

Determine if:

[a] the external system boundary is defined;

[b] key internal system boundaries are defined;

[c] communications are monitored at the external system boundary;

[d] communications are monitored at key internal boundaries;

[e] communications are controlled at the external system boundary;

[f] communications are controlled at key internal boundaries;

[g] communications are protected at the external system boundary; and

[h] communications are protected at key internal boundaries.

Analytics (from page 43 of CMMC Level 1 Final Draft 20211210_508):

Determine if:

[a] the time within which to identify system flaws is specified;

[b] system flaws are identified within the specified time frame;

[c] the time within which to report system flaws is specified;

[d] system flaws are reported within the specified time frame;

[e] the time within which to correct system flaws is specified; and

[f] system flaws are corrected within the specified time frame.

While regulatory requirements may be unique in the extent to which they call for these controls, most align in a similar manner to the points illustrated here.

To further complicate regulatory adherence and compliance, some networks may still be considered as a connectivity mechanism to services. These "extranets," or business service networks, typically focus on getting as many endpoints onto the network as possible, with enforcement being an afterthought. That said, these networks will be subject to additional scrutiny as they put multiple organizations at risk and may be the driving factor behind compliance with regulatory requirements.

Threat Mapping

Threats to the network come in all shapes and sizes, including malware, ransomware, worms, viruses, phishing attacks, denial-of-service attacks, and intrusions. These threats may be a significant driver in the need for segmenting and implementing a Zero Trust Architecture, solely based on the threats that are posed to critical systems that enable business as usual. Threats such as ransomware have been known to shut down hospitals, financial institutions, and government offices.

What drives many organizations toward a need for implementation of Zero Trust principles is insurance related to the business, requiring an understanding of potential threats to the network and their likelihood of occurring. After these potential threats, their likelihood, and where they exist are understood, the cost of exploitation versus protection measures must be calculated and compared. Much of this process will rely upon the identity and understanding of flows for endpoints in the organization. As one example, some organizations claim to enable the business by allowing it to use endpoints that are most conducive to accomplishing the output required. This may include the use of personal machines on the network, which greatly increases the likelihood of potential ransomware. This likelihood would offset the convenience of allowing personal device use, potentially influencing policies stating what is required for endpoints to be joined to the network, what restrictions on noncorporate devices should exist, and whether additional spend on devices that would be comparable would be more aligned with a threat mitigation approach. In these cases, the output of the threat map may influence the objectives for design in alignment with Zero Trust.

Data Protection

Data is critical to any organization. Data protection is a focus of Zero Trust. This protection includes data at rest or in motion. Data protection is generally seen as a trifecta of evaluation criteria, including whether the data's confidentiality, integrity, and availability can all be guaranteed. For organizations, especially in the research and development fields, which are most at risk of data loss or inaccessibility, the protection of this data and understanding of who or what is accessing it become the priority for their Zero Trust architecture. Ensuring that information is confidential and accessible only by authorized identities in a sanctioned way, that the data will be complete and accurate to what was entered when the identity accesses or changes it, and that it is available during the time and in the manner expected are all measures of data protection. For many organizations, unauthorized access to data has been the focus of exploits in recent years, and for those for whom it has not, the accessing or exfiltration of this data could have regulatory, monetary, contractual, or reputation impacts. The need to focus on protecting data has never been greater and is the focal point of many audits and policies.

Reducing Attack Surfaces

Zero Trust is an ongoing approach to networking that progresses through the five Zero Trust pillars outlined in this book. For many organizations, in combination with the other drivers and goals, just reducing attack surfaces and securing the business to avoid undue focus on mitigating risk may be the driver for applying Zero Trust pillars to their network. This alignment can imply additional policy adherence and improvement, visibility, vulnerability management, enforcement policies, and analysis and can be done to better reduce overall attack surfaces of endpoints, users, and workloads within an organization.

Plan: Segmentation Design

A key aspect of Zero Trust is the application of enforcement mechanisms, which must be influenced by the Policy & Governance, Identity, and Vulnerability Management pillars. Segmentation needs to be planned for, encompassing the potential impact, how the impact will be tested, and which entities within the organization will be affected by the segmentation policies as applied. Segmentation design has two primary schools of thought: top-down and bottom-up. Both are covered as approaches within this section.

Top-down segmentation design creates a broad view of segmentation as it would apply to the entire enterprise, focused on business alignment for each segment. Throughout this process, it is imperative to define the business drivers and understand the goals that were determined in the previous section. This understanding of what the goal for the broader organization is will aid in determining the segmentation scope, level of segmentation, and granularity of segmentation. Generally, to approach segmentation in a top-down manner requires an understanding of not only contextual identities, as explored in Chapter 6, but also how those contextual identities align with lines of business. With top-down segmentation, a broad business goal drives a need for segmentation and limitation of access as the central priority of the architecture. Devices and identities within the architecture are then aligned in accordance with business goals.

For those organizations that are driven by regulation, for example, endpoints that are subject to that regulation must be treated differently than those that fall outside the regulation. This may mean that a user who belongs to a business and utilizes two separate devices (such as a PC and an iPad) may have different access between the devices because of the functional use aligned with the business for the respective devices. The same may be true for two IoT devices on board the same chassis, with a PCI classified payment system requiring complete separation from the maintenance computer on the same soft drink machine. This treatment disregards anything related to communication patterns in the initial classification of devices and focuses strictly on business use, with traversal as a secondary or even tertiary step.

After policy and approach are determined related to the top-down segmentation design, technical artifacts may be collected to aid in planning for where and which method of segmentation is used. These technical artifacts may detail which business units belong to individual segments or enclaves, demonstrate flows and traffic traversal between or within enclaves or systems, consider the gaps in traversal mapping, and create a plan for how segmentation will be applied in a phased manner, typically within the applicable segment. Based on this plan, a technical application of segmentation can be applied, and an outcome strived for via a technical means.

The bottom-up approach focuses on traffic collection and analysis first, with sorting through flows, logs, and policies to have a definitive output. It determines segmentation strategy based on traffic patterns, typically with an alignment to the goal of reducing the attack surface or addressing mapped threats within an organization. In this method, segmentation planning is directed based on what sets of users, endpoints, and workloads are communicating with other sets of users, endpoints, and workloads. This method is most effective when both identities and traversals are known as the primary step, treating the business units to which these identities and traversals belong as a secondary or tertiary priority.

Tools used in the bottom-up design process typically integrate with other data sources to bring additional context to traffic streams. This will typically start with an asset identification mechanism, preferably an asset management database containing devices unable to authenticate, but may also begin with a passive identity system such as Cisco Identity Services Engine (ISE). Even a passive identity system enables an organization to integrate with identity sources such as Active Directory or LDAP and utilize these identities to inject into NetFlow records through integration with products such as Cisco Secure Network Analytics or Secure Workload. Where identities are known, an organization also can benefit from firewall log analysis by mapping a currently known IP address to an identity rather than requiring a second step to resolve the identity for traversal mapping.

From a practical perspective, the implementation of segmentation may require that both of these strategies be utilized for the best results to be achieved. For models where the attack surface must be reduced due to regulatory requirements, for example, a common approach is to classify identities based on their business unit within the organization and then map their communications to create additional segmentation within the enclave. Using the two approaches in conjunction allows high-level architectures to be created using data and input from the various impacted teams while validating plans and developing policy for implementation from low-level traffic collection and analysis. Key to success is mapping out where either approach might best succeed based on tribal knowledge of the organization.

Top-Down Design Process

Executive and leadership buy-in links the ability of the organization to create an architecture and implement it. Architects and engineers need that support when designing and implementing Zero Trust. This support is especially important for a top-down, or business-aligned, segmentation strategy.

The purpose of the design must remain relevant to leadership and clearly define the business value and the operational advantages as they relate to the organization. The top-down design approach takes items that relate directly to broader objectives to help achieve buy-in. The following nonexhaustive list identifies some of the considerations and steps in designing from the top down:

- **Define business drivers and segmentation scope:** This effort focuses on upper management and executive sponsors of the segmentation effort. Work done here will typically focus on collecting and understanding an organization's business goals, drivers, and priorities. During this effort, overall organizational scope will be determined (for example, classified uncontrolled information may be in scope, but classified information may be out of scope) and current and planned projects that may impact any segmentation efforts.

- **Define impacted teams:** This effort varies depending on the scope and industry vertical. As a general rule, for any segmentation strategy, there must be cooperation between the team that enables connectivity, the team that secures connectivity, the team that troubleshoots connectivity, and the team that owns the applications or endpoints that rely on connectivity. In many organizations, these teams can be translated as network engineers, security engineers, operations, and applications teams.

  Segmentation project teams may consist of a subset of the following:

- Network engineering, architecture, and operations

- Security engineering, architecture, and operations

- Applications architects and owners

- Systems and database administration

- Risk and compliance

- Key user groups, such as

  - Operations technologies support teams

  - Biomedical support teams

  - Research department representatives

  - Individual application support teams

- **Define use cases and workflows:** This effort typically consists of interviews and conversations with impacted teams and focuses on workshop discussions, as covered in Chapter 9, "Zero Trust Enforcement." At this stage, an organization is evaluating what has been collected in the previous step and is trying to add both context and completeness to the collection of data. This work clarifies the impact of application or access outage and the range and scope of use cases, users, applications, and endpoints. This effort should also be seen to inform the impacted teams of the effort underway to implement segmentation and how this segmentation might affect the various groups. Building relationships with the impacted teams is key to success.

- **Determine security controls and capabilities gap analysis:** This effort is focused on determining the current and future state of security control capabilities deployed. The overall intention of this effort is to determine which controls are deployed, where they are impactful, plans for future control deployment, and where gaps exist that may impact segmentation deployment.

- **Define segments:** This effort varies somewhat by industry vertical where specialty segments can be identified and created. Generally, segments are defined by categorizing users, endpoints, and workloads and are typically grouped by function and by risk and/or impact. In this step, the organization can define the desired end state from an overall segmentation plan perspective.

- **Collect technical artifacts:** Identifying and classifying enterprise assets are foundational to achieving segmentation. This effort consists of the collection, categorization, and analysis of an organization's intellectual information as it pertains to its broad network and security hygiene and typically consists of

  - LAN, WAN, data center, and cloud topological and architectural diagrams

  - Application inventories

  - Asset inventories (CMDBs)

  - IP address allocation schemas

  - VLAN assignment schemas

  - Host-naming conventions

  - Business continuity and disaster recovery classifications

  - Data classification standards

  - Audit and test findings

Note that the definition of the segment to apply Zero Trust tenets to is key to the top-down approach. Each segment consists of its own set of use cases, data, or endpoints contained, and therefore, the boundaries and the approach for this phase of the Zero Trust journey may differ as separate business units within an organization plan for their Zero Trust journey. Due to this, the approach that each business unit takes may differ or be gradual in approach from top down to bottom up, and can be considered in either direction, depending on the organization's approach to Zero Trust.

Bottom-Up Design Process

As the name implies, the bottom-up design process is opposite in its approach to deploying segmentation to the top-down design process. In this approach, because of its common alignment with reducing attack surfaces, understanding contextual identities and how they interact is paramount. In a bottom-up design, it is assumed that endpoints will be used across business units and are rarely able to be divided into discreet segments. For consulting firms, for example, a single consultant may be part of multiple business units due to the nature of this person's knowledge set as it applies to technology as opposed to a single vertical or regulatory requirement. The consultant's device, therefore, must have access across organizations and to various assets, making a better approach to segmentation be based on traffic traversal rather than organization. The same goes for organizations whose physical servers host multiple business unit virtual applications due to resource restrictions. Because users across business units must all reach the physical server for individual applications, a better approach is to focus on understanding that traversal and enforce allowed traversal and traffic patterns rather than creating large numbers of exceptions or investments in dedicated environments per business unit.

In a bottom-up design, limited knowledge typically exists into the interactions between business units or their owned applications due to political challenges within the organization or ignorance of the endpoint or application owner as to its behavior on the network. Especially in organizations that have separate funding buckets, applications, and projects that are strictly controlled by the department, there is rarely an appetite to understand the full picture of how devices interact across departments, because departments would be motivated only to understand the aspects of the interaction that they fund. Therefore, it takes a technical team not bound to either department or business unit to understand the interaction and ensure the interaction continues to function as expected, even after segmentation controls are applied. Attempting to apply the top-down, business-related approach to this scenario would result in limited success and typically only result in finger pointing on the fault of an interaction not working as expected or who funds the interaction and therefore troubleshooting.

Once contextual identities and traffic traversal are understood, enforcement mechanisms that are related to the business unit can be applied. These enforcement mechanisms consist of management abilities that are known to be required of the owning business unit or department and are enforced based on membership in that department. At this point, definitions of segments, gap analysis, and similar steps can be taken in the opposite direction of the top-down approach.

Implement: Deploying the Segmentation Design

Deploying segmentation is the result of data collection, regardless of the model used to collect this data. With an understanding of organizational layout, contextual identities, traffic traversal, gaps in enforcement, and similar concepts, an organization can begin to deploy the segmentation design. However, approaches for deploying segmentation differ between organizations. Different approaches are detailed in the following sections with considerations for each.

Creating a Segmentation Plan by Site Type

Creating a segmentation plan across sites and site types first requires defining sets or categories of use cases that could be found at the respective site or sites. This discovery will typically take place as part of the segmentation workshop, an approach to which is documented in Chapter 9. This workshop will determine use cases, capabilities, gap analysis, scope, and priority in alignment with the segmentation model that will best fit the organization. For those organizations that are undergoing net-new architecture designs for individual sites or that need a Zero Trust application on a per-site basis, a segmentation plan based on site type may be the best fit.

When an organization is approaching an application of segmentation based on site type, the best approach is typically to classify sites into common categories, either based on impact to the business for the proposed segmentation design or other site characteristics. Commonly, one characteristic in determining which sites have Zero Trust applied to them earlier in the process is the technical ability of users to describe specific results of their actions. For sites that host technical users who can describe the result of attempting to connect to the network and not receiving an IP address, for example, more impactful lessons learned can be built and used to influence success in future sites. In other examples, sites that generate the most revenue for an organization may have Zero Trust applied well after others so that lessons learned can be generated and utilized to ensure little to no downtime is experienced in revenue-generating sites.

During the discovery of site-based use cases context is identified, with the goal to design templates with reusable patterns. When an organization is applying aspects of a Zero Trust strategy, these patterns allow reuse based on lessons learned on previous sites to classify, evaluate, or enforce restrictions applied based on use cases.

Some commonalities found in site-based deployments of Zero Trust are discussed in the following sections, as also documented in Figure 8-1. While many of these segments may not exist in combination at any one site, the following discussion aims to provide a starting point for classification of segments that could exist across sites for many organizations.

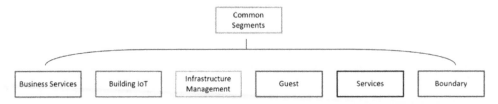

Figure 8-1   *Sample Healthcare Administration Building Segment Mapping*

Business Services

Business services endpoints are any endpoints that are managed and used to conduct "business as usual" for the organization. While this may differ between different verticals or types of businesses, the typical intersection of business services may include corporate managed workstations, managed BYOD devices, printers, phones, and conferencing and collaboration services. These resources are typically easier to identify, determine the vulnerability posture of, and apply enforcement to because they have an active user who either directly interfaces with the device or a GUI residing on the device. Resolution of the need to remediate vulnerabilities or send information relating to the behavior of the device is also typically easier. Due to the managed nature of the device and ability to configure it directly or remotely, it can typically be configured to send any logging information available to a centralized SIEM. These devices are typically considered lower risk to apply enforcement to due to their ability to provide feedback to the user on what it is unable to do but high in impact due to being common user-required devices for business functions.

Building IoT

Typically, building IoT devices are connected to the network but may be simplistic in their ability to be interacted with, meaning they may not have a direct GUI or easily accessible configuration modification ability outside of their management system. These devices can be any size, from that of a microchip the size of a fingertip, all the way up to control boards in HVAC or manufacturing units. Identification of this category of device may be a challenge due to age. In many examples, such as medical or manufacturing devices, these devices may have been created decades ago and included a USB 1.0 or 1.1 protocol port to which a wired or wireless network interface card could be connected. Therefore, with a bulk purchase of network interface cards, any devices connected to the network with the same make or model of NIC could look the exact same while being unique devices. Examples of devices in this category include physical security, badge readers, HVAC, lighting controls, and other general building automation and security functions.

Infrastructure Management

Infrastructure management includes devices that maintain network devices, applications, and overall traffic flow on the network. While having a slight overlap with IoT devices, this category typically includes managed power strips, battery backups, temperature sensors found in data centers, humidity sensors, voltage sensors, and the multitude of connected devices that ensure the network runs as expected. They are a combination of devices that can be easily interacted with but not always managed and non-GUI devices that must be managed through a management system. These devices are typically easier to identify, but care needs to be taken when blocking access from them due to potential notifications and environmental impact by not being able to reach their required resources. Successful implementation in infrastructure management can produce KPIs measured in less frequent incidents of compromise sourced from IoT environments to other segments. Because they are the connectivity conduit through which users access the network, applying segmentation controls to these devices is typically higher risk.

Guest

The chief information security officer (CISO) of one of the largest auditing firms in the United States was once quoted as saying, "I believe Internet is a birthright, and I am of the opinion that we should afford that right to all who enter our premises." While a generous view of the offerings afforded nonemployees, guest networks and devices are encompassed in this sentiment. A guest device should be considered a device in the network that should have no abilities to interact with internal systems. For most guest endpoints and networks, dedicated services—for example, domain naming, time, address allocation, printing, or presenting—are all segmented off the corporate network to prevent exploitation or unauthorized access. While devices may drastically differ, most organizations restrict the guest network to those that can interact with a guest registration system of some sort, typically by web GUI. Therefore, expected devices, such as Windows endpoints, Mac endpoints, mobile devices, and tablets, should all be easily identified, and enforcement applied via a dynamic access control application.

Services

Also known as "shared services," the services enclave is one that exists in almost every organization. To ensure that DHCP services, DNS services, NTP services, and management services are all treated with priority and are grouped together into a common area, networks are architected around the services enclave. Organizations rely on the services enclave for most of the core network protocols that allow endpoints to traverse the network or be troubleshot because many IT organizations keep remote desktop–permitted services in this enclave as well. This enclave should be considered a key business structure and treated with priority when it comes to maintaining business as usual. The reliance of all devices, including network connectivity devices, on these shared services makes enforcing segmentation methods on them very high risk.

Creating a Segmentation Plan by Endpoint Category

Another logical approach to deploying segmentation within a site is focusing on endpoint categories that exist at that site. The ultimate goal for deploying a segmentation plan based on endpoint category is the assumption that endpoint categories will typically be similar between sites. For those sites that have a more homogeneous population of devices, applying segmentation to those devices is generally assumed to be less impactful after enforcement is tested on a small number of test devices.

One example of this approach is the hospital endpoint categorization for segmentation design seen in Figure 8-2.

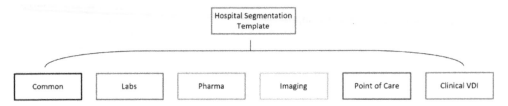

Figure 8-2   *Common Healthcare Endpoint Types*

In the specific case of a Hospital Segmentation Design Template, clinical use cases typically include similar types of devices with similar needs for traffic traversal. For example, imaging devices, including MRI, CT, and radiology types of devices, have similar traffic patterns and communicate with dedicated management systems found within the same segment. Only for external services, such as streaming music for patient entertainment, or backups to secured cloud storage repositories will imaging machines communicate outside of the enclave. Therefore, creating a segment for imaging functioning devices can be a successful approach in these environments.

For this categorization methodology, focus should be related to functions and services offered at a typical hospital and where these categorizations of functions and services can be further differentiated by device types and traffic flow requirements. One common challenge that many organizations run into is getting too granular in the categorizations from the start, creating "nested" subcategories that may start to describe endpoint characteristics that are irrelevant or impossible to identify based on contextual identity mechanisms. One organization went so far as to attempt to describe endpoints based on age, a futile attempt to segment devices from one another given their need for the same access.

From a segmentation perspective, the clinical categorizations may share common services (out of the DC or locally from the Common Services category) but would typically be expected to not communicate between categories. Examples of these categories are provided in the following sections.

Common or Shared Devices

The Common category is similar to the services category and represents shared services that exist for the enterprise, as opposed to a singular site or unique segment of the overall network. As opposed to classifying the services related to their unique location, of which there may not be one, this category represents the shared services as an endpoint type that is then shared across many, if not all, sites. By doing so, devices that exist in a finite number of data centers in a centralized model can be classified as a high-level category that is understood to be consumed by all sites, and potentially endpoint categories. Similarly, application of enforcement technologies to these devices can be very high risk.

Labs

Previously in the chapter, labs were presented as a category of site and functionality for nonproduction testing of network-connected devices and endpoints. However, the healthcare vertical utilizes the labs verbiage as an area of the organization where diagnostic tests can be carried out on medical samples. The Labs category of endpoints is intended to support sets of endpoints and systems with specific capabilities to support various lab use cases. Lab instruments, instrument workstations, and terminal servers would be typical endpoint classifications to be segmented in the labs enclave. Application of enforcement technologies within labs is considered relatively low risk.

Pharma

The Pharma category of endpoints is intended to support services and functions specific to delivering pharmaceutical services within a hospital. Medicine stations, anesthesia systems, pharmaceutical safes, and medication carousels are endpoint classifications that would be segmented through the pharma enclave. Commonly, these types of endpoints are among the first to be considered for an enforcement mechanism due to the sensitive nature and potential impact on customer welfare that they pose. Medicine stations, or drug cabinets as they are colloquially known, dispense all types of medicine, many of which could be abused if they fell into the wrong hands, or could impact patient health if improper dosage is provided to the patient. Application of enforcement technologies in this segment is typically a medium risk and should be tested thoroughly in the lab before deploying.

Imaging

The Imaging category is intended to support sets of endpoints and systems with specific capabilities to support various imaging use cases. Imaging modality, administrative, and viewing workstations are endpoint classifications that would be segmented through the imaging enclave. Due to the peer-to-peer traffic traversal nature of these types of endpoints, they will typically need to be more robust in their segmentation policies as applied, ensuring that real-time backup, viewing, and logging of information is constantly available without interruption due to their long use times. Application of enforcement technologies in this segment is typically a medium risk and should be tested thoroughly in the lab before deploying.

Point of Care

The Point of Care categorization of endpoints is intended to support patient point of care devices. Infusion pumps, heartbeat monitors, and blood pressure meters are endpoint classifications that would be segmented through the point of care enclave. For many point of care devices, the limited customization and modification abilities to change their network configurations on the fly make them one of the last endpoint categories to have policy enforcement applied. In many cases, newer devices that are more easily customizable become a separate subcategory of devices within the endpoint parent category to ease enforcement and even testing of enforcement. Application of enforcement technologies in this segment is typically a high risk due to direct patient impact of not being able to communicate.

Clinical VDI

One aspect of layered security not outlined in detail is the potential for limiting access to critical information through the use of virtual desktop infrastructure (VDI), which has little to no abilities to allow information to be exported to an external device. The Clinical VDI categorization of endpoints is intended to support thin client terminal endpoints for exactly this business case. Exam room and nurse station terminals would be segmented through the clinical VDI enclave, and segments containing these VDIs will commonly have policies applied at the VDI manager level, dictating which access the virtual desktops have, as opposed to attempting to segment these virtual devices via a physical network access device.

Creating a Segmentation Plan by Service Type

Categorization based on service type provides a method to identify the services that an endpoint provides to the organization, such as use cases and traffic flows traversing the enterprise boundaries. As with the other design templates, the categorizations of use cases defined is expected to be a super-set of all categorizations that exist for an organization. An example of this approach to categorizations shown in Figure 8-3.

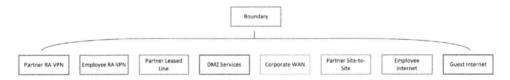

Figure 8-3   *Healthcare Boundary Service Segmentation Service Mapping*

Boundary services categorizations are better defined as policy enforcement points than segments or enclaves, hence why this example is used to illustrate the design in alignment with service type. These specific use case definitions are used to categorize traffic flows entering and/or exiting from an organization's physical infrastructure.

Partner/Vendor Remote Access VPN

The Partner/Vendor Remote Access VPN categorization is intended for organizational partners with semi-trusted access to defined internal resources. While broad in its description, the number of endpoints and services that belong to this category can be just as broad. Ranging from anything related to soft drink machines that need remote administration throughout the campus to elevators, escalators, and human safety devices such as smoke detectors, all sorts of endpoints may belong to this category. The level of access granted to this category of service is highly dependent upon which services and how robust the services are to which partners are accessing them. While medical devices or human safety devices may number in the thousands, and they may all be accessible through a singular portal or singular port per device, more limited numbers of elevators or escalators may be accessed on a larger number of ports and protocols for reporting and safety tracking. Because of the potential for service-level agreements related to partner or vendor interactions, the level of risk for applying enforcement mechanisms in this segment varies between low and high risk.

Employee Remote Access VPN

For organizations that allow employees to work from home, there is an inherent need to allow connections into internal systems to flow from an untrusted area, typically the Internet, into a trusted area via a virtual private network after proper authentication and authorization. In many ways, one of the first major considerations within most organizations' Zero Trust journeys will be the secure access provided via the VPN medium. Employees are typically expected to authenticate in a definitive manner, and may be provided granular access to specific resources, based on resource categorization, as defined by the administrators of those endpoints and services. The process to provide this access varies significantly, and the level of access may also be wildly disparate between organizations, but this model is like that which is applied to internal endpoints accessing applications via the wired and wireless mediums. With the explosion of work from home abilities, the application of segmentation enforcement has increased on remote access to be medium to high risk; however, if done outside of standard business hours, this risk can be minimized.

Partner Leased Lines

While many vendors and internal employees may access data via a specific client or hardware set, terminating in a specific area of the network, many organizations have areas of the network dedicated to traversal of external entities that are trusted, having access to broader amounts of information without a need to use a specific client or device. These terminations will typically be part of the demilitarized zone (DMZ) of the network but warrant their own category of service based on the common design decision to have a secondary or tertiary uncategorized area of the network. This "trusted DMZ" or "partner DMZ" allows devices from third parties to access information contained within the enclave, merely by maintaining a contract with a service provider for a leased line termination for both organizations. A subcategory of this enclave could include VPN-based partner terminations, which typically occur via dedicated hardware connected to the public Internet. Because of the potential for service-level agreements related to partner or vendor interactions, the level of risk for applying enforcement mechanisms in this segment varies between low and high risk.

DMZ Services

For a business to survive in the modern era, some presence on the public Internet, whether self-hosted or third-party-hosted must exist. The demilitarized zone services categorization could also be classified as inbound from the public Internet. The DMZ services enclave is designed for publicly accessible web pages and services, which then have a secondary or secured connection to information that may be proprietary to consume this information without exposing it to untrusted consumers. Inbound traffic into this area from the Internet is intended to terminate through an application front end where no direct access to internal services is supported. Because of the potential for web servers facing the public Internet and being an organization's sole presence on the web being found in this category, applying segmentation enforcement could be considered high or very high risk.

Corporate WAN

The corporate wide area network (WAN) categorization provides backbone services supporting communications paths between corporate locations. These circuits are typically trusted but may have an overlay encryption placed on them, depending on how they traverse between sites, specifically through dedicated lines or even via the public Internet. They represent a key policy enforcement point for containing traffic flows allowed between locations, making them a prime area to allocate firewalls or intrusion prevention systems to analyze traffic and traffic patterns. They may also contain access methods or connection points to cloud services, especially as shared services begin to move to cloud hosting platforms. Because of this backbone connecting sites and potentially data centers, applying segmentation enforcement on this medium is very high risk.

Employee Outbound Internet

Almost every organization has a service provided to its users for outbound Internet in some fashion. Whether it's to access information for research purposes, share documents with fellow employees and partners, or to access Software as a Service offerings the organization subscribes to, most organizations allow some level of outbound Internet access. This outbound service termination point provides for a prime area to filter and limit access to what the organization considers relevant access or cache commonly accessed resources to limit bandwidth consumption. This area may also have considerations to unmanaged devices and applications to consume services, such as updates, software, patching, and synchronization services. Should employees require Internet for their job functions, applying segmentation enforcement could pose a high risk.

Guest Outbound Internet

The Guest wireless service enclave is defined to support guest wireless Internet access only. It is expected that this zone will support guest wireless anchor controllers, dedicated DNS services, and outbound web proxy capabilities. For most organizations, it is a wise and common approach to physically separate guest Internet from corporate/employee Internet access via physically separate hardware and services allocated to the service. Being a convenience offered by an organization to its guests, application of enforcement technologies is typically low risk for these devices.

Unknown

An Unknown category was created to catch anything that missed all other classification. Expect that not all endpoints and devices will be identified in the early stages of deployment. Initial unknown policies will, by necessity, be open, permitting traffic to most segments. Over time this open policy becomes more restrictive as more devices are identified and categorized, with the eventual goal being that any device that is unknown is placed in a provisioning network where identity can be established and categorization assigned.

Regardless of the model used for the segmentation strategy, understanding the business, endpoints, applications, workloads, and sites is critical to forming the segmentation model enabling the Zero Trust architecture. To create the overall segmentation model, all business units involved must collaborate, and they must complete aggregation of technical artifacts before analyzing what needs to be enforced and how. These models are meant to provide a high-level plan for segmentation that spans between multiple virtual boundaries, including sites, data type, and business units. Figure 8-4 shows a high-level segmentation mapping and design that combines the methods discussed.

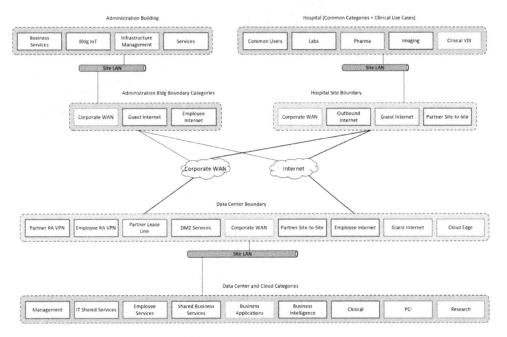

Figure 8-4 *Segmentation Model*

Implement: The Segmentation Model

The outcome of the dedication to collection and analysis of data related to the segmentation functional model best for an organization is an evaluation of the dependencies and interrelationships found within the business. By understanding these relationships in as much detail as what has been described here, an organization can build a segmentation plan as a foundation to determine and describe the expected interactions between entities. This segmentation plan, seen in Figure 8-5 as a matrix of communications, helps to highlight where simple permit/deny controls could be deployed as opposed to where tighter controls based on port and protocol would be applied between entities. The Trust matrix in Figure 8-5 shows interactions between business units that vary between a simple permit/deny of all traffic between the two entities, and more restrictive port and protocol-based policies applied, ensuring that traffic, even between peers within the same segment, can be restricted in their communication. Note that in XY axis graph (Figure 8-5), X is the source and Y is the destination. In some cases, traffic is expected to be initiated in one direction only.

ENCLAVE TRUST MAPPING		TO	Enterprise		Facilities		Digital Edge		Cloud		Common Services			Business Services	
			Branch Endpoints	Corporate Endpoint	Physical Security	Building	Proxy to Third Parties	API Gateway	Private	Public	Identity Services	End-User Services	Administrative Services	Retail	Back-office Systems
FROM															
Enterprise	Branch Endpoints		■	Y	N	N	Y	N	Y	Y	Y	Y	N	Y	Y
	Corporate Endpoint		N	■	N	N	Y	N	Y	Y	Y	Y	Y	Y	Y
Facilities	Physical Security		N	N	■	Y	N	Y	N	Y	N	N	Y	N	N
	Building		N	N	Y	■	N	N	N	N	N	N	N	N	N
Digital Edge	Proxy to Third Parties		N	N	N	N	■	Y	N	N	Y	N	N	N	N
	API Gateway		N	N	Y	Y	N	■	Y	N	N	N	N	N	N
Cloud	Private		N	N	N	N	N	N	■	Y	N	N	N	Y	N
	Public		N	N	Y	Y	N	Y	N	■	N	N	N	Y	N
Common Services	Identity Services		Y	N	N	N	Y	N	Y	N	■	Y	Y	N	N
	End-User Services		Y	N	N	N	N	N	Y	Y	N	■	N	N	N
	Administrative Services		Y	Y	Y	Y	Y	Y	Y	Y	Y	Y	■	Y	Y
Business Services	Retail		N	N	N	N	Y	N	N	N	N	Y	N	■	N
	Back-office Systems		N	N	N	N	Y	N	N	N	N	Y	N	N	■

Figure 8-5   *Policy Decision Matrix*

There will likely be multiple matrices across different places in the network. For example, intra-data center segmentation and/or inter-site segmentation would warrant a similar exercise.

Summary

For many organizations, the hardest part of a Zero Trust journey is which direction to start in, given the massive undertaking that Zero Trust is to the uninitiated. An overwhelming amount of information relating to identities, traffic traversal, and assets on the network requires some structure to work within and make decisions on how to implement Zero Trust. As part of the planning subsections, this chapter covers how to develop a plan, including an evaluation structure for what tools are within the environment, their purposes, gaps, and potential to help understand where the organization currently is, and what improvements need to be made to align to those Zero Trust goals. It then covers implementation steps and approaches to deploy segmentation, with considerations for each. The evaluation of these implementation approaches can help define a timeline for both the initial steps as well as subsequent steps that need to be taken for Zero Trust to be a success, unique to the organization.

It should be noted that testing this approach and understanding potential capabilities in a nonproduction environment is a major step in evaluating what improvements needs to be made within the organization. Finally, after planning and testing have concluded, implementation of the segmentation plan for preventing access based on the evaluation of potential controls can take place.

References in This Chapter

- US Department of Defense, "Cybersecurity Maturity Model Certification," https://dodcio.defense.gov/CMMC/.

- PCI Security Standards Council, www.pcisecuritystandards.org/.

- International Organization for Standardization, "ISO/IEC 27002:2022, Information Security, Cybersecurity and Privacy Protection—Information Security Controls," www.iso.org/standard/75652.html.

Chapter 9

Zero Trust Enforcement

Chapter Key Points:

- The most practical first step in planning for Zero Trust and segmentation is to discover which entities exist on the network and the policies governing those entities. To do so, the organization should implement a discovery or monitor mode for as long as possible, and in parallel to other enforcement tasks being executed.

- Monitoring of endpoints is most effective where large varieties of entities exist, to get a better cross section of suspected identities. Having on-site representation can help determine what entities are when they cannot be dynamically classified or classified through tribal knowledge.

- The enforcement paradigm for endpoints on the network has changed to no longer be focused on a single appliance, but rather distributed throughout the network among multiple enforcement points.

- While approaches to implementing enforcement differ between greenfield and brownfield environments, careful planning and documentation of lessons learned regarding profiling during monitor mode can ease any impact when moving toward an enforcement mode.

- Authorization of entities should be considered the most important outcome of the Zero Trust journey. This authorization has specific considerations that need to be addressed regardless of whether the entity is positively identified, is part of a greenfield or brownfield environment, or requires special considerations such as unified communications devices.

For most organizations, implementation and operationalization of a Zero Trust strategy is the goal. The aim is to ensure that endpoints are neither prevented from executing business as usual nor allowed to access resources they are unauthorized to do so. Zero

Trust inherently moves organizations from connectivity to a security mindset. Still, its implementation must be completed in stages to ensure that these goals can be successfully achieved, and thus, careful planning must be undertaken for each of these stages. Throughout the chapter, we discuss a practical plan for how an organization might align with a stepwise approach and ensure that when an enforcement mode for a security-based mindset is reached, the organization can have confidence that as much due diligence as possible has been done to be successful. Most importantly, this chapter provides a written account of what has been accomplished to show the political powers that be where any gaps in the process may have occurred and what can be done to overcome them.

A Practical Plan for Implementing Segmentation

Continuing with the principles that have been defined throughout this text, implementing Zero Trust and segmentation as part of Zero Trust must start with the Policy & Governance and Identity pillars. This implies a need to start with understanding contextual identity and traffic flow between clients, between VLANs, and external to the organization, and aggregating as much information as possible on how and why flows occur. The biggest mistake that most organizations make when it comes to implementing segmentation is assuming that by sampling endpoints in small quantities in a strictly lab-based environment, they understand the full traffic flow the endpoint utilizes. This approach neglects the external interactions performed by an endpoint for its business-relevant functions and how external devices may interact with the device for their business purposes.

While this explanation is not to imply or explicitly state that devices should not be monitored and mapped out in a lab or some other nonproduction-type environment, it does add a second set of tasks or subphases to testing in which the device is first proved out in a lab, but is then monitored in production for as much time as possible or practical to verify and understand behaviors when the device is placed into production, outside of the "clean" lab network. This is especially true for most organizations that lack a definitive asset management database, knowledge of where devices are connected to the network and via which medium, or a combination of all of these approaches. One positive side effect of the Zero Trust journey is that the explicit identity of all endpoints on the network can be built out and understood.

Endpoint Monitor Mode

After the policy is accepted and deployed, some existing policies allow the discovery of endpoints on the network in a nonimpacting manner. The first step in the discovery journey related to identity is what many organizations and vendors refer to as "monitor mode," "visibility mode," or "unenforced discovery." The idea behind monitor mode is that endpoints coming onto the network can be detected and interrogated via the protocols they inherently use while on the network, such as DHCP, DNS, Active Directory login, CDP, LLDP, or even open port and protocol scans with NMAP. This is meant to allow organizations to understand what is on the network well before enforcing any restrictions. While in this mode, a network access control system may still be used to determine the identity of the devices and even allocate an authorization result to the endpoints; however, this result is not enforced. The lack of enforcement allows devices to continue to behave in a business-as-usual fashion. At the same time, knowledge is acquired through the connection of the devices and insights that the network access device can provide the network access control engine.

The advantage of still allocating an authorization result to the session for the contextual identity is that this authorization result, in and of itself, can be used as part of the classification, validation, and discovery of endpoints. In the case of Smart Building Central (discussed in the appendix), the manufacturing branch of Smart Building Central had a problem that was not easy to solve. While most of the devices SBC Manufacturing used in daily operations were networked, very few of them were originally manufactured with built-in networking hardware. The hardware contained a USB slot natively, allowing external peripherals to be connected to the device. This USB slot was, in turn, used to attach a USB-to-Ethernet network interface card, allowing the device to be networked and to communicate with central control modules and other devices as the need arose. However, when the contextual identity was explored for all these devices, they were all seen as the same type of device: a USB to Serial NIC manufacturer's device. No fewer than 20 different types of devices were connected via the USB to Serial NICs.

In this case, it would have been easy for SBC Manufacturing to assume there were many USB to Serial NIC manufacturer devices on the network and allocate the same authorization result to all of them. Only through the ongoing analysis and determination that a substantial number of devices all looked like the same contextual identity within monitoring mode was SBC Manufacturing able to prevent what could have been a significant outage. This outage would have been caused by the allocation of a single authorization result preventing access to many of the business-as-usual critical systems for these similarly profiled devices. SBC Manufacturing overcame this challenge by implementing two additions to its contextual identity analysis. The first was an allocation of the USB to Serial NIC profile to each identity, indicating that it was a legacy device without native Ethernet connectivity built in. The second was additional context provided by traffic analysis and network protocols, which were then factored into the contextual identity to understand better what the device was.

Initial Application of Monitoring Mode

The two biggest mistakes that organizations make are assuming that the monitor mode phase of a Zero Trust journey is a finite period and not allocating enough time for the initial discovery of devices. In most organizations that lack a robust asset management system, monitor mode is a function of how much staffing the organization can allocate to validate and resolve discrepancies in the results. In the case of Smart Building Central

Manufacturing, a network of 1600 devices took approximately four months with a team of three mapping out assets present on the network full time. Tasks that the team performed throughout these four months included

- Identifying the suspected type of device utilizing visibility and profiling technologies, resolving the "what" aspect of contextual identity

- Determining the business functionality, owner, and support team for the device to understand its ability to support a secured network, potentially adding 802.1x to the device configuration

- Utilizing traffic analysis to understand and create a baseline for the device to help understand when the device deviates from the expected baseline

- Documenting all of this information into an asset management database, ensuring that this information is quickly and readily available during both operational tasks and during incident response, where the need arises

For organizations with a significantly larger footprint, it is not unreasonable to expect that initial asset discovery could last for 12 to 18 months, depending on allocated staffing. While significantly underrated in its importance, monitor mode is where most organizations spend the most extended amount of time within the Zero Trust journey because of their need to understand endpoints beyond just network access control means, such as auditing, and risk mitigation means.

However, the tasks taken to identify the device, determine business functionality, analyze traffic, and enter the information into an asset management database are wins or accomplishments for the organization. The lack of this information should be considered a significant vulnerability and risk resolved through these activities. Identifying which devices exist out on the network will assist with troubleshooting and incident response. Therefore, each of these accomplishments should be capitalized on within messaging as it relates to the value of the project as it is relayed throughout business entities and functions. The minimization of unknown devices should be used as a security advantage and the operational advantage documented here.

Many organizations also assume that once the monitor mode transitions to an enforcement mode, there is no more extended room to monitor endpoints and traffic on the network. Most organizations that work toward a fully enforced Zero Trust–capable network find that having a remediation policy or quarantine policy as the default policy on their network access control enforcement engine assists with remediating "hard denials" of endpoints. A remediation policy can allow limited access to business-critical services within the organization, such as service request ticket engines, remote access, and control applications. Using a profiling engine can be used to assure users that they can request support after the device is connected to the network. This ensures that provisioning of devices can happen anywhere on the network, even in the small office/home office where users can reside hundreds of miles from their local organizational helpdesk. This same approach is used in many organizations as a provisioning technique, where onboarding of new devices starts in a monitoring mode that is enabled at the local helpdesk. At the same time, enforcement exists everywhere else within the network.

For most organizations, any changes to the network devices through which endpoints are connected will occur phased or rolling. It is typically most effective to start deployment of monitor mode in an area where two main conditions exist:

- A large variety of devices exist on the network. Where locations exist on the network with a large variety of different endpoints that will be connected and able to be profiled or identified, powerful lessons learned can be built out and applied to a more significant number of future sites, minimizing the amount of work that needs to be done in a net-new fashion for those sites. For example, in previous examples citing multiple camera models that had similar contextual identities within SBC Manufacturing, the presence of these devices within a single location made it easier to identify them uniquely when they existed singularly at other locations while looking similar to one another.

- An on-site presence can visit and identify devices as sampling is occurring. Tribal knowledge (or the knowledge that is present throughout a team about their purchases, use cases, and probable manufacturers or traffic patterns of devices per use case) is extremely valuable within the monitoring and profiling processes. As with the consideration of a large variety of devices existing within the starting location for the application of monitoring mode, having an on-site presence that can identify or validate aspects of the contextual identity and report this information back to the network access control administration team will ease much of the guesswork that naturally occurs during the process. An ability to have this resource visit the endpoint via "sneaker net," identifying the what, how, and where aspects of contextual identity can lend itself to creating a standard profile that can then be applied across the rest of the network to similar devices.

Monitor mode overall should continue to be used throughout the entire process of Zero Trust, given that network and security teams are constantly going to introduce new endpoints and use cases for support. The use of monitor mode, even if only done in a lab or provisioning area where the onboarding of endpoints occurs, can help determine what devices are out there and help an organization decide on when to transition into an enforcement model.

Endpoint Traffic Monitoring

In parallel with the contextual identity of endpoints being determined, the allocation of an authorization result that is not enforced can be allocated to the endpoint session. By giving an authorization result to an endpoint's session, any information applied with that allocation, such as unique tags for the device, device-specific identifiers, attribute-value pairs, or even the received identity, can then be consumed by endpoint traffic monitoring systems, which add further color to the identity of the endpoint. In the case of Cisco technologies, the ability to create enclaves as part of the Overlay policy determinization, which will later serve as the basis behind segmentation, allows the expected broader, or parent, tags to be applied within the authorization result and then consumed by traffic monitoring tools. Tools such as Cisco Secure Network Analytics consume the endpoint's identity, including the authorization TrustSec tag applied to the session via Platform Exchange grid (PXGrid) when integrated with Cisco Identity Services Engine. The NetFlow records, used to determine the baseline for traffic as it traverses the network, will contain identity and enclave tags in the form of TrustSec tags, which further helps understand how endpoints communicate within a given enclave or across enclaves.

To further augment the answer of where monitor mode should be deployed to be most effective, the organization should also consider an additional factor of how many common enclaves that are expected to be mapped out exist within a given site. Given a site that has a vast majority of the enclaves that are going to be used throughout the Zero Trust journey, such as a campus of buildings or a headquarters, the variety of devices that exist in that campus or headquarters, and then the expected business units used to develop enclaves will provide for a massive value to the Zero Trust journey. A variety of traffic flows and an extensive set of communication patterns, while seemingly overwhelming in their process and analysis, quickly becomes a game of pattern matching based on identities communicating between one another. This becomes significantly easier given the injection of identity when DHCP IP addresses can change sporadically and leave little remanence of their historical endpoint owner unless scrutiny is applied to DHCP logs. As opposed to relying on legacy addressing for creating these communication patterns, the consumption of identity provides for an identity–to–identity-based traffic pattern with the ability to map which identity attributes should be used for a given user to assist in mapping out that identity communication pattern.

Monitoring of Additional Sites

Organizations typically run into the next common challenge, which is selecting how to progress their rollout of monitor mode to minimize timelines while maintaining business as usual should an errant configuration change be made. Especially early in the monitor mode, organizations commonly question whether the application of monitor mode will truly not impact the business-as-usual processes and are correct in doing so. Configurations on Cisco switches utilize very few commands to differentiate between ports that are in a completely open state, monitor mode state, low impact (limited enforcement) state, and closed (full enforcement) state. Specifically, these commands will include in part

- **Authentication open:** Strict monitor mode with any authorization results sent to the switch port not enforced

- **Authentication opens with the addition of a preauthorization ACL:** Limited enforcement, which allows devices to reach critical resources deemed necessary before authentication but limited otherwise

- **No Authentication open:** Fully enforced, preventing all protocols other than Extensible Authentication Protocol over LAN (EAPoL) and TFTP for voice domain devices.

For Smart Building Central Financial, a matrix was created that considered two different aspects of a given site to evaluate where in order it would have monitoring mode applied:

- **Business criticality of the site:** The business criticality of the site was evaluated based on the number of users, business entities, and financial impact the site would have should it lose at least 10 percent of the devices located on its network. The 10 percent should be considered a controlled 10 percent because authentication would be applied on a port-by-port basis for wired mediums, user-by-user basis by introducing new SSIDs for wireless, and a user-by-user basis for remote access tunnels as they were configured with a new authentication server. While many organizations will maintain that "all sites are business critical," business criticality being equal across all sites implies there is no priority for any devices on the network. Therefore, all endpoints and locations can be treated the same.

- **Variety of endpoints or business units existing at the site:** Where an organization has a relatively homogeneous site in its device types, there may be few lessons learned that will contribute to the overall success of the Zero Trust journey. As a transition is implemented from monitor mode into enforcement mode, sites that have a large population of similar devices should be enforced with a common pattern or ruleset.

Smart Building Central classified its financial sites into this combination of factors to determine which sites could be monitored first and could potentially be moved to enforcement sooner than others, especially when implementing enforcement in parallel. The implementation plan looked like the one illustrated in Figure 9-1.

| | | Business Criticality | | | | | |
		Very Low	Low	Medium Low	Medium	Medium High	High	Critical
Expected Endpoint Entropy	> 25 Device Types		Mystic, CT Salem, MA Rochester, NY					Dallas, TX Newark, NJ
	< 25 Device Types	Buffalo, NY Rochester, MI Durham, NC			New York, NY Brooklyn, NY Pittsburgh, PA		Boulder, CO Montville, NY Mondtville, CT	
	< 10 Device Types							
	< 7 Device Types			Virginia Beach, VA San Jose, CA Portland, OR Vancouver Island, VC		Richmond, VA Orlando, FL Colorodo Springs, CO		Chicago, IL Santa Clara, CA Dunedin, FL
	< 3 Device Types	West Palm, FL Marlboro, MA Kansas City, KS						

Figure 9-1 *Implementation Plan*

In the case of Smart Building Central Financial, teams determined that the most valuable sites where they could begin monitor mode started with Buffalo, New York; Rochester, Michigan; and Durham, North Carolina, so they could identify the most significant number of required profiles on the network, with little chance of interrupting business-critical services within the organization. These sites were followed by West Palm, Florida; Marlboro, Massachusetts; and Kansas City, Kansas, which all had their required profiles built out after the preceding three sites due to overlapping device types existing across the sites. This allowed West Palm, Marlboro, and Kansas City to be put in monitor mode much more quickly, shortening timelines to determine any unique endpoint profiles present.

Enforcement

After extensive analysis and monitoring, any organization should consider and apply enforcement to its network access devices in any form. In the legacy world of open access layer with a secured edge, it was common to have a working session with the firewall team due to limitations that exist in network device documentation stating exactly which ports, protocols, and communication patterns devices use when attached to the network. This analysis was further eased for organizations with a lab-based network where limited traffic could be sent through the firewall, instead of hundreds of thousands or millions of connections per day through a production firewall. Throughout monitor mode, including both the identity phase and the traffic monitoring phase, this traffic should be determined to ensure that accurate policies can be written. When an organization is writing policies, there should be a focus on applying policies as close to the endpoint as possible to offload enforcement abilities to areas close to the endpoint where they might be most effective.

Smart Building Central's corporate offices meant having four separate enforcement areas that teams could apply enforcement to be most effective. To coincide with the production legacy network, they used the firewall at the end of the network to block external communications out to the Internet and had broad policies about which subnets or VLANs were allowed to flow out to Internet resources or external client sites. One side effect of the redistribution of policies to be a more layered approach was a need to evaluate which rules on the firewall were still required per the enforcement plan, because the firewall as a single point of enforcement had well over 350,000 rules present on it, allowing individual IPs and endpoints to others externally. This redistribution of these protection and enforcement mechanisms meant that firewall rules had to be audited, many of which were years old. With a lack of an asset management database and the inability to determine when devices were retired from service on the network, many of the firewall rules were built with various use cases in mind, inserting explicit allows where they seemed to "best fit."

The auditing process had to analyze what rules were present on the firewall and could potentially be removed and needed to evaluate the best place to put the restriction that the rule was meant to provide to the business. With the ability to audit and minimize core firewall rules, Smart Building Central Corporate could distribute rules and re-architect the network so that it did not require VLANs all being sent through firewalls or routers to apply restrictions between them. With this revelation, Smart Building Central was able to maintain rules related to inter-VRF traffic on firewalls, move rules for inter-VLAN traffic to switches where VLANs terminated, restrict intra-VLAN traffic to switch ports utilizing TrustSec tags, and apply restrictions to virtual machines using agents that modified the local firewall, preventing access within the same chassis.

This distribution of protection, as well as auditing, resulted in a 50 percent drop in the number of firewall rules present on the edge firewall, all of which were subsequently labeled as to their purpose as part of the audit. With this ruleset, it allowed for dynamic rules to be applied per client session, which, even with Cisco's recommendation to limit access control lists to 30–35 lines, meant each endpoint type could be restricted for its access across VLANs as opposed to defining all rules in a singular area. A side effect of this dynamic distribution was a minimization of firewalls throughout all Smart Building Central; as enforcement mechanisms were distributed, firewalls could be combined in purpose and minimize capital and operational expenditures.

Like monitor mode, however, enforcement mode should not be considered a finite accomplishment, because policies will continue to evolve. As new endpoints and use cases are discovered within any organization, additional rules will be required to prevent communication in any way referenced previously: externally, across VRFs, across VLANs, or within VLANs. Integration with identity and the asset management database established throughout the identity phase of the Zero Trust journey is critical to ensure an understanding of how endpoints interact with each other, regardless of their IP address or location in the network. The building of a robust and layered identification mechanism must not fall back to legacy approaches to segmentation that utilize only firewalls; otherwise, the entire enforcement architecture of Zero Trust will suffer.

Network Access Control

The network access control (NAC) system will play a critical part in both the monitoring mode of the Zero Trust journey and enforcement mode. With a properly architected network, NAC will be the identity engine from which all mediums send their endpoint access requests and be the decision point where access requests are granted, granted with an authorization result, or denied. Within the monitor mode phase of the Zero Trust journey, NAC should be a single source of truth when accessing the network and determining endpoints' contextual identity related to the who, what, where, when, and how aspects. After the device has been identified, identification will be further augmented with additional information from traffic traversal tools and vulnerability management tools. The challenge with many NAC systems is that they provide for various authorization results, which are then processed differently depending on the network access device to which the endpoint has connected. For example, a Cisco Wireless LAN Controller (WLC) can't implement to pass traffic while not considering the authentication and authorization result, which most would deem "monitor mode." With the WLC, an endpoint must be granted an authorization result, and that result is applied as soon as the RADIUS session completes. A VPN termination point has similar limitations.

On the other hand, a wired switch can use various configurations to enforce a policy either completely, with exceptions, or not at all. While this can play into the Zero Trust implementation plan, whether an organization considers multiple policies across multiple mediums a feasible implementation strategy or not will be organizationally specific.

Which medium an organization starts with on its Zero Trust journey is also organizationally specific. For most customers, a wired medium, for which the connection does not have to be changed, is the most conducive place to start. The wired medium allows users to connect to a switch port and never know that anything has changed while their contextual identity is being monitored. This provides an advantage to network administrators looking to understand the network. They do not have to prevent devices from getting onto the network or change the connectivity aspects of devices connecting to the network to gain visibility into who and what are connecting. Even before group policies are applied to configure managed endpoints to enable their supplicant and identify which credentials to use to authenticate against the network, a wired switch that sends protocol information such as HTTP, DHCP, DNS, Active Directory login information, and CDP information can be used while passively observing the endpoint and not modifying its access. In addition, many organizations find that while most endpoints that are wired may also be wireless, the opposite is far from true. This situation lends itself to lessons learned and the ability to determine which contextual identities are on the network, providing information that can be consumed when wireless mediums are added into the Zero Trust architecture by understanding the types of devices and locations that they typically exist in.

When it comes to the wireless medium, the organization can ease the challenge of network access control enforcement being applied by utilizing alternative mechanisms for authorization result applications. There is the ability to create a makeshift monitor mode, providing access to the network for endpoints that may not be profiled or identified yet, while incrementally restricting access via the enforcement mechanism as traffic patterns are determined. This makeshift monitor mode comes in the form of a singular interface on the wireless controller. The traffic flows out onto a particular VLAN and with an access control list that applies an explicit "permit any" to any devices connected to the SSID. The most significant challenge related to this medium, in general, is that when RADIUS is applied to the SSID for enforcement, endpoints are forced to authenticate and be authorized somehow. This implies a need to touch endpoints to change their network settings if the authentication mechanism that is employed differs from the one already used.

While authentication can be set to be open and no protection is present on the SSID, this configuration is far less common than a preshared key (PSK) or EAP-type authentication mechanism. Should a preshared key be used without an authorization server, such as that in an iPSK model, the endpoint's configuration may need to be changed to accommodate the Zero Trust implementation for the wireless medium. One advantage of using Cisco Wireless LAN Controllers to broadcast the SSID is the ability to enable profiling on a per SSID basis, sending this information in addition to the standard authentication and authorization that is allowed under the SSID.

In many scenarios, organizations might find that standing up a new SSID to fulfill their Zero Trust requirements may be a better option, and migration to the new SSID for managed devices is the first step. Locational data and information based on APs and their mapped locations can then be used to determine where devices that have not moved over to the new SSID—perhaps being applied via a group policy or management ability—still exist. If an organization knows that all managed devices were moved over to the new SSID, it can assume that these devices are not managed or up to date with management policies, which can provide valuable information related to the contextual identity. While this ability to determine whether devices are managed or not can be without NAC, a lack of explicit profiling abilities by not utilizing NAC limits the level of visibility and enforcement that an organization can determine and apply.

In the broader picture of gaining visibility into the contextual identity of endpoints, VPN terminations are midway between wired and wireless in terms of difficulty in gaining visibility and enforcing restrictions. With Cisco remote access, a user connects to the network through a tunnel group and must authenticate regardless of where the tunnel group looks for its authentication database and database containing credentials for users connecting to the remote access system. Therefore, the migration of an authentication source can be considered trivial and is applied as three lines within the tunnel group configuration related to authentication and accounting. Like wireless, a "permit any" can be used to the authorization result to ensure no impact or change in the endpoint's access to the network. VPN is therefore considered "mid-difficulty," and organizations will typically tackle this either as a bellwether to determine their ability to roll out network access control as part of their Zero Trust journey or as a second priority behind either wired or wireless.

Environmental Considerations

For most organizations that look to deploy Zero Trust and pursue the Zero Trust journey, typically, the driver is a regulatory or senior management decision to do so. Still, commonly this consideration is combined with an interest in implementing Zero Trust as part of a refresh or new build related to network hardware. While many organizations pursue a one-for-one swap of networking gear to accommodate higher throughput and minimize end of support challenges, either scenario can be a fantastic place to start the Zero Trust journey. However, the approach to how Zero Trust has implemented changes is based on the deployment methodology. The differences between greenfield, or net-new implementations, and brownfield, or one-for-one swap, are presented in the following sections.

Greenfield

About a deployment that is currently underway, a greenfield environment is a "start from scratch," or new standup, of the network, infrastructure, or policy altogether. A new building that will be the proving ground, a hospital without current patients, or a network refit would be examples of this concept. The benefit that a greenfield implementation lends to an organization pursuing a Zero Trust journey is that it can be systematically implemented, and certain types of devices added to the network in order. Where timelines allow, a greenfield implementation also provides for all devices with an incomplete contextual identity to be remediated before moving to new groups of devices, providing for the limited operational overhead of devices that need to be investigated because of not hitting a definitive policy. This also lends itself to traffic mapping, as only known identities would be present on the network, and limited ports can be allowed to flow based on known traffic patterns and vulnerability management because this behavior could be in response to a security incident.

For Smart Building Central Manufacturing, a greenfield approach was a great way to implement Zero Trust with limited needs to test endpoints in a lab. SBC Manufacturing had the major challenge of systems being critical to business and building operations not being available to disconnect from the production network to determine their contextual identity or how the endpoint presented itself to the network. As new devices would need to be ordered to implement into a new manufacturing plant, coordination with the team to support these devices, networking teams, and security teams allowed for configurations to be put onto the expected switch ports to which the endpoints would be connected, and during blocks of implementation and testing time, the devices plugged in and the results shared between teams.

For devices that could operate as expected based on documentation and being profiled with required probes, this easy process was definitive in its ability to identify the devices. For those manufacturers that had minimal reference information for ports and protocols for traffic traversal contained in their documentation or for devices that did not have a built-in profile within SBC Manufacturing's network access controller, this was a bit more difficult because of their chosen method to deny devices that were unable to match an authorization rule. However, after singular devices were defined, profiled, and traffic mapped, generally all the rest of the devices were allowed to connect without issue. Therefore, as many networking teams will do for standard changes across multiple devices, SBC Manufacturing connected a singular device, then three devices, then increasing quantities to validate that the methodologies to identify and provide access to the device were consistent and effective throughout the process.

Brownfield

A brownfield network is typically defined as a network already in place that has policy applied on top of the current network or deployment. Most times, this type of network results from a network device swap, where configurations are carried over from one network device to another, and endpoints previously connected reconnected. This is an addition of configurations to an already-deployed switch in other scenarios. The challenge with this sort of Zero Trust rollout is that there is an expectation that all devices that were previously connected continue to work when reconnected or when the new configuration commands are added as if nothing had changed. This means working through evaluating devices that were reconnected well before an understanding of what the devices are and providing for differentiated access based on their contextual identity. This scenario typically results in a need to take extra time for analysis of devices, which, as opposed to greenfield networks, may triple, or quadruple the amount of time for implementation to ensure that devices are not impacted in their connectivity but also can be identified and policy applied or evaluated.

This situation was precisely the case for Smart Building Central Emerging Tech, whose focus was developing semi-conductors in a fast-paced market that could suffer little to no downtime. SBC Emerging Tech was planning to re-outfit its smart building, which included testing facilities and manufacturing facilities for the semi-conductors with the expectation that devices could be swapped from old hardware to new hardware with little to no downtime during concise change windows in the wee hours of a weekend morning. To prepare for the swap, which was not uncommon to SBC Emerging Tech, switches were staged vertically adjacent to the legacy switches with the understanding that swapping cables could be an upward or downward motion, and a typical 48-port switch could be swapped in less than 10 minutes. However, SBC Emerging Tech was put under pressure by regulatory agencies, including governmental agencies, to ensure they could protect themselves from a data breach, unauthorized devices, or interference in their manufacturing processes by other technologies connected to switches throughout the organization. The fear of a slowdown in manufacturing critical components to some of the world's most critical energy and infrastructure-based devices made for a challenging need to balance functionality with security. To address these needs for understanding what was on the network, SBC Emerging Tech used operations staff to document—to the best of their abilities—which devices were currently connected to ports, including attempts to map out MAC addresses, IP addresses, and potential hostnames, where each of these factors could be determined.

After the mapping of devices was completed utilizing more manual means, devices were added to Cisco Identity Services Engine and statically assigned to buckets meant to identify them based on the information that SBC Emerging Tech could determine. These buckets provided full access for each of the endpoints, with the team understanding that unneeded ports would be removed at later stages of the project. For unidentifiable devices, between both tribal knowledge and profiling abilities, the device was placed into a remediation bucket for later identification. These devices became the highest priority to identify after being moved to a new switch. However, this effort extended the amount of time for identification significantly. While SBC Manufacturing was able to identify devices based on groupings and add them into switches, with complete policy application being applied within approximately one month of dedicated analysis and application, SBC Emerging Tech took almost three full months because policies could be used due to the number of remediation devices that required analysis. Following the methodologies presented in this text, there were discreet stages for identification, traffic analysis, vulnerability management analysis, and eventually enforcement. However, these four stages required serial application across identified groups based on the preceding stage. For example, where a soldering iron was identified, data for identifying the soldering iron needed to be fed back into the analysis process and identification database and run against all observed devices. This was a recursive process for every unique device found.

Practical Considerations Within Contextual Identity

While covered extensively throughout this text, contextual identity has several practical application considerations that should be contemplated when deploying onto a secured network. Remember that contextual identity is a combination of attributes that can be gathered from the endpoint unobtrusively to determine and validate that the identity is what it says it is. These issues are considered:

- Who is the user who is utilizing, managing, owning, or interacting with the device in some capacity? The device may be "headless" or not require user interaction, which can be accounted for.

- What is the device? The device may be identified with some confidence through signature-based profiling techniques based on the device's interaction with the network or other devices on the network.

- Where is the device? Where the device is located when it is being used can be a valuable attribute to determine what access it should have to resources within the network. A user with a device in the parking lot of a building, for example, may or may not be a valid use case, as opposed to one in the lobby or office area.

- When did the device interact with the network? A device accessing the network well outside of business hours may be a higher risk to the network if it typically accesses the network only within business hours.

- How does a device attempt to interact with the network? Both the medium through which a device attempts to connect to interact with the network and the protocol and interactions a device attempts to execute can indicate the device's identity and how it intends to use the network.

- What is the Device-level profile? Sometimes referred to as threat analysis, the evaluation of an endpoint's configuration, file structure, and potential risks posed to the network can be used to determine what access it should be given to align with risk tolerances.

Authentication (AuthC)

Depending on the use case for a given organization, authentication can be a compelling aspect of the contextual identity. Most organizations that begin the Zero Trust journey must start by determining the organizational capabilities—both present and future—for applying an authentication mechanism. Even the smallest of organizations typically have a domain controller with Microsoft Active Directory Users and Computers setup, providing an ability to classify users based on their business function. These groups can be used as part of the authorization result application; however, they do little to authenticate the user or device against the network. Active Directory Users and Computers focuses on two significant aspects of the contextual identity: the username and password for that user to validate the user belonging on the network and the machine identifier allocated when it joined the domain. In most scenarios, this is plenty of information to validate that the machine belongs to the organization and the user is organizational. However, many organizations are moving toward allowing users to use mobile devices on the network as either a primary or secondary work machine. This situation presents a challenge for the use of Active Directory because these devices are rarely joined to the domain, if they even can do so, and therefore need their authentication managed via some other means.

The more common authentication method that organizations use is a certificate issued to the device from the organization's Active Directory certificate authority. This certificate authority can rely on the username or machine ID allocated and consume this from Active Directory Users and Computers to insert this identity into the certificate's canonical name or subject name. Other aspects of the user's or machine's identity, such as email address, phone number, unique ID number, or alternative ways of identifying them, can be used in the certificate as the authentication method. This capability provides alternatives to a user's first and last names to be used as their identity; it also provides a registration ability for mobile devices that can then be associated with a user, to then present that identity to the network in the form of a certificate. It is becoming more common for organizations to move away from on-premises management consoles to enroll devices, instead preferring to have a cloud-based mobile device manager with the ability to register and apply certificates and other device settings across a much larger set of devices. For a sample operating system supported by a cloud-based mobile device manager, see Figure 9-2.

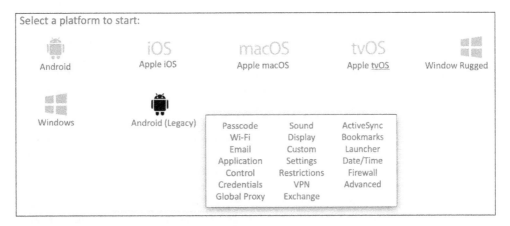

Figure 9-2 *Common Mobile Device Manager and Its Endpoint Device Abilities*

One aspect that would be remiss not to mention is that the certificate applied to a device can contain information relating to the Active Directory Users and Computers, such as username, which can then be validated against Active Directory to determine whether the account for that user is in existence, suspended, or requires additional action to be taken. This capability adds one more layer to the layered security model discussed in the preceding chapters. For example, while the same user may have a Windows PC, Apple iPad tablet, and Android cellular phone, separate device names or attributes can be embedded into the certificate present on each to provide differentiated access, even when profiling is unavailable.

Authorization (AuthZ)

As mentioned in the preceding sections, authorization is based on the successful authentication of a user or device. One common mistake that many organizations and administrators make is to assume that a device can be authorized or provided differentiated access somehow, without ever understanding the contextual identity. Contextual identity is reinforced with a method of authenticating the endpoint prior to being able to provide it any access on the network whatsoever or change that access once applied. Access that considers contextual identity typically comes in one of two forms.

The first is when an endpoint has its supplicant enabled but does not have correct—or any—credentials for the endpoint to present to the network. In this scenario, organizations commonly have an issue where the endpoint drops from the network due to misconfigurations on the endpoint. A misconfiguration issue is caused by the management system for the endpoint not applying the proper configurations in most scenarios or the device being disconnected mid-policy download. When a misconfiguration scenario occurs, a remediation policy cannot be hit, as this would be an authorization result. The only resolution would need to be to turn off the supplicant or connect to a medium that an alternative supplicant can successfully connect to.

The second comes in the form of administrators within an organization who want to create a "workaround" for users who fail authentication, allowing them to get "some" access to resources within the organization, despite their failure to authenticate. This is the wrong approach. Should a user fail authentication based on their credentials being incorrect, typically, the risk is far too high to allow that user to connect to the network, with the potential that the user is a disgruntled or former employee intent on causing harm wherever they can find a hole in the network defenses. Instead, the user should be forced to connect to another medium or network that allows MAC Authentication Bypass only, allowing the user to interact with a web page, forcing login before access is granted. A registration process can be built into this process, forcing the user to enter details about themselves and verify those details via email, SMS, or similar mediums while restricting what domains can be used to eliminate one-time-use email accounts from being able to register. The combination of the user's login to the web page, locational data provided for by the network access device port or AP to which they connected, the time at which they connected, and validation of this information through active confirmation (SMS or email link confirmation) can enable users to get Internet-only access by applying an access control list, based on their authorization, even if authentication is done in a less-than-recommended manner.

Segmentation

For most organizations that implement segmentation, conversations will inevitably devolve into a need for granular segmentation at any level of the organization. A permit/deny policy will turn into a need for port- and protocol-based policy. Five endpoint groups will turn into 100 endpoint groups. Singular tags within the 16-bit Cisco Metadata field within the frame will turn into a need to "stack" or combine tags to provide a group with subgroup permissions as they join the network based on their group membership. For any organization implementing segmentation, it needs to consider how to be most successful with implementing segmentation, based on both operational abilities and feasibility of the technological solution in general. This is where the layered security approach should be considered most heavily.

A practical approach to segmentation involves the classification of contextual identities into no more than seven groups to start with. Where the need is, these seven groups may differ if all groups communicate within the same site and not across sites. Many organizations have attempted to bypass this recommendation but inevitably find themselves in the "analysis paralysis" stage of Zero Trust, where every detail is considered for the segmentation policy, whether all those details are relevant to the identity's ability to be exploited or not. For example, such as shown in Table 9-1, most customers can fit their endpoints into a combination of seven of the following groups, at least at a broad level.

Table 9-1 *Endpoint Mapping*

Corporate Endpoints	Contractor Devices	Data Center Devices
Medical Endpoints	Security Devices	Branch Devices
Manufacturing Endpoints	Media Devices	Quarantined Devices
Research Endpoints	Demo Devices	Remediation Devices
Lab/Nonproduction Endpoints	Network Devices	Shared Services Devices
Servers	Infrastructure Devices	Unified Communications Devices
IoT Devices/Sensor Devices	Headless Devices	
Guest Devices	Authenticated Devices	

The combination of seven of the listed groups will very much depend on the policies and use cases of the organization and their endpoints discovered throughout the visibility phase. However, it should be noted that to an operations team, many of these groups may look the same related to the contextual identity, except for an Active Directory group. A headless device and a data center device may be the same: each is authenticated via MAB because there is no user logged in, each exists on the wired medium, each exists in the data center, and each can be a Windows device. Therefore, the organization must ask,

"How will someone who does not have tribal knowledge of the architecture and design team differentiate this device from any other on the network?"

The second question that then needs to be answered is "How does the policy for this device differ in a significant manner from other devices and their interactions?" For example, when two devices are classified—a security device and a media device, for example—both may use shared services, and both may communicate within each other's tags. Based on this analysis, a risk assessment should be undertaken to determine whether the level of access each device needs differs significantly between the two groups before separating them into separate policies. For example, during discovery, if a security device was determined to need access to shared services, port 443, 8443, 80, and 6667, while a media device required access to shared services, 443, 8443, and 6668, the gap between the two device categories is two ports. If the risk is minimal for those two ports, such as the devices not listening on those ports or authenticated via a third party on those ports, the endpoints should be grouped together at least for the preliminary classification to minimize the number of tags required. It should also be noted that minimizing the tags in use would be most beneficial when security and media devices exist on the same subnet and require tags versus the ability to distribute enforcement between tags within the subnet, ACLs across subnets, firewalls across sites, or in other use cases.

Greenfield

A greenfield deployment of endpoints is typically the easiest to start the Zero Trust journey with. However, unlike the brownfield site, buy-in from upper levels of management needs to be obtained and socialized for endpoint owners within the greenfield site. Due to human psychology, a natural reaction is to be upset that access over a given port or protocol has been gotten rid of, especially when this was used as a convenience. This is typically regardless of the potential for exploitation and security concerns related to the access. During the implementation phase, whether combined with the visibility phase to enforce immediately or separated out to gain visibility before enforcing, there will inevitably be concerns that the way operations teams previously undertook tasks is no longer available. The organization should explore options for how to correctly approach challenges that operations teams encounter as opposed to compromising security for convenience.

Brownfield

A brownfield environment is typically the harder of two options to begin the Zero Trust journey. However, the same lessons apply here as to the greenfield environment. The first is to ensure there is buy-in from upper-level management to deploy enforcement. Critical to this success will also be to ensure workarounds for getting users back onto the network after they have determined challenges related to access do not include removing configurations. While good intentions reign supreme in most corporate scenarios, they are often forgotten about and create a patchwork of policies and enforcement throughout the network. Should an operations technician be provided permission to remove configurations from a port just to get an endpoint onto the network, they will inevitably forget that the configuration was removed, or the political structure will prevent the configurations that prevented that device from its business purpose from ever being applied to the port configuration again.

This same lesson learned goes for an exception process. Exceptions should be critically scrutinized and explored, no matter how much time it takes to reach a decision on a potential workaround to get an endpoint working as expected. For most organizations, as soon as an exception process can be filed and granted, the exception process is almost guaranteed to become the rule and put the organization right back where it started in connectivity over security.

Unified Communications

Commonly, Unified Communications (UC) devices are expensive in the ports and protocols they require to interact with other Unified Communications devices. Because of this, UC becomes a perfect opportunity to utilize tags within subnets or events potentially across subnets. The challenge with UC devices comes when a combination of physical phones, softphones, and mobile softphones are all utilized on the network. This need to interact across most mediums on a wide variety of ports causes a need to broaden policies and how those policies dictate traffic traversal. Where possible, classification of UC devices into their own category during the segmentation phase during later stages of enforcement, separate from Corporate PCs and further separate from mobile devices, provides for the most flexibility and more significant quantity of options for endpoint interactions during technology refreshes where physical or softphones may be purged or reintroduced to the network.

Data Exchange

As discussed in the visibility and vulnerability tenets of Zero Trust, data exchange between systems to disseminate identities and vulnerability analysis is highly recommended. Methods and protocols such as PXGRID and STIX/TAXI provide a structure to exchange this information. Even if not utilized in policies, these methods can offer a massive amount of data exchange and therefore value to determine the additional context in a device's contextual identity. As more products accept visibility information, identity can become more pervasive and available for enforcement purposes, and can include access to applications based on the type of device and vulnerabilities observed.

Summary

The practicality of deploying Zero Trust has real-world implications that need to be accounted for and considered. Whether it's the environment to which Zero Trust is being designed for or added, information exchanged between tools within the environment, policies in place to dictate access and capabilities of a device, or just the methodology to ensure that sites are added in based on criticality and lessons already learned, there is much that can be considered as part of practically implementing Zero Trust on a network. Organizations should consider all these aspects and plan accordingly for potential stumbles in the process with an attitude of acceptance should there be a need to fall back to a previous stage when unexpected journey elements are encountered.

Chapter 10

Zero Trust Operations

Chapter Key Points:

- Organizations that have an integrated or close-knit network and security operations teams are more likely to be able to operationalize throughout their Zero Trust journey. Centralized buy-in for both teams is key to success.

- Breaking down deployment areas for Zero Trust into groups, such as early adopters, early majority, and late majority, can help determine obstacles and buy-in criteria that may need to be overcome to execute the Zero Trust journey.

- When an organization is considering the operationalization of Zero Trust implementations, it should consider onboarding not only new entities but also new support staff. Without the ability of new staff to support the technology used to execute the Zero Trust goals of an organization, the organization will be prevented from conducting business as usual.

- One of the most significant challenges any organization will run into on its Zero Trust journey is the maintenance of the components and best practices of Zero Trust. Maintaining the mechanisms put into place for discovery, asset management, and policies is the only way to ensure the Zero Trust model that is implemented can be maintained.

- Designing an attribution schema to consistently maintain contextual identities is key to understanding how any changes made related to those contextual identities will impact operations, support, and the ongoing Zero Trust journey.

- Maintenance will rely on onboarding, discovery, and ongoing application of distributed enforcement found throughout the Zero Trust journey.

Depending on the methods and constructs used to implement Zero Trust Segmentation into the organization's ecosystem, there are several considerations to manage. These considerations include but are not limited to policy changes; control changes add moves or changes of devices or workloads, services, and/or applications. The key to managing the post–Zero Trust implementation is processes and teams that work to agree to modifications to the existing implementation with well-established product owners.

This chapter discusses the methods to maintain Zero Trust after the teams have designed, tested, and implemented the Zero Trust strategy discussed and defined throughout this text. We discuss a few pitfalls to avoid and ways we have seen it work best in today's environment. We use examples to help illustrate the best practices or things to avoid.

The cornerstone of a Zero Trust cybersecurity strategy is the implementation of least privileged access controlled through defined enforcement policies. Zero Trust strategies can succeed only if security policies are in place and remain effective. It is the "remains effective" that becomes critical once a Zero Trust solution has been implemented. As a result, security policies must be maintained and refined on an ongoing basis.

When your Zero Trust environment enters the steady operational state, the network and assets are still monitored, and traffic is logged and audited. Responses and policy modifications are often based on input from monitoring data traffic and assets. Other sources of input that may result in policy changes can come from external sources such as current threat intelligence and industry regulatory or standards changes. A company's users and stakeholders of resources and processes should also provide feedback to refine security policies and performance.

Additionally, when changes occur to the workflow, services, assets, or architecture, the operation of your Zero Trust architecture and its policies needs to be reevaluated. New devices, major software updates, and organizational structure modifications will change the current security policies.

Zero Trust Organization: Post-Implementation Operations

Of course, an organization's journey to achieving Zero Trust is never complete; new controls, policies, or modifications of existing controls or policies are required as new products, services, or businesses are obtained. Many changes can be implemented more readily in a software-defined Zero Trust Organization; however, these changes will happen smoothly only if the organization uses well-developed processes, well-managed organizational change and architecture review teams, and well-informed product owners.

We find organizations trying to navigate the adoption issues within their organization to achieve Zero Trust. Several teams or groups often own the concept of Zero Trust but are not moving forward to implementation. Sometimes leadership will fund only the network team projects but not the security team projects, or the other way around. The reason for this lack of resource allocation may be that the different challenges within the business only enable growth and exclude protective controls that lead to funding or resource allocation gaps.

We find the best way to navigate these challenges is to gain authorization and sponsorship of leaders responsible for the security and network activity. By using this method to gain sponsorship, the Zero Trust implementation team removes many of the silos or barriers within the organization where resources are short, funds are scarce, and teams are fighting over the same amount of funds to gain more resources by going higher in the organization. This method also understands that movement must occur, and both groups are trying to achieve something that requires all hands working to make Zero Trust possible within their organization.

Looking from the outside of an organization and having been within many organizations, we can easily see how politics and budgets get in the way of being able to move forward. Removing obstacles to position the organization to implement Zero Trust is essential. The current threat landscape should help focus organizations on what can be achieved when their teams all work together and everyone is in the same boat, rowing in the same direction.

One of the critical components of operating a Zero Trust organization is representing security, network, applications, and operations to establish control and ownership within each of these teams. See Figure 10-1 for illustration. These teams need to work together, collaborate, and cross the boundaries of having an organization to support the Zero Trust Organization. The number-one issue organizations find today is a siloed mentality between teams, which causes competition or lack of motivation to move forward with initiatives that other groups have sponsored and put forward. This is a failure of leadership at the very top.

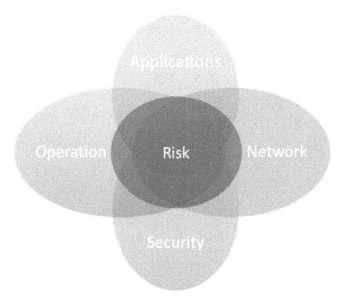

Figure 10-1   *Zero Trust Segmentation Cross-Team Alignment*

One of the critical features of a siloed environment is that one team does not know the names of other essential team members when asked in "should be" partner organizations. Another feature is that when a group creates a great idea, another unit copies the same idea and competes against the other team, dividing leadership's focus and goals.

Creating this cross-pollinating collaborative space for employees should be the number-one objective of organizational leaders. Suppose everyone is going down the field in the same direction, and everyone is aligned to the same set of goals trying to achieve the same thing. In that case, organizations will find that their budgets are well spent on initiatives that are put forward. Cross-team oversight of organizational health and individual contributor mindsets matters to the organization. This mindset also matters to having a Zero Trust organization.

If an organization has silos, some information will not be shared across the various teams in a Zero Trust situation. And the organization that does not move in the same direction may have cross-competencies for segmentation implementation tools supporting one group but not working for another group. This situation can lead to chaos inside the organization or a complete stop. The most important thing about an organization is to be an ongoing concern. An organization must move forward past the status quo to be a constant concern.

Adoption Barriers

In his book *Crossing the Chasm*, Geoffrey A. Moore talks about the various phases of adoption for multiple groups of people. As an illustration of "the chasm," see Figure 10-2. We believe early adoption is a fundamental goal, but crossing that chasm and getting teams who may be more likely part of the Early Majority, Late Majority, or even the last group, the Laggards, to change and be brought on board are very important. Inside an organization that chasm can be broad, especially with teams being very siloed.

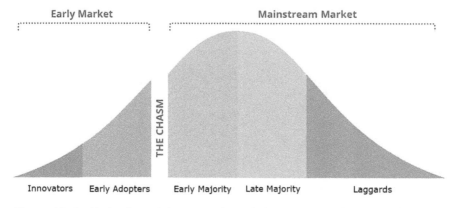

Figure 10-2 *Technology Adoption Life Cycle from* Crossing the Chasm *by Geoffrey A. Moore*

Operationally, an organization that is divided into hardened silos will fail to be able to work toward a shared vision of what must get done. Inside an organization, a critical task of leadership is to establish collaboration and a shared vision. Organizational behavior has repeatedly enabled or disabled businesses. We can name many companies that are no longer at the forefront or no longer the ones in the lead because they could not either address change or develop a well-balanced organizational behavior structure.

This adoption life cycle plays out within departments, teams, and even silos. With each personality type, programs may be strengthened, or adoption may even fail. Understanding the types of adopters and how program teams may support them in adopting the new strategy is critical.

Innovators and Early Adopters

Using the "crossing the chasm" scenario, the innovators are the teams that either sponsor, create the design, or develop the Zero Trust policy. The early adopters are the teams that support the pilot or testing within the Zero Trust environment. They tend to be the teams we work with to get programs off the ground and move into full organizational adoption.

Sponsors are the "venture capitalists" within an organization. They are innovators or early adopters and critical to ongoing success. Sponsors of a Zero Trust program must continually evangelize the plan within the organization as leaders move, change, or leave the organization.

Maintaining executive support to have a budget for critical solutions and teams within an organization is also a factor for determining success. Keeping focus on the Zero Trust Segmentation Program within an organization may be difficult, especially when elevated levels of turnover, change, or organizational restructuring motions occur.

This group is responsible for understanding how important a particular set of solutions are within an organization and how critical they may be to control access and push overall policy. It is the responsibility of the overall governing team that supports Zero Trust. They must have this understanding if funding is to remain in place to support the Zero Trust program.

This group is best served by building the Zero Trust Strategy into overall governance documents, and policies are critical to the success of any Zero Trust program. Embedding the strategy into the organization's mindset by building Zero Trust into the rules, methodologies, and processes that govern the organization will help address concerns that the remaining adoption groups will have.

The Early Majority

Moving past the innovators and the early adopters, we have the early majority adopters, who will begin adopting a Zero Trust mindset. They have more questions and expressed doubts but are interested in seeing where this new idea will take the organization after their questions have been satisfactorily answered. These questions are like those the sponsor addressed with executive leadership when seeking funds or resources. Addressing these questions earlier in the implementation cycle will help gain the early majority's support.

The early majority's questions tend to be more in depth and may require updates to plans before this group will successfully adopt the necessary changes to support Zero Trust. Many want to be a part of the solution, so making minor updates or changes may be all that is needed to get them on board. The early majority are the teams responsible for supporting the overall organizational migration and onboarding of innovative solutions or business units into the overall strategy and design over the long haul. The success or failure of the comprehensive program of Zero Trust lies within this group's adoption success. The continued operation and maintenance of the solutions supporting Zero Trust segmentation within the organization are usually the responsibility of this adoption group.

The Late Majority

Interestingly, the late majority have the greatest experience with change and seem to know that the details have hidden issues or concerns that need to be addressed. They tend to want to see the outcome before there can be an outcome. They can be frustrating to implementation teams who want to complete the project as it has been defined and approved. Sometimes implementation teams may have to "restart" the project or repeat "kickoffs" to get this adoption group moving forward.

Tendencies in this group lean toward finding obstacles at every turn and asking the implementation teams to remove the latest identified obstacle to their satisfaction. Many in the late majority adoption group like it when others have tried and failed at implementation to prove their point; there is too much risk to move forward.

Organizational leadership will have to meet this challenging group and address what can be addressed, but in the end, they will have to "take on all the risk" for this adoption group. The group will be happy to proceed if the movement ahead has been sufficiently de-risked for themselves or their teams.

Laggards

Laggards tend to be told what to do from the top. They are generally afraid to make a mistake or to have any errors. This fear leads them to be stuck in "analysis paralysis." They like to admire problems, as one leader likes to say, from every angle. This admiration process ensures that no action is taken. They hope the implementation team will forget they ask for their support or assistance.

To implement Zero Trust Segmentation, the most challenging of all adoption styles is when the entire organization adopts change from a laggard's viewpoint. This means that their competitors are always ahead of them, customers are always looking for other organizations to move to, and other organizations offer better features that their shareholders or stakeholders would like to see or achieve.

The laggard organization is frozen, and so are its teams, due to fear of making a misstep or significant mistake, or expending resources. Generally, it takes a change in leadership or core teams to begin the thaw to move, change, and implement new ideas or methods. Leaders who are agents of change find organizations with this adoption style very frustrating and will move on to other organizations quickly.

Applications Owners and Service Teams

With many adoption pitfalls identified, we need to discuss the shape of an organization that supports Zero Trust. Let us talk about the application and operations teams that are critical to the success of Zero Trust.

Application teams build systems and solutions inside of the infrastructure that holds the critical assets of the company, the intellectual property, the data, the customers, the strategy, the numbers, and everything without the application management team being on board. Many Zero Trust segmentation programs are implemented without application team engagement.

As with any team left out during the initial stages of a program, typical organizational behavior says that the team's likelihood of being willing to jump through hoops at the very end of implementation is exceptionally low. Engage application teams early. Bring in the application ownership teams to orient them and keep them involved and engaged. Doing so is essential to the success of the overall program. To ignore them would bring unplanned interruption and complexity to the business due to misunderstanding the interoperability and requirements of these applications.

Operations and Help Desk

Operations teams need to support the adoption of Zero Trust Segmentation to ensure that the infrastructure to support the enforcement of Zero Trust may be functional and operational. These teams must be included at the beginning, with clear ownership established with the operations teams.

Critical to the success of operations' adoption of Zero Trust is the development of operational guides and runbooks needed to support the solutions, address alerts with critical teams, and update contact information routinely.

Policy manuals and internal rule sets must be updated to support the operational teams. Well-established governance documentation will enable round-the-clock support teams to function equally with their daytime counterparts. The consistency of the operations team is critical to operational success and the ability to satisfy customers or stakeholders.

Network and Security Teams

Either the network team or the security team may be the team that initiates the Zero Trust program but may not be the team that oversees the program after critical solutions have been implemented. One or both teams will become key stakeholders after implementing key infrastructure components. The network and security teams will enable the business to adopt Zero Trust. Still, over the long term, the operations teams, application teams, and the group responsible for oversight will handle day-to-day migrations and internal adoption.

Governance teams or security teams may be responsible for policy development and oversight. Identity and access management teams, generally part of the security team, are essential in establishing the services needed to support critical infrastructure elements.

These teams must collaborate to make the business gain the most from their organization's Zero Trust Infrastructure. Zero Trust implementation fails, stalls, or is only partially implemented due to dysfunction between these teams.

Having worked in large enterprises, this team has seen positive, productive relationships between network and security. It takes work and communication at the top and every level. Suppose teams in organizations are having collaboration issues. Start there to resolve the problems before the journey is undertaken to create a Zero Trust Organization.

The Life Cycle of Zero Trust Policies

Maintenance of the Zero Trust policy impacts various components across an organization. Each of these may have different capabilities to establish and maintain trust. One of the primary functions described in NIST 800-207, "Zero Trust Architecture," is the policy decision point made up of a policy engine and a policy administrator whose operational intent is to be the arbiter of policy decisions for all connections established within the Zero Trust environment. In practice, at least at the time of this writing, a single off-the-shelf product or set of products performing this function is a conglomeration of various components, all potentially under the management aegis of different departments and/or organizations.

For example, there may be a network access control solution managed and operated by the network team on campus. At the same time, in the data center, there may be a Privileged Access Management solution managed and operated by the systems administration team and a remote access solution managed by the security team. Each solution has a role in a Zero Trust Architecture and fits into the architectural models presented through 800-207. However, the management and maintenance of policy could be significantly different for each use case because each use case is unique, with other goals applied to access policy.

As has been discussed throughout this book, Zero Trust is not intended or expected to be a wholesale exchange from processes and technologies incorporated in today's enterprise network infrastructures. Zero Trust operationalization is expected to be an evolution to an infrastructure support model where trust determination and trustworthiness evaluation are included, using many of the same infrastructure components and processes currently employed within the enterprise.

Understanding that Zero Trust concepts will impact all consumers, providers, and facilitators of IT services makes business sense to create or augment existing governance bodies to guide practices that will improve an organization's ability to migrate to Zero Trust policies.

One of the primary sources of information for organizations to derive trust and trustworthiness to establish access policy is inventory management and attribution. Inventory management systems such as configuration management databases ingest information from various sources. They should be intended as the sole source of truth for assets and configuration items (CIs) across the enterprise. CMDBs are utilized by existing change advisory boards (CABs) and/or configuration control boards (CCBs) to establish, maintain, and manage configurations and identify connected assets and their dependencies across the organization. Integrating these governance practices related to Zero Trust is fundamental to identifying control attributes that might impact access policy decisions.

From a Zero Trust policy maintenance perspective, organizations should look toward creating standard attribution schemas that can help standardize trustworthiness measurement criteria across the various enterprise use cases. It is expected and natural that an enterprise would have numerous use cases that drive different Zero Trust architectural solutions. These solutions can be driven by common trustworthiness criteria that allow endpoints to connect to a campus network, administrative access to workloads and workload infrastructure, or remote access solutions.

There are essentially two ways of determining the trustworthiness of users, devices, and applications (subjects) that are accessing data (resources), both of which can be used independently or in conjunction with each other to determine access policy:

- **Attribution:** Criteria that can be presented to policy enforcement points (PEPs) and are measured against policy decision points for access policy granted to an individual connection request.

- **State:** Criteria presented to policy enforcement that are measured against policy decision points but use information derived from external sources such as threat intelligence and CVE reporting sources.

Creating a common set of criteria that can be applied across multiple use cases gives the different policy engines and policy administrators a common methodology for evaluating trust and access policy. Incorporating an attribution schema into asset and inventory management tools and processes supports engaging multiple teams with disparate operational requirements, data sources, and business outcomes. This method will help foster a broader knowledge and acceptance of Zero Trust goals while creating an environment where shared goals are expressed and incorporated into Zero Trust policy and access decisions.

Zero Policy Management

The attribution schema described in the following paragraph, and illustrated in Figure 10-3, is an example for organizations wishing to establish a methodology for consistently representing contextual identity. The schema is made up of sets of independent variables that can be used to uniquely identify characteristics of users, devices, and workloads. These characteristics can then be used to derive identity-based, context-aware security policy. This attribution scheme is further intended to be leveraged to support automation and programmability for various aspects of software-defined network infrastructure and security policy.

Each attribute defined could apply to a user, endpoint, or workload. It is likely that some attributes are more applicable to a specific category but are represented here within a single master list. Each attribute is intended to be objectively defined and would have a standard definition regardless of the asset category (user, endpoint, or workload) to which it is applied.

Understanding and categorizing the who, what, where, when, why, and how as they relate directly to a Zero Trust access policy helps drive trust decisions and can provide a means for visualizing trust of an individual access request based on attribute evaluation.

NOTE   It is not expected that all attributes will be applied to all use cases, assets, or CIs. Access and trust criteria should be made against the fewest attributes possible.

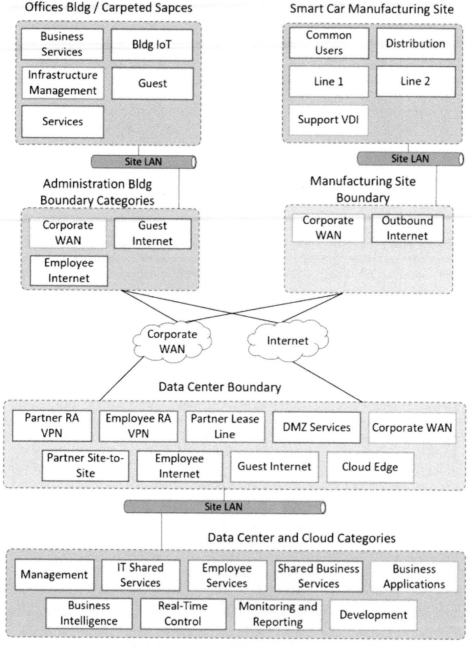

Figure 10-3   *Manufacturing Segmentation Plan*

In a sample environment, as illustrated in Figure 10-4, the following use cases are intended to provide examples of how attribution can be translated into Zero Trust policy assignment. Policy enforcement points throughout the network path are expected to act on different condition evaluations. Also, throughout this network path, it should be expected that other policy engines and policy administrators will govern policy for different PEPs. In the use case represented later, various attributes of endpoints, users, and workloads are evaluated and used as criteria for policy assignment.

Use Case: SBC Owned and Managed Device Connecting to Dashboard Tech Wireless, Dashboard Development Engineer Connecting to Dash DevEng Workload

Security Policy: IF Endpoint is SBC Owned **AND** Endpoint is Workstation **AND** User is SBC Dashboard Team Member **AND** Workload is DashDevEnv THEN PERMIT

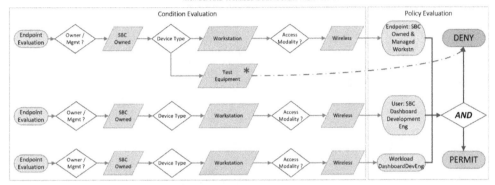

* Representative example that a change in any attribute may immediately halt policy evaluation and cause a DENY Result

Figure 10-4   *Zero Trust Attribution Decision Flow*

Practical Considerations: Cisco Network Architecture

From a Zero Trust policy maintenance perspective, tying attribution to policy creation allows for a clear definition of conditions to be met by all the components involved in connection establishment (endpoints or devices, users, and application workloads). Collection and evaluation of attributes will likely happen at more than one PE/PA and may be enforced at different PEPs along the transmission path.

Understanding traffic flows as they apply to each use case, where attribution is evaluated, and where the various policy enforcement points relate to the overall network architecture is another key component of maintenance of a Zero Trust policy and architecture.

The use case example in figure 10-5 maps where the policy engines, policy administrators, and policy enforcement points would be in a Cisco network architecture. We can see that there are three primary domains where attribute evaluation occurs and where policy can be enforced: the local area network, the WAN edge, and the data center.

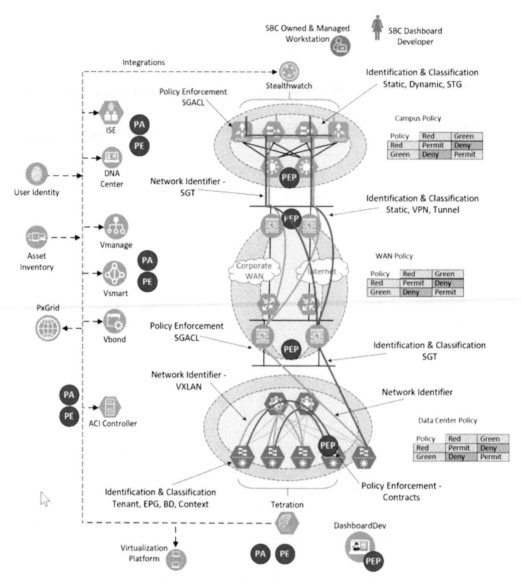

Figure 10-5 *Policy Maintenance: Where to Look*

In the LAN, DNA Center for SDA fabric deployments, in conjunction with ISE, provides PA/PE functionality where access layer interfaces are the typical PEP for TrustSec-enabled segmentation. At the WAN edge, attribute evaluation is performed through the vManage infrastructure and can be based on tag value, VXLAN headers, or application parameters. SDA virtual networks can be allocated to tunnels provisioned across the WAN, and PEPs can enforce based on VXLAN header information, TrustSec tag value, or standard IP-based controls.

At the data center where the APIC controller manages, the ACI acts as the PA/PE for the data center fabric, where policy enforcement can be implemented through VRFs, tenants, or endpoint groups and contracts and will likely work in conjunction with a Cisco Secure Workload solution to provide traffic visibility, PA/PE, and PEP capabilities through host-based native FW capabilities.

Moves, Adds, and Changes in a Zero Trust Organization

Within an organization, onboarding new types of devices becomes a new process flow for Zero Trust segmentation to be successful. If an organization has a strong, robust onboarding process for new solutions or devices, it could be as simple as adding a couple of steps. One of those key steps is to identify the solution or device's life cycle, what it complies with or does not comply with, and how it supports the organization from a strategic or operational perspective. After these definitions are applied to this solution or device, then as a part of the robust onboarding process, some attributes should be well established to support this new technology coming into the environment; however, if this new type of solution or device is significantly different from anything in the infrastructure, then an architecture review board should be engaged to define this new solution or device type. This new solution or device type will need to be assessed and tested to approve it being brought into the environment.

All these steps might seem overbearing or overconcerning; however, they will save the organization issues and troubles in the long run. This due diligence will be rewarded at the following audit or the time of the subsequent incident knowledge of this new device. It's critical to the success of a secure environment and, therefore, the implementation of Zero Trust. On the other hand, if an organization does not have or does not support a well-defined onboarding process for new types of devices, establishing an architectural review board becomes a critical first step today.

The ongoing process should be well defined, but we would not recommend having a complex process that overwhelms anyone engaging in bringing new services, devices, or opportunities to an organization. An initial assessment to validate that it is a new device should occur. Users should proceed with that solution or device type template if that initial assessment can align the new device to existing framework devices. However, these new solutions or devices may often align 95 percent to the current template. Still, with additional tweaks or changes required, that change process should be part of the architectural framework review board, and that change process should not create an undue burden on those using the method.

Heavy processes lead to shadow processes bypassing organizations that have adopted Zero Trust but have shadow processes that will not be successful in their overall journey to achieving Zero Trust.

Summary

In this chapter, we discussed the organizational methods to maintain Zero Trust after the teams have designed, tested, and implemented the Zero Trust strategy discussed and defined throughout this text. We discussed pitfalls to avoid or mitigate and ways we have seen them work best in today's environment using a real-world example.

The key takeaway is that ownership of the Zero Trust strategy and solutions is essential to establish as early as possible within the organization. This ownership must be maintained over the life of the Zero Trust program. The teams that own the program must be focused on the organization's business success and overall business strategy.

Zero Trust policies and procedures should not be considered static. These policies should evolve and refine as your systems, workflow, or company requirements change. Zero Trust policies are the backbone and foundation of an effective cybersecurity solution. These policies effectively define your priorities for protecting resources and information.

Regular policy maintenance may occur as a proactive or reactive response to risks or threats. Proactive changes to security policies may be performed due to recommendations or alerts based on information from threat intelligence sources about a zero-day vulnerability announcement. Reactive changes to security policies may be required due to an actual occurrence of a security event or anomalies identified from monitoring or data traffic to assets.

Everyday activities within a company can cause changes to systems or the environments of operation and can significantly impact the security posture of assets. Examples could include installing new hardware, changing a system's configurations, and installing patches outside the established configuration change control processes. When your technology or services change how systems are used or operated, it should be required to review and revise security policies as needed.

Make the necessary policy review and updates to prevent potential threats, minimize risk, and stay compliant with laws, contracts, and regulations.

References in This Chapter

- Geoffrey A. Moore, *Crossing the Chasm*, 2021, www.crossingthechasmbymoore.com.

Chapter 11

Conclusion

Chapter Key Points:

- Throughout this text, a model for Zero Trust and its considerations for success for any organization have been discussed. This model assists in helping an organization start down the path of Zero Trust.

- Key to being successful in Zero Trust is having the right people and buy-in from executive management within the organization. Without a singular level of escalation to assist in easing political challenges, the Zero Trust journey will be much more difficult.

- Utilizing the five core principles of Zero Trust presented here is a great starting point. However, continuous improvement and reuse of each principle throughout an organization's journey will be key to the ongoing success of Zero Trust.

The key question most organizations are asking is twofold, and one that they see as relatively simple: How does an organization start down the Zero Trust journey, and how does an organization benefit most from that journey? Key to answering this question is the linchpin of gaining buy-in from executive levels within the organization to support the journey and understanding of the benefit that will result in using the journey to secure the business. This buy-in helps in the journey by lending executive authority, or even board-level authority, to a need to validate that overlay and policies therein will allow for the evolving journey, not to mention allocation of budget and funding to accomplish many of the tasks required for Zero Trust to be successful.

Critical to this buy-in is also ensuring that the right people are "on the bus," that is, are engaged from business-critical areas to help set direction, collaborate with one another, and understand the broader business functions of the organization so that they might make an informed decision relating to all the Zero Trust principles to directly benefit the business. This effort includes understanding the network, tools already present that may become critical to the success of the Zero Trust journey, responsibilities of those involved within the journey, and that implementation of Zero Trust concepts will need to be a long-term goal, not something immediate and without gradual application. This goal should also be predicated on an interest by the parties involved to implement Zero Trust vision correctly, as opposed to what has been done in the past and operating under restrictions dictated in the past. This implementation may mean redesigning parts of the architecture, developing new processes, or retraining staff and the impact on their daily work.

The next key consideration is the need for understanding contextual identities throughout the network, which is typically the greatest benefit due to the impact it has on the ability to apply controls throughout various enclaves, segments, and business units. An understanding of contextual identities on the network can bring with it a more informed ability to determine what controls, what granularity of those controls, and which are the right controls applied to the contextual identities based on their business functions and the unique business challenges they may encounter. These challenges will never be a "one-size-fits-all," and will be unique per organization and business vertical; therefore, this analysis and understanding become critical to determine where challenges exist within an organization. What is common across industries is a need to understand the contextual identities and how they interact with one another on the network. While this task is challenging due to the number of endpoints in most large organizations, it can be approached piecemeal, with a "big bang" approach not necessarily being the right direction in most cases, but rather using small groupings of assets to determine much larger themes throughout the organization.

For most organizations, once an understanding is complete, decisions must be made about the level of enforcement that can be applied to help abide by the policy dictating the need for Zero Trust. While many organizations require a broad policy that minimizes the impact of malware infection within a network while still allowing for business as usual to thrive, others will prioritize protection over business by implementing granular methods to prevent devices from communicating with one another, except for the strictest port and protocol communication rules. In many cases this will result in further decisions being made as to the location of restrictions that would best benefit the organization, minimize impact, and be distributed in such a manner that a single point of failure does not exist. This effort may require redesigning of the architecture used to ensure that required mechanisms can be applied in the most effective way possible. Once again, the buy-in from executive or board-level resources who support the Zero Trust journey can ease the pain related to time, budget, and buy-in for these tasks.

Execution of all steps, in a gradual manner and based on the risks calculated throughout the journey, must be implemented in a calculated and precise manner to ensure business as usual is not interrupted. Implementing identity visibility, mapping flows through the collection of NetFlow data and correlating it with identity, enforcing in phases ranging from permit and deny to port and protocol, all need to be executed, typically while ensuring the business continues to operate. The modeling of impact, testing at low-risk sites, building of lessons learned, and maintaining an eye for the goal are critical to this success.

Finally, using new information learned throughout the entire Zero Trust journey to shape the future of access and leveraging a common Zero Trust methodology is what keeps Zero Trust successful. Many organizations reach a point where they begin to find new information that challenges the successes created by the Zero Trust journey by introducing policy exceptions. Zero Trust relies upon the consistent application of processes and technical means to ensure that the organization continues to be as secure as possible.

Zero Trust Operations: Continuous Improvements

The Zero Trust journey is one that most organizations are interested in pursuing, but many do not know where to start. Throughout this text it has been illustrated how expansive Zero Trust can be and what the building blocks are that make up the Zero Trust journey. It could be easy for organizations to reach a conclusion wondering how they could ever be fully Zero Trust compliant, but as with every journey, Zero Trust starts with singular steps. Organizations should first map out Zero Trust and what it means to them. As illustrated in Figure 11-1, this will be a continual and gradual process.

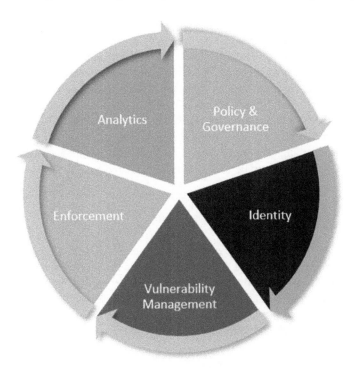

Figure 11-1 *Zero Trust Operations: Continuous Improvements*

Policy & Governance

Based on the Zero Trust Capabilities outlined throughout this book, an organization can begin to map out what its needs for the network are, and how each of the capabilities can be implemented across the organizational structure. While policy is specific to the organization and its business functionalities, commonalities can be found in the need to allow only corporate assets onto the network and provide them access to business-critical resources, while segmenting off areas where unauthorized contextual identities might sit, such as guests, contractors, and even high-risk devices.

Policy & Governance is a function of the buy-in that is gained from executive leadership, propagated down to individual contributors, but is abided by all in the organization.

Identity

Once the policy is in place and signed off, approaches to the Identity pillar can vary throughout the organization and across organizations. Identity can be an inconsistent aspect of the Zero Trust journey given the number and variability of that identity across users, devices, organizations, and detection mechanisms. In general, some mechanism to force the contextual identity to authenticate and then be authorized based on aspects of that contextual identity must exist.

This identity also needs to be considered when devices are newly purchased, acquired, or merged into the network with an explicit onboarding process being performed, easing in the future needs to rediscover endpoints as part of the initial identification phase. As part of the overlay policy, not only should considerations be taken for which devices that are currently on the network to access restricted resources critical to the business, but how to ensure that future devices present an identity that is conducive to determining what access they require when introduced onto the network. This policy typically results in a discreet onboarding process, detailing what purchasing, devices, configurations, and policies are all acceptable for devices that are to be used on the network and have access to restricted data in any form.

Vulnerability Management

For every device that is connected to a network, regardless of the user owning, managing, using, or troubleshooting it, there is an inherent risk posed by having the device present on the network. To minimize this risk, an analysis of how the device behaves as opposed to how it is expected to behave while on the network needs to be done. This analysis is highly reliant upon the contextual identity of the device, considering the authentication information or profiling information related to the device, to ensure context can be factored into this risk analysis.

Developing a baseline of which resources a device connects to allows variations within that baseline to be detected and understood if a new feature or functionality of the contextual identity was enabled. Meanwhile, the understanding of this communication pattern can be used as the basis for an enforcement policy to be applied, preventing this communication outside of the known required ports and protocols.

Enforcement

While determining identity and vulnerabilities within the network should undoubtedly be considered the proverbial "long pole in the tent" for Zero Trust, enforcement through a variety of mechanisms is the goal. The art of enforcement is ensuring that the correct methods of enforcement are applied in the correct areas to minimize risk that vulnerabilities can be exploited or that contextual identities are introduced into the network that are unable to be accounted for. This enforcement needs to be layered and present throughout the network, and in areas where the vulnerabilities inherent to the devices participating in that area of the network can be best controlled in the most effective manner.

The layered enforcement mindset ensures that a singular device is not overloaded with the breadth of enforcement needs that a given contextual identity has and protects against having a single point of failure, either by preventing or allowing access.

Analytics

Analytics, both analyzing device behavior and the policy it hit when it came onto or changed its disposition on the network, are fed into all other Zero Trust capabilities to validate the functionality of those objects and improve how they are applied to contextual identities.

The analytics capabilities should consider information gathered from each of the other security capabilities, such as using the identity to validate against an asset management database to determine whether a device present on the network was retired and dormant for months and has been reintroduced onto the network recently. While everything may look in accordance with that identity, further analysis applied will indeed show it to be out of the ordinary. The same goes for being able to build lessons learned and valuable information relating to device behaviors, user behaviors, and success or failures related to each to ensure false positives and true negatives can be more easily noticed. External feeds or information on these devices and their expected behavior, or behaviors seen in the wild that go against expected behavior, also need to be part of this analysis.

The Zero Trust journey is cyclical in nature with a need existing for ongoing analysis and understanding of not only the devices on the network and how their access may change throughout their life cycle, but also understanding and analyzing new devices or contextual identities that will inevitably be added to the network over time. This analysis feeds the rest of the Zero Trust strategy in that understanding of devices and contextual identities may influence changes to the overlay policies, may add more information to be used in the identification of devices and users, may uncover previously unknown or undetected vulnerabilities, or may determine when enforcement needs to be restricted or loosened to allow an identity to fulfill its business function.

The analysis therefore should be fed from all information available to be gathered on the network, ranging from application logs, to switch counters, syslog from devices throughout the network, and identity accounting information. This information then needs to be aggregated, analyzed, sorted, and presented in an effective manner based on the business goals an organization has, which often requires further analysis of the data and its conclusions to modify and get the correct data per those goals.

Summary

The expansiveness of Zero Trust should not discourage an organization from pursuing application to its architecture. As the world moves toward a security mindset, as opposed to a connectivity mindset, the five pillars of Zero Trust Capabilities along with the methods and best practices outlined by the team, minimize impacts on organizations as a result of malicious actors. While many offerings exist related to Zero Trust and the controls that can be implemented to become "Zero Trust compliant," the application of the five core principles found here—Policy & Governance, Identity, Vulnerability Management, Enforcement, and Analytics—has been proven to be successful within organizations. There are many compliance frameworks that get added or updated each month as a part of the Zero Trust journey. We have worked to enable organizations to be able to apply any or layer compliance frameworks by using the core Zero Trust Capabilities outline throughout this book.

Every day, working with organizations around the globe, the concepts and ideas surrounding Zero Trust grow and develop. With each organization, more information leads to updates and growth. The strength of design for an organization is that Zero Trust is all encompassing and the designs created for an organization will have a lasting impact.

Applied Use Case for Zero Trust Principles

Business Problem

Smart Building Central Inc. (SBC) was embarking on a state-of-the-art building, slated to be its new headquarters and be "A place that people would want to work." The new headquarters, deemed Smart Building Central, was slated to be a smart building with the goal of making working from the office as close to working from home as possible. Every system in the building, with few exceptions, would be connected to the network, with the backbone of the building being based on Cisco switching and wireless technology. With those endeavors, SBC Inc. also wanted to avoid being the next cybersecurity incident headline by ensuring that devices would only communicate in a manner that was sanctioned by the system's owners. This meant developing a secure communication bus between interacting systems, ensuring that the communications were mapped, controlled, and secured for daily operation within Smart Building Central.

The risk was significant. Smart Building Central's interconnected campus consisted of Internet of Things–based devices, mobile applications to interact with IOT devices, and a wealth of applications and middleware to control systems across the building. With this goal of creating the ultimate work-from-home experience, and the assistance of Cisco Security Services, Smart Building Central began its journey toward "the art of the possible." The knowledge that the approach would need to be as structured in its application as it was in its goal served as the guiding light toward success.

Goals and Drivers

The goal of Smart Building Central was to make the headquarters building a place where employees would want to work but also to show off the technologies to SBC's end customer in a sort of "art of the possible" partnership between Cisco and SBC Inc. SBC's line of building enablement technologies—including elevators, escalators, cameras, HVAC systems, lighting systems, irrigation systems, and security systems—would all be the central showcase of Smart Building Central, along with custom-developed integration software and brokering systems.

With breaches of recent years top of mind, SBC knew that there would be a need to understand how a centralized mobile app could integrate to change environmental factors around the individual worker. It would need to be able to locate users within the building on the scale of feet, and help them navigate to building services, both in normal times and during emergencies. Combined with the expected functionalities of any office building, including scheduling conference rooms, payment system integration, and even ordering from the resident Coffee Shop, smart technologies were meant to link users to services in a seamless manner. However, unauthorized communications had to be prohibited from high-risk systems, such as HVAC systems communicating with point of sale. The largest challenge to be overcome was going to be the flat nature of the network, designed for no more than a couple thousand users. SBC Inc. defined new goals:

- Priority Goal #1: Understand all devices within an environment or building, their users, and network access devices.

- Priority Goal #2: Evaluate the ability for all devices to be authenticated and dynamically authorized to the network through testing of sample devices, identified within the discovery process.

- Priority Goal #3: Determine communications required externally for each device as identified.

- Priority Goal #4: Determine the internal communications required for each device identified.

- Priority Goal #5: Ensure that all devices are onboarded into the asset management database, providing a single source of truth for devices unable to actively authenticate.

- Priority Goal #6: Force authentication for all devices capable of authenticating.

- Priority Goal #7: Exchange authentication data with peer systems within the environment.

- Priority Goal #8: Apply differentiated policy for actively authenticated devices.

- Priority Goal #9: Apply differentiated policy for devices unable to actively authenticate.

- Priority Goal #10: Provide metrics to prevent authentications that were not legitimate in nature.

Application of the Principles of Zero Trust

Like many deployments, Smart Building Central was designed by its technical architects in alignment with classic networking aspects, aligning with a common "hard perimeter with soft, gooey interior." Their classic design focus had as its key tenet that any device could get onto the network and have its communication limited only at the perimeter firewall. All other connectivity internal to the network was allowed with few enforcement mechanisms utilized within the "network trust boundary." This was described by Cisco's architects as a "connectivity over security" model. Due to the nature of its business, SBC Inc. found itself in a position where it would need to align with multiple regulatory requirements, including a need for authorized access, understanding of contextual identity, prevention of interactions between devices with no business interacting internally, and understanding of interactions with external entities. SBC not only had to account for devices interacting on behalf of business as usual but also had to plan for periodic review, auditing, and attempted exploitation of the devices and network as part of their future considerations.

The first step toward implementation of Zero Trust at Smart Building Central was a workshop, as described in Chapters 1–3. In its first attempt to hold a workshop, SBC started by inviting director-level talent from its networking and network security teams. As seen in Figure A-1, within the greater reporting structure of SBC Inc., networks fell under the chief technology officer, while network security fell under the chief information officer.

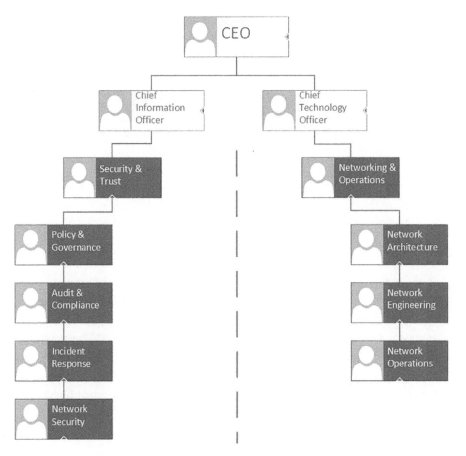

Figure A-1   *Organization Chart of SBC Inc.*

Within the SBC Inc. culture, this hierarchy made for challenging interactions for a multitude of reasons. To begin, the two teams had different motivations and definitions of success with relation to those motivations. The networking team, which was within the same reporting structure as the network operations team, was focused on getting devices onto the network. Their primary goal was ensuring endpoints were able to conduct their business functions. The burden of doing so was already challenging. The typical process for an endpoint that was added to the network was distributed across multiple functions with no definitive process defined for the exact requirements the endpoint, user, or department must follow to gain network access. Unfortunately, this presented itself to a fair number of additional challenges, short timelines, and removal of any roadblocks that prevented a device from getting onto the network for a legitimate business purpose.

The network security team was admittedly often at odds with the networking team. Being responsible for audits, penetration tests, incident response, and misconfigurations, the network security team was quite a bit more conservative in their approach to allowing connectivity on the network than the networking team. Throughout the policy and governance phase of the Zero Trust engagement, it quickly became clear that a singular mission statement and some level of personnel to facilitate that mission statement had to be defined. So long as both teams conflicted in their view of the definition of "success," no practical progress could be made. SBC needed to avoid the inevitable use of timelines alone to dictate the approach to the problem statement of "excessive access and connectivity." SBC Inc. wanted to avoid making the same mistakes by implementing the same methods as used in all other architectures. Due to the need to align with regulatory requirements that would be unique to Smart Building Central, the same approach would fail in its ability to align with these regulatory requirements, causing loss of government contracts, manufacturing grants, and in-house payment systems.

The first task agreed upon between the attendees within the initial workshop was a need to define the outcomes required for the successful deployment of Smart Building Central. This definition of the successful outcome needed to be solely defined as the success criteria, not considering the current processes or governance that existed within SBC Inc. at the time. Five goals were determined to define success for Smart Building Central, all to be shared across organizations within SBC Inc. These goals included

- The ability to definitively identify a device as it was connected to the network, resulting in the device being provided only the access it required to fulfill its business purpose.

- Prevention of unauthorized devices introduced from within Smart Building Central to access any key resources within the building or within SBC Inc. data centers.

- Minimization of impact of any one device being compromised within Smart Building Central or the greater SBC Inc. preventing business as usual within Smart Building Central.

- The ability to enable next-generation smart capabilities with devices allowing for both comfort as well as health and safety alerting for both administrative and individual authorized users within the building.

- Metric-based re-evaluation of priorities of Smart Building Central's implementation of these technologies to define whether additional adjustments to tactical approaches to solving these challenges needed to be implemented, or whether the charter was infeasible for SBC Inc. as a company.

- The collective agreement across SBC's management that these goals were their guiding principles ensured no one entity could dictate the approach or metrics upon which the outcome could be measured.

Policy and Governance

The first determination made by attendees to the Smart Building Central Zero Trust deployment meeting was that a change in culture had to occur for the implementation of any additional restrictions to be introduced. Knowing that conflicts in the past had prevented similar projects from getting off the ground within SBC Inc., leaders within both the network and network security teams agreed that changes to the organization well "above their paygrade" would need to occur. An understanding of the business impact of not doing so would need to be well articulated to leadership within the disparate organizations to drive this change. The largest challenge to be overcome was separate measurements of success for network and security teams, specifically being uptime for business-related applications versus resources spent on responding to threats on the network, respectively. With the requirement to identify, understand, and enforce access for identities throughout the Smart Building Central campus being a key success factor for the implementation of Smart Building Central, priorities and metrics had to change. This change seemed drastic: an evaluation respective to whether security would inhibit the goals of the business versus SBC Inc. having the business at all. Without success in the form protecting the network from threats, SBC Inc. would lose its contracts to do business—the lifeblood of the company.

Throughout introduction to this use case, the term *initial* has been used in a purposeful manner. With the realization and agreement between network and network security teams that decisions to be made had to be made at a higher authority level, the ability to succeed without having this charter in place was prevented. Internal meetings, alliances at the highest levels, and mutual understanding of success across the business units within SBC Inc. had to be accomplished to enable this success. Over the course of three months post-workshop, SBC Inc. determined changes that needed to be implemented to ensure success of the Smart Building Central project. The first was a move of the network security team into the same organization as the network team, falling under a separate leader reporting through the chief technology officer. It was determined, based on business culture, that having teams report to separate executives with differing metrics of success would continue to inhibit success. This success applied to not only the Smart Building Central project but also future projects that would be influenced by the technologies required to make Smart Building Central a success. With Network Administration, Network Security, and Network Operations all reporting through the same executive management, a singular authority could provide edicts for successful implementation of technologies that would fuel Smart Building Central.

It is important to note that teams concerned with audits, penetration testing, incident response, and policies governing each of these aspects continued to report through the chief information officer. This alignment provided for an independent body that could help influence the technologies and controls required when applying them to the Smart Building Central project. In addition, this alignment gave the network and network security teams the ability to define their largest pain points that must be overcome to accomplish the goals set out before them. Those pain points included

- The inability for either team to track, determine, or influence new purchases of devices that would require network connectivity.

- The lack of any communication to either team on the requirements for a device on the network before new devices were connected to the network.

- An inability to validate that devices were properly configured or onboarded with proper settings to connect to the network.

- A culture of consistent exceptions that allowed for the loudest or most influential users to connect devices to the network without question as to the merits of the connectivity or business purposes.

- A lack of visibility into what was currently on the network and, more importantly, whether those devices belonged on the network.

A large aspect of Smart Building Central's success would be overcoming the pain points as defined by the network and network security teams. To do so, the collaborative team could now present a need for definitive policy to require which devices were provided what access and how. This information would be communicated to the newly formed corporate security team. Then, the corporate security team, made up of policy writers, auditors, penetration testers, and incident response engineers, could now act in an advisory role to the network team. The team would maintain a separated responsibility of ensuring the compliance of users to corporate standards, while the network security team merely had to build in the controls to validate that compliance.

The corporate security team, now with this newly defined responsibility, created policies aligned with Zero Trust core principles:

- All users who wish to partake in network communications with any device, application, or username must agree to adhere to policies for the protection and control of data flow within the SBC Inc. network.

- All devices must be clearly identified through network discovery means before being allowed to participate on the network in any manner. Identification of the device must include

- Who owns, manages, troubleshoots, and maintains the device, including its respective life cycle and vulnerability management techniques.

- The type of device, its purpose on the network, and assurance that it adheres to the identification policies defined for participation.

- The expected location or locations for the user or device when interacting with the network.

- The expected life cycle of the user, device, or application as it interacts with the network, including whether it is constantly connected, or intermittently connected.

- The medium that the user, device, or application expects to be connected over.

- The expected interactions, ports, protocols, and communication patterns that a user, device, or application had regarding other identities within the network.

- The exception to this policy is guest users who do not belong to SBC Inc., its partners, affiliates, or authorized network users.

- All devices that interact with the network must have validation by the owner, manager, or operational technician that the device has been properly onboarded in accordance with onboarding standards for SBC Inc.

- Any unauthorized device added to the network will be removed from the network with haste, and the responsible owner, manager, or technician prevented from reintroducing the device until all previous steps were validated by the network audit team to ensure compliance.

These simple but clear policies ensured that respective teams were made responsible for devices on the network, as opposed to overloading two teams with responsibilities that should be distributed across the company. As a result, these policies also increased the collaboration between network teams who would be responsible for ensuring a device could get on the network, and network security teams who ensured that control mechanisms were put in place to allow only required connectivity. This collaboration allowed for the respective teams to focus on properly onboarding and identifying devices, as opposed to auditing and ensuring that repeat offenders or application owners who disagreed with the policies were all held to account. In Smart Building Central, following policies would be the only way to add devices to the network.

Understanding the Business

Post-reorganization, Smart Building Central still had one major gap: When it came to the devices, users, and even applications that used the network, SBC was reactive in removing unauthorized devices. With regulatory requirements being a net-new addition to the building, its infrastructure and endpoint management, changes in processes would also need to be considered to better identify and act in a proactive manner to remove threats as soon as they were identified. The first step in this process was to better understand the business of SBC Inc., and specifically how the business was broken down. The understanding for which business units, their purpose within the company, and their reliant endpoints, users, and applications would ensure each business unit could fulfill its purpose. In the second workshop held to plan for the implementation of Smart Building Central, senior leaders were invited to participate to work through what their business was responsible for, key systems the business relied on, and known interactions for those systems.

Considering the needs of Smart Building Central to be a headquarters building with enabling technologies, it was agreed that the leaders from current Corporate Operations would be invited to an identity-focused workshop, including business units with allocated space with Smart Building Central. These Corporate Operations departments, including Finance, Human Resources, IT, Marketing, and Partner Sales, were assigned into the corporate endpoints category, which would later become one of the enclaves used to organize and enforce policy. Each department within the corporate endpoints category was asked a series of questions:

- How do your users typically access resources to do their jobs?

- What types of endpoints do you, your employees, and your partners or contractors use when they connect to the network?

- Through which medium do your users connect when they connect to critical resources?

- What are the critical resources that you rely on to do your job?

- Is your department active only during standard business hours, or do you regularly have long shifts? Do these shifts differ per time of year?

- Do your employees utilize their mobile devices at work for either personal or professional reasons?

- What systems within your standard working environment could be improved to make your use of the office more effective?

As would be expected, these questions, even when provided ahead of time to department heads and senior leadership, resulted in a variety of answers. The most common answers were small handfuls of application names or IP addresses being provided, especially by nontechnical resources. The answer to what could be improved, however, was broad and varied. Users needed the ability to present in an ad hoc manner devices that were most effective to their working patterns, an ability to easily find available collaboration spaces, and an ability to move to collaboration spaces most suited to brainstorming for the project at hand.

It was found that SBC Inc. had standardized on Lenovo laptops for all employees and had a stringent exception process to prevent the use of any other brand of laptop accessing corporate resources due to exploitation the company had suffered years prior. At the same time, other laptops could connect to the wireless guest network while on site for Internet access, and data could easily be transferred to them via physical means. Employees commonly utilized this tactic to work on laptops with larger screens, less stringent requirements on installed applications, or on machines where they were less likely to have their activity tracked. This behavior was typical of IT and Marketing users, both departments containing technical users who understood workarounds to policies that existed preceding the policy rework.

It was also found that most users split their time accessing resources on their corporate devices between wired and wireless networks, mainly because those employees who were in the office would dock their laptops when at their desk. This activity would cause the laptop to prefer the wired connection but switch to wireless when attending meetings, sales briefings, or events away from the employee's desk. The wireless network, being solely preshared key authentication, provided a medium over which third-party devices could be joined with little control over the owner or purpose on the network. There was also significant disregard for hiding the password needed to join the SSID. So little caution was given to the preshared password that plastic placards could be found throughout IT cubicles with a "frequently asked questions" list, including the key for anyone to observe and use.

Both aspects of security policy limitation were directly contributed to by the lack of identification techniques for any resource on the network. Most identification of endpoints was both reactive and done via tribal knowledge or manual lookup efforts. For many of the applications that employees utilized to do their regular jobs, there was little understanding of how these applications interacted between themselves, with application owners having left the company sometimes over a decade ago. With these application owners gone, the management of the application was left to no one in particular. If an application broke, technicians would log in to it with either default credentials that had never been changed, or with credentials that were static and part of a knowledge base that anyone on the network could gain access to. The significant risk of these practices being common across departments created a renewed sense of urgency with senior management of SBC Inc. to secure business processes and to identify devices and applications. Truth be told, senior resources within SBC Inc. did not realize how large of a risk the network and its connected devices had become.

The next aspect of the identity workshop for each of the respective corporate departments was an ask about roadblocks to doing their daily work or encouraging employees to come into the office. With Smart Building Central being slated to be an innovation forum for new ideas and enablement technologies, SBC Inc. wanted to hear from its business units what would encourage employees to want to come into the office, as opposed to being remote or working from home. The most desired aspect of working from the office was to network, socialize, and build their relationships with coworkers to feel more aligned with the business and the team that they worked on. Many of the participants alluded to "conversations around the water cooler" being an aspect that they valued most about being in the office but complained that the office was commonly far too noisy and distracting. One of the largest asks was to have collaboration areas where employees could work together on projects without the need to shout over cubicle walls. However, a major aspect of this collaboration was being able to seamlessly share ideas digitally without the need to find or schedule a conference room, which was already a very difficult task. It also was not guaranteed that the collaboration was best suited for laptops with standard mouse and keyboard layouts. Many employees noted they would rather be able to effortlessly share their tablet or phone screens with each other than to whiteboard with smart pens, enabling them to better share, edit, and save ideas for future development and expansion. This meant providing areas that could be easily accessed, connected to, and collaborated within, without distracting others or needing to clear multiple technological hurdles to do so.

With these asks, understandings, and recommendations from those occupying the building, the company's innovation engineers were invited to the workshop to illustrate their vision for Smart Building Central's future technology enablement. The innovation team, focused on employee experience as well as marketing of SBC's products, painted a futuristic picture of a headquarters that the market leader in smart buildings should provide:

- Ensure that there was as little downtime in the workday as possible; this effort was mainly a function of ensuring that employees could get to meetings and destinations as quickly and efficiently as possible. This innovation was enabled through a vast array of technological solutions:

  - For employees to get to another floor and meeting as quickly as possible, the longest amount of time spent was waiting for an elevator to climb multiple stories. To mitigate this wait, the SBC Inc. innovation engineers had created an application that would inform a centralized controller of an employee's need to take the elevator to another floor. This controller worked the same way that rideshare services did: an employee could use a web page or mobile application to inform the controller that they needed an elevator to another floor. After the employee enrolled in this need, location tracking was enabled for their mobile device and tracked in relation to distance from the elevator. This location tracking both provided a GPS-like navigation path within the application for the user to get to the closest elevator and their ultimate destination, as well as scheduled one of the six elevators in Smart Building Central to arrive with a destination of the employee's floor already programmed in. This location tracking was able to factor in calculations of where the user was at a given time, their walk speed, and distance from their destination for the application to schedule their elevator ride.

  - Resembling common coffee shop mobile applications, Smart Building Central incorporated a mobile ordering system to the building's coffee café and cafeteria. With full menus provided within the app, employees could order their most common orders on the way to a meeting without having to worry about whether fresh coffee was available or food was provided at the destination conference room floor.

- Ensure that meetings were most successful and collaborative through seamless interaction. Technology was used to ensure that conference rooms were both available and easy to use regardless of the technology an employee possessed:

  - From within the same application as navigation and food ordering, conference rooms could be scheduled on demand with a click of a mobile phone button. Virtual meetings, provided by Cisco WebEx, were automatically joined as soon as the user entered the physical room, as detected with motion-sensing abilities. If the user elected to invite others to the virtual meeting, they would be automatically notified of the virtual address for the room.

  - Conference rooms were outfitted with sharing technology that was compatible with all Apple- and Android-based phones, providing the ability to share or mirror screens from any device on the building's Wi-Fi network and display content to the series of TVs found within the meeting room they were invited to participate in.

  - The mobile application, recognizing the owner of a conference room, would allow change in temperature, adjustment of shades, change in overhead lighting, and volume of the virtual participants on the screen in the room.

  - For Smart Building Central's centralized conference space, able to accommodate thousands of visitors for the exploration of innovative ideas that SBC Inc. sold, audio/visual systems could be used to broadcast to internal television networks within Smart Building Central as well as companywide.

- Ensure the comfort of all who would visit Smart Building Central:

  - In conference spaces, thermal imaging cameras were used to calculate the number of attendees, determine the ambient temperature, and adjust the conference room temperature to maintain consistent audience comfort.

  - With Smart Building Central being in a sunny geographical area of the country, one of the greatest complaints was the temperature and light in other building offices. While having a corner office was a privilege, the glare and heat generated by windows surrounding the office made it unbearable in the hot summers. The same went for conference rooms full of participants in physical meetings. Like the temperature-sensing technologies in conference rooms, temperatures could be adjusted on a per room basis. This was combined with lumen-sensitive windows that could detect direct sunlight and change the tint of the window through electro-chromic glass inserts, saving both energy and time of pausing due to glare or heat concerns.

  - All conference rooms, private offices, and the employee gym were outfitted with online music streaming built into the building mobile app.

The ideas presented within the workshop were futuristic, innovative, and concentrated on creating an employee focus for Smart Building Central. However, in the spirit of Zero Trust, SBC Inc. knew to align with the newly created policies for endpoint participation on the network, large changes would need to be made ensuring the security of not only critical resources within the SBC Inc. network, but also to maintain the comfort and safety of employees. The first step would have to be introducing a definitive identification mechanism into the building's infrastructure.

Identifying and Vulnerability Management

To break the massive undertaking of identifying devices on the network into practical amounts, Smart Building Central first was broken into five Virtual Routing and Forwarding (VRF) instances: Corporate, Building Management Systems, Labs, Guests, and IOT. For each Virtual Routing and Forwarding instance, 100 VLANs were allocated in a fashion that could provide predictability to a device's initial category on the network. For all corporate PCs, tablets, and managed mobile phones, for example, devices were allocated to the Corporate VRF. However, how could SBC Inc. be sure that just because a device was connected to a switchport that belonged to the Corporate VRF, that it was a corporate-provided device?

Smart Building Central deployed Cisco's Identity Services Engine to identify devices throughout the network, while also aligning with new policies that would require that the device be definitively identified. For IOT devices specifically, Identity Services Engine was complemented by Cisco CyberVision, specializing in operational technology identification. The greatest advantage that SBC Inc. had working in its favor is a culture of consistent corporate endpoints, all of which were centrally managed. PCs managed through group policies were already the standard workstation of choice after the removal of third parties that were unmanageable. This allowed SBC Inc. to push new group policies to managed endpoints that would enable the device to present its username and device credentials to the network. These credentials were subsequently verified by Identity Services Engine and referred to Active Directory for validation. Once validated, endpoints would be actively probed for software installation related to endpoint management agents being enabled, anti-malware agents being up to date, and the presence of the Thousand Eyes clients was utilized for measuring network response times. The use of vulnerability techniques such as "posture checking" verified that the largest portion of devices on the network in Smart Building Central, the PCs that users were issued, were validated in both their management status as well as ownership. All PCs that could not be identified or verified being up to date were prevented from accessing the network, with a resulting need to visit IT staff to remediate any management issues.

For applications and servers that had to exist on Smart Building Central's network and be local to the building itself, the initial step in identifying them was via their physical location on the network. Smart Building Central had a centralized main distribution facility (MDF) within the building where all servers were required to be located. In addition to being physically secured from other areas of the network, the MDF contained switches only allocated to servers that were required to be mounted in server racks allocated to the department. Policy enforcement could therefore consider this physical location as one attribute of the contextual identity used to enforce policies associated with these servers and applications.

For applications or servers connected to these devices, switches were unable to identify themselves using a native supplicant on the devices. As a result, the owner of a device had two options. The first option was an acknowledgment from the application owner that the device must be added into an asset management database, including properties for the device such as its owner, manager, troubleshooting contact, purpose, life cycle, interactions, protocols, and ports utilized to fulfill its function. All of these attributes were utilized to track the asset and to write strict policies for its interactions on the network. The risk incurred by the application or endpoint owner was that while the application may be business critical in nature, its inability to be identified and enforced would incur potential impact to SBC's contracts, and therefore, it would be prevented from executing functionality not explicitly documented.

The alternative second option to populating the asset management database manually was to provide SBC's IT department the ability to collect this information automatically using an agent installed on the server. This agent, which was part of Cisco's Secure Workload solution, collected behavior from the device's communications and provided for the ability to enforce policies or alert on deviation from those policies while not enforcing for critical applications. Upon the device's deployment, initial information would need to be populated, including the owner, manager, troubleshooting contact, purpose, and life cycle for tracking the device and ensuring it was understood who the responsible party would be should the device change its behavior. However, the behavior tracking ability of the Secure Workload agent lessened the burden of understanding all protocols and ports and ensured that a mechanism to enforce these policies existed as close to the server as possible.

Comfort-sensing devices were classified into the IOT Virtual Routing and Forwarding instance. Comparable to devices that would enable other aspects of the business, these devices would need to be classified in an equivalent manner to servers, ensuring that the identity of the device could be determined in a programmatic way. Ownership of the device was documented, and expected behavior of the device was understood. However, it was immediately accepted by the owners of the devices, the network engineering department, and the Smart Building Central innovation team that most of these devices would not be able to have an agent installed on them. Especially for small sensor devices with minimal memory onboard, limited network stacks present, and often a proprietary interface required to configure and change settings on the device, there was no way that a standard method of deploying an agent or evaluating that the device's behavior could be done local to the device. After accepting this limitation, SBC Inc. created a "tiger team" deemed "The Key Masters" inside of SBC Inc. network engineering to overcome the challenge.

The Key Masters' charter was to be an onboarding, analysis, and troubleshooting team specifically for IOT devices within the Smart Building Central environment. With the newly created asset management database as their source of truth, all devices must be onboarded and evaluated by the Key Masters before being allowed on the network. This process was tedious but required collaboration with the owner, manager, and troubleshooting contact for each device, typically being identical. The device was first connected within a secured, hardened environment and would need to be connected alongside its systematic dependencies. For example, for smart thermostats that were connected to the network, the entire system that could influence or communicate to or from the smart thermostat would need to be built out within the hardened lab. Much of this knowledge came from product owners, who either had already implemented this system in other areas of SBC Inc. or were subject matter experts on the product itself and its ability to perform functions on the network. Knowing that devices within a system must interact for successful functionality, each device was entered into the asset management database and categorized into a unique system name, specific to its function, with each device also having a role within the system.

The identifying aspect of IOT devices was found to typically be solely in the devices' unique MAC address. The MAC address was therefore used to authenticate the devices in a passive manner, given their inability to actively identify themselves. This MAC address was documented in the asset management database and then exchanged into Identity Services Engine. Utilizing the organizationally unique identifier (OUI) of the MAC address, the address was classified into its product and manufacturer category for use as part of the applied authorization policy. The device was then passively identified regarding its expected posture, or how the device should look to the network. Aspects of the device's interaction with the network—for example, headers contained within its HTTP requests, contents of its DHCP address requests, the hostname either provided or configured for the device on the corporate DNS server, and whether the device responded to queries via SNMP—were all considered to create a scoring system for whether a device was what it represented itself as.

With a profile of what the device looked like within a controlled and verified environment, the next challenging task was to fully understand not only the interactions documented within the system schematic for the devices but also how these interactions occurred between each product in the system. The innovation team for Smart Building Central did as much due diligence as they could in determining the systems to be implemented into Smart Building Central, including tracking the system deployment notes and documentation from the manufacturer. These schematics were provided to the Key Masters for their consideration in their documentation on the expected behaviors. Many of the guides offered as documentation additionally included a list of ports and their expected usage when a system was deployed on a network. What the Key Masters quickly found, though, is that developers for the software or firmware utilized by most devices rarely had a networking background or skillset. This issue became evident through the collection of interaction traffic utilizing Cisco Secure Network Analytics and tracking the conversations found within NetFlow. What the Key Masters determined was that obvious interactions that may be prevented by a firewall (such as access of cloud services, shared services such as DNS and DHCP, and even identity services such as Kerberos) were documented, as seen in Figure A-2.

However, most manufacturers of devices that would be found within the IOT VRF didn't plan for their interacting systems to be prevented from communicating openly with the

IOT devices. Smart Building Central's desired application of validated traffic flows and enforcement of any communication outside of those flows was not a consideration. Therefore, manufacturers rarely documented the interactions within the system. This required that the Key Masters collect and document what equated to 10 times the number of connections provided by manufacturers, and create records for each of the interactions, protocols, and ports within the asset management database for later consumption.

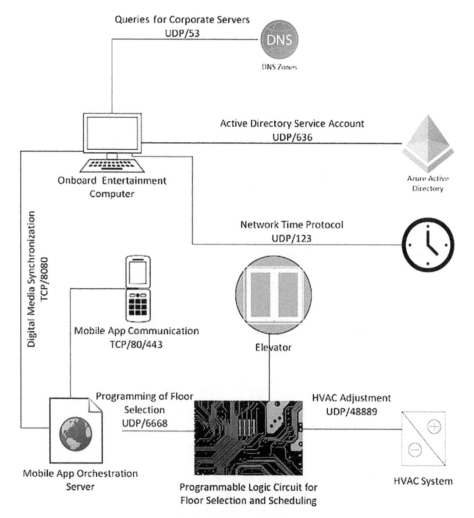

Figure A-2   *Elevator System Interaction Diagram*

The documentation of these interactions served two purposes for Smart Building Central. The first was to ensure that policies could be written in a distributed manner, across multiple enforcement points to prevent communication to or from the device as required. The use of TrustSec as a Layer 2 enforcement mechanism between devices that were expected to be deployed within the same VLAN resulted in a policy that would be configured within Identity Services Engine. This policy allowed only those communications in a protocol and port manner. Devices that would be required to be part of separate VLANs could have their VLANs dynamically assigned to them through a RADIUS "push" containing the VLAN. Further restrictions were applied in the form of downloadable ACLs, also configured within ISE. For devices that needed to interact across VRFs—a thermostat to the chiller or heat pump that would cool or heat a room, for example— policies would be deployed to a firewall. Any devices that would need to interact with cloud-based resources could have their policy applied directly to the cloud server they were interacting with via the IP tables mechanism modified with Cisco Secure Workload.

The second purpose of documenting the behavior of each of the devices within each system was to develop a baseline communication to understand whether the device was behaving differently in the field than what was observed in the lab. This change in behavior was thought to potentially indicate some level of compromise. As the Key Masters found out very quickly in the testing process, utilizing vulnerability management and evaluation tools on IOT devices with limited network stacks can easily, and without warning, cause the devices to stop responding to any network communications. The programmable logic circuits that control chillers and tell them to turn on for only as long as the thermostat indicates that temperature is incorrect in the room, for example, will stop responding when an NMAP or vulnerability scan is run against them. To resume normal operations, the device required a reboot, typically predicated by complaints by those in the room that was facilitated by the chiller were far too warm or too cold. This was a direct dichotomy with the goals Smart Building Central had for the smart systems. Therefore, the traffic mapping and interactions associated with each system were tracked with custom-built scripts that would fire alerts based on the NetFlow telemetry ingested by Cisco Secure Network Analytics. These alerts would indicate to administrators that the baseline communication was not conforming with known patterns, or had completely stopped, which would indicate a problem. The alerts and information provided could be macro (system-to-system ongoing communication) or micro (header content change) in nature.

Application of Enforcement

Even with identification of devices done and mapping of communication baselines being complete, the criticality of systems within Smart Building Central caused anxiety across all aspects of the business. With demonstrable impact that could be incurred by inadvertently shutting down a chiller merely by attempting to evaluate it for vulnerabilities, senior management was even more concerned about the balance of business as usual, with the ability to adhere to regulations allowing the business to function. Throughout the identity phase of the Zero Trust testing, the Key Masters applied varying levels of enforcement techniques to each system and evaluated what impacts each would have on the system. Knowing that some devices within the building management system were never meant to be networked when originally developed, there was a known risk to applying authentication at all. This phase yielded an additional discovery into which enforcement technique would work best for each system.

For many of the devices that ran building management systems—programmable logic circuits specifically—the original system was built as a series of components that could be easily swapped in and out of their case using PCI ports, some also having USB 1.0 ports.

The assemblers of the devices, having assembled some of the components in the mid-1990s after the initial introduction of PCI and USB to the market, would never have expected that wired or wireless LAN cards would be attached via the connection bus. Therefore, logic used when sending signals to and from the connection bus was simplistic in nature, some devices being found to interpret any level of enforcement or prevention of access at the access layer switch port as a disconnection. This result made for a need to work around these devices and apply lesser security to the type of device at the initial connection, in favor of moving the enforcement technique to a higher layer in the network topology, such as the firewall. Key to this understanding and determination was the use of the Identity and Vulnerability Management phases, as the device did not present any sort of error to the network based on the application of this enforcement. It simply shut itself down and stopped responding until it disconnected and reconnected.

With this need for distributed enforcement in mind, the network security team for Smart Building Central designed a plan for application of security across each VRF and throughout the network, as shown in Figure A-3. The major components of the enforcement application included a series of technologies, including TrustSec for intra-VLAN communications, downloadable ACLs for inter-VLAN communications, firewalls for inter-VRF communications, firewalls for external communications, and DNS policies for external resolution.

Figure A-3 *Distribution of Enforcement Mechanisms*

Firewalls

The firewall continued to be Smart Building Central's perimeter security device of choice. However, the standard for deploying firewalls for remote sites, regardless of their function, was what some would consider far too complex. SBC Inc., being a manufacturing company and having several innovation centers throughout the world, had many contractors who partnered with the company to administer and update various types of devices. Elevator computers, thermostat logic, and sensor monitoring by emergency services companies were major focuses and would be required within Smart Building Central. Therefore, agreements were created with vendors to allow set IP addresses and sites to access these systems inbound through the firewall. In addition to the inbound rules required, some contractors had a physical presence within the SBC Inc. offices, but it was unpredictable where these contractors would work from at any given time. Their technician responsibilities often brought them to various offices with a working agreement with the contractors to allow them to work from any SBC Inc. building, giving them a temporary "home base of operations."

With this agreement in place, the SBC Inc. standard for deploying firewall rules was to replicate the inbound and outbound exceptions for these contractors to every firewall in the company's firewall fleet, in addition to local rules for site-specific business purposes. When the initial template was provided for the Smart Building Central application of firewall rules, it was found that the sheer number of rules would overload most vendor firewalls for the scoped size of throughput and endpoints found within the building. The company's network security team provided 350,000 rules that would need to be populated onto the firewall for these purposes. Given the burden these rules would have on firewalls to be implemented, another approach had to be taken.

The first step in reducing firewall rules was to revisit the Identity phase of the Zero Trust principles to identify what rules applied to which contractors and whether some of the rules could be removed. Comparable to the realized risk of not having a definitive asset management database, each corporate firewall of the SBC Inc. fleet had thousands of rules without any identifying characteristics, remarks, or understanding of their purpose or life cycle. To reduce the firewall rules and, in extension, distribute the enforcement techniques, SBC Inc. had to evaluate which rules were required. Many of these rules should have been removed long before and could be applied to endpoints via a different mechanism. Therefore, an effort was undertaken to understand firewall rules through a series of evaluations:

- Each firewall rule was first evaluated against the DHCP scopes internal to SBC Inc. to determine whether a suspected owner could be identified. The overall architecture of SBC Inc. being distributed branches that must connect back through campus or data center sites did provide some identification abilities. DHCP scopes could be linked to smaller offices with only a handful of business units. For these sites, and the business units identified, team also attempted to identify destinations through tribal knowledge, or knowledge that existed within teams already, as opposed to relying solely on DNS records.

- For connections that could not be readily identified using DHCP scopes specific to a site, DNS lookups were performed into the last known endpoint that occupied the address that was being allowed access through the firewall. One significant advantage that SBC Inc. had in this regard was a centralized SIEM system that logged 13 months' worth of data per corporate requirement, giving them a lookback on the activities of any given endpoint or user for the last year.

- For rules that were unable to be identified using DHCP tracing, tribal knowledge, DNS lookup, and log analysis, the rule was incrementally disabled on each of the company's four campus firewalls, while remaining active on data center firewalls. An expectation that users would complain when they were unable to access destinations via one data center but allowed to access it through another was accounted for. The effect of disabling the firewall rules only on campus firewalls incrementally ensured limited impact to the business while waiting for these complaints. In addition, which firewall was disabled could be planned around business priorities, such as the number of contractors flowing through each firewall on a regular basis.

The result of the analysis completed for 350,000 firewall rules was that only approximately 125,000 were used actively within the organization. This included removing nearly 50,000 that were overlapping rules, having little or no effect. As these rules were cleaned up as part of the process, the number of rules shrank significantly. Of the 125,000 rules implemented and used, it was determined that many were duplicate rules that existed for all 175 campuses and branches that SBC Inc. allowed contractors to visit. Most of these rules could therefore be simplified and applied on a device category basis with downloadable ACLs—a more simplistic and distributed approach.

Identity Services Engine (ISE)

For the firewall rules that pertained directly to overlapping subnets traversing to a small number of destinations, Identity Services Engine policies were written to accommodate this access. With the age of the firewall estate, it was safely assumed that SBC Inc. did not use the next-generation features of its firewalls. Features such as TCP randomization, TCP normalization, or even intrusion prevention policies were not applied to individual connections. While SBC Inc. had IPS systems deployed separately from its firewalls, it was determined this would be combined into the next-generation firewall offering of Firepower Threat Defense. This also enabled identity to be directly exchanged with the firewall for further policy enforcement.

With this determination made, access control lists were built, allowing access from endpoints outside of the Smart Building Central network into one of 24 jump hosts used to permit this access based on contextual identity. The results of this access were rules consisting of a combination of who, what, where, when, and how, and more specifically rules could be written that allowed for authenticated contractors' differentiated access. The policy applied looked comparable to the following:

> *A contractor found within a contractor's active directory group (who), authenticated via a VPN client into Smart Building Central (how), accessing the VPN*

from outside of Smart Building Central (where), via a laptop running Windows or Ubuntu (what), within business hours only (when), could traverse to one of 24 sites used as jump hosts for customer devices for administration. This comparatively simple rule, based on contextual identity, further reduced the rules to be applied to contractors by almost 10,000 rules, with at least one wired and wireless subnet in each of 174 external sites being allowed access to these jump hosts.

With firewall rules minimized and well within the quantity of rules that any firewall vendor could accommodate, focus shifted to corporate endpoints, collaboration endpoints, and guests. Within Smart Building Central, the innovation teams had a dream of a paperless building. All signage was easily updated and presented on screens strategically positioned within the building to allow information sharing as well as an automated emergency function that would change all signs to point to their nearest emergency exit in times of emergency. Similarly, when entering the building, all guests were registered on iPads, and all badges were reusable and linked to the identity registered on the iPad and were used to identify and track users throughout the building. There was an interest in ensuring all presentations were digital, files hosted centrally for consumption on mobile devices, and presentations done wirelessly to also minimize the number of cords required within the building. Both goals played into a clean, conservation-focused, and sustainability goal.

As mentioned earlier in the appendix, Smart Building Central utilized Android- and Apple-based presentation products to allow any devices to connect to them and share the entirety of a user's screen or a singular application. The challenge came when this goal was applied to both corporate endpoints, as well as guests. It was well established that all collaboration endpoints would be part of the Corporate VRF of the network, especially given the nature of full-mesh traffic connectivity needs between softphones. A similar communication pattern applied to video collaboration devices within the building. But the use of Android and Apple presentation devices provided a distinct advantage to the collaboration and security solution, because it allowed these devices to be treated as a separate input to the collaboration devices altogether. This input was switched to when a shared screen triggered the device. These devices therefore existed in a "shared services" VRF of the network, with enforcement applied to allow communication to these devices via a firewall and identity-based policy for both corporate endpoints as well as guests.

This identity-based enforcement mechanism was a combination function between Cisco Identity Services Engine and the inter-VRF firewall of choice, Cisco's Firepower Threat Defense platform. As each corporate user connected to the network, regardless of medium, the endpoint was required to authenticate to the network, and an authorization policy applied. Within this authorization policy, a TrustSec tag was applied, identifying the user as a corporate user on a corporate endpoint. The same procedure occurred for SBC-managed mobile devices, with a similar Corporate Mobile TrustSec tag applied to the endpoint's session. Guests were provided with login credentials when they entered the network as part of their registration via iPads at the physical security desk. This credential was then associated with their badge and the device used to log in to the guest network.

Corporate users with personally managed cell phones were treated similarly, just with a use of their Active Directory credentials to log in to the guest central web auth portal, as opposed to credentials provided at registration. This methodology provided a required level of accounting and attribution of behavior for each guest, with the ability to revoke access to the guest network should the user leave campus with their badge or take other nefarious actions while on campus. Both identities, in the form of tags, were exchanged from Identity Services Engine to the Firepower Threat Defense platform. This exchange allowed for creation of a rule allowing for corporate endpoints and corporate mobile devices, found in the Corporate VRF, as well as guest devices, found in the Guest VRF, to communicate through the firewall to the Shared Services VRF based on their contextual identities. In addition, this methodology allowed for limitation of any guest or corporate device from communicating with others within its peer group, preventing the potential spread of malware. This rule similarly prevented communication between corporate endpoints and guest devices to prevent sharing of information between trusted and untrusted sources. This rule ensured that while functionality had to be allowed from the three groups to perform the same action, the three were prevented from communicating in undesired ways.

A similar approach was used for the administration of IOT devices, which were determined to have a management GUI. IOT devices existed within the IOT VRF of the building and typically included thermostats, sensors, IP cameras for both security and temperature sensing, and the programmable logic circuits for elevators, escalators, and smart glass. Each set of separate systems had to interact with some sort of management controller, including the mobile application processing unit, and their respective controllers for system functionality. These controllers were all consistently placed in the Building Management Systems VRF, which was separated from the sensors themselves by the Firepower Threat Defense firewalls.

Like the identification and authorization methods used for collaboration units, endpoints that needed to communicate with their management systems were configured with credentials where supported and profiled to determine the functionality of the device. For devices that were known to not have the ability to actively authenticate to the network with credentials, their MAC addresses were onboarded into an asset management database as part of the new responsibilities of the Key Masters post-completion of the system interaction testing. If the endpoint's MAC address was found in the asset management database and should have a device profile, or "look" like it should when participating on the network, it was provided its respective IOT tag. These tags were controlled in their interactions with building management systems via the Firepower Threat Defense firewall, and only known and validated protocols and ports allowed to traverse.

TrustSec Tags

One aspect of the initial goals that Smart Building Central had for endpoints within its network was the minimization of impact for any exploitation that was observed within the network. This meant ensuring that should a device be compromised within a system, a series of measures was used throughout the enforcement mechanisms to ensure that the potential impact on the rest of the network was minimized. These measures resulted in the use of TrustSec tags within the network, assigned to each unique device as it joined to the network, and associated with a unique session ID created when the device joined the network. However, one common mistake that many organizations will make, as noted in Chapter 7, is focusing on all endpoints as unique groups, increasing operational efforts through the number of policies written for endpoint interactions. While TrustSec tags were used within Smart Building Central, the Key Masters were very careful not to overwhelm the network operations team with hundreds of potential tags and settled on a maximum number of 10 tags that would be deployed throughout the network. Within each of these 10 tags, additional "sub-tags" were planned for, and they were typically associated with the separate endpoint groups but were planned to be implemented only when absolutely required, and well after Smart Building Central's go-live date. One aspect that had to be considered for the 10 tags to work was the required interactions between devices within each VLAN and which communications were considered critical.

Key to ensuring Smart Building Central did not expand beyond its capabilities for TrustSec was carving out the exact use cases that would require TrustSec. This plan included those which could potentially have endpoints that could be exploited within the same VLAN. The ability to control the communication in some other way, such as downloadable ACLs, separate VLANs, or a VRF termination on a firewall, was paramount. It was determined that the TrustSec tags to be created for Smart Building Central would be of the following types:

- Corporate endpoints (PCs and managed mobile devices)
- Collaboration endpoints
- IP security cameras
- Printers
- Print servers
- IOT
- Guests
- Building management systems
- IT

During the identification and traffic mapping phase, the most challenging endpoint that the Key Masters had to map out was that of IP cameras. IP cameras were found to serve two purposes within Smart Building Central—both physical security, as well as thermal imaging and measurement of ambient temperature. While cameras differed in firmware, their behavior was identical when connected to the network: when the device was newly connected to the network, it would first reach out to its peer group within the VLAN via a multicast message, followed by a broadcast message, asking which network video recording system it should connect to for sending its video feeds. Whenever the device's firmware was corrupted due to rapid power on/power off events, or in the event of a power surge, the device would reset all information previously configured on it relating to a statically configured network video recorder and perform the same action. For security purposes, it was determined by the SBC Inc. corporate security team that in lieu of losing access to physical security cameras and visibility into any area of the network, they would much prefer the dynamic ability for cameras to discover their network video recorder dynamically and be statically configured after the loss of connectivity than have a loss of connectivity until a technician could visit the physical device. A risk analysis of this behavior had to be undertaken to determine the best course of action.

On one hand, leaving all IP security cameras open to peer-to-peer communication could lead to a loss of physical connectivity within the building if exploited by a device on the same VLAN. At the same time, preventing this communication had a similar effect, where devices were lost during an event that was determined to potentially happen significantly more frequently in nature. It was determined that IP security cameras, needing to communicate on port 6668, would be restricted to this port local to their peer group to exchange configuration information, as well as multicast and communication toward the firewall to communicate to their controller. However, because of the critical role these cameras played within the network, and their respective behavior, they were "carved out" to be a separate TrustSec tag and have a unique policy applied to them.

Other devices, such as thermostats and sensors, were classified as IOT sensors in a more generalized enclave mainly because the loss of configuration for each of these devices would result in a need to visit the device, but there was less risk of impacting daily operations of the building until that visit could be completed. These devices also having a limited number of unique ports used to communicate within their peer groups resulted in a shared set of ports that would be allowed to communicate on. This result was applied, keeping in mind that some devices would be able to communicate on erroneous ports to their operation, regardless of whether devices within the group listened on all the allowed ports or not.

Most other peer-to-peer traffic flow within Smart Building Central was prevented with TrustSec tags, because the need for devices to communicate in this pattern was limited. One of the major goals Smart Building Central had, for example, was to change the culture as it related to communication to printers. To ensure that data loss prevention mechanisms, centralized printer authorization, and ease of use were all implemented for print jobs within Smart Building Central, IT operations teams wanted to ensure that any given PC could communicate only to a centralized print server. This print server would then relay printed documents to the required printer of the user's choice, which could also be recommended based on location within the building to which the print job was sent from. Knowing that PCs, printers, and the print server would all exist in the same VLAN in many cases, TrustSec tags were once again the optimum application of enforcement to be applied. A policy was implemented with corporate machines able to communicate only to print servers and explicitly blocked from communicating with printers directly. Printers would then be allowed to communicate to print servers, forcing the print servers to function as a centralized middleman to printers and PCs for control purposes.

With the need of Smart Building Central to move away from classic networking techniques, such as allocation of blocks of IP addresses to certain types of endpoints or departments, the general layout of PCs, mobile devices, printers, print servers, and corporate devices was to distribute them all within a single VLAN. This further caused a need for TrustSec tags as an enforcement mechanism. However, for digital signage devices that would utilize static IP addresses for easier management, there was a need to allocate a set of IP addresses that would be reachable by IT systems, not reachable by the standard corporate system, and unable to infect other digital signage should the device become compromised. This need was approached by laying security enforcement mechanisms on the endpoint's session.

The first layer of security was to dynamically assign these devices to their respective VLAN so that if they were moved between network ports, especially in the case of a conference where large densities of signage would be required in the conference area, there was little to no overhead by operations teams. To do so, digital signage devices would authenticate to the network with a unique credential to the device, be profiled based on its unique endpoint attributes, and be applied a VLAN specific to digital signage in a dynamic manner. The switch the endpoint was connected to, having the VLAN existing but not assigned, was configured via RADIUS to assign the VLAN to the session. On top of the dynamically assigned VLAN, the IOT tag was applied to the digital signage, preventing peer-to-peer communication between IOT devices; and finally a downloadable access control list was applied, allowing the device to access its two digital signage controllers, residing in the building management system's VRF at two singular IP addresses.

DNS

The final challenge for enforcement that Smart Building Central ran into was the vast use across all platforms of cloud services, both internal and external to the company's public cloud. Throughout the Key Masters' discovery phase and traffic analysis done to determine communications, they found that 93 percent of all endpoints within Smart Building Central utilized the cloud for hosted dynamic content of some form. Not only did popular smart assistant devices rely on the cloud almost exclusively for content that was served to them, but on-site gym devices with streaming services, PCs accessing websites within the cloud, IOT thermostats that received updates to their firmware from the cloud, and sensors that sent readings to a cloud server owned by SBC Inc. all presented a significant risk to the success of Smart Building Central. The largest concern that Smart Building Central had with regards to its systems was that of the potential for a device to reach out to a cloud server that was eventually deprecated or no longer available. The potential for attackers to re-create this resource to serve nefarious means, including malware or ransomware, was significant in its potential. While security mechanisms were used internally to prevent the spread of this malware, there was still a necessary risk that needed to be mitigated around the potential for exploitation from within the cloud.

Smart Building Central, to mitigate this risk, stood up its own DNS servers for the smart building, as opposed to relying on the exclusive use of corporate DNS services. These DNS servers acted as a subsidiary of corporate DNS services but then forwarded all external resolution requests to Cisco Umbrella for resolution. Cisco Umbrella, seeing more than 170 million DNS requests per day, provided a level of intelligence to DNS resolution for Smart Building Central that the corporate DNS services of SBC Inc. did not have. For each DNS request being sent to Umbrella, the request was evaluated for a set of criteria around the trustworthiness of the website that was being requested. These criteria included

- The age of the DNS record as registered

- The owner of the DNS record according to its registration

- Whether the website presented a secured certificate upon request

- The content observed by Umbrella DNS that the website served up

- The business relevance of the content being served

The advantage of Umbrella DNS seeing so many requests daily is that it contains information on commonly accessed malware and ransomware cloud resources so that they can be classified and actively blocked before any traffic even traverses to the site in question. For Smart Building Central, this meant the ability to prevent sites that may have been spoofed, as well as an enforcement ability within Umbrella DNS to filter out content irrelevant to the business while presenting a warning page to the user, such as traffic with strictly adult themes, violence, sites used strictly for data sharing, or those that were considered overtly political in nature. This filter was applied strictly to corporate PCs, IOT devices, and other corporate devices and was not applied to the guest or personal mobile phones areas of the network.

Analytics

As can be imagined, the distributed authorization and enforcement mechanisms throughout Smart Building Central made for a massive analytics data set to be consumed and utilized, both to influence policy as well as troubleshoot traffic traversal issues where dynamically applied controls were present within the network. Smart Building Central had a SIEM for consumption of security events, including passed and failed auth, firewall allowed and denied flows, and syslog events for attempts to log in to systems throughout the network, but one major gap still existed within the architecture. The management of SBC Inc. was very interested in evaluating how well their security was working in relation to the number of threats that were potentially dangerous to Smart Building Central that we blocked. While one aspect of this was the number of devices that were prevented from communicating based on being blocked from accessing the network altogether, another was the number of flows that were blocked in transit due to the application of TrustSec. TrustSec, not being a stateful firewall, will drop communications between endpoints within the same VLAN; however, on some network access devices it lacks the ability to indicate that this drop occurred. This inability makes for a challenge in both evaluating where these drops occurred and troubleshooting when flows that were expected to occur were unsuccessful.

To mitigate this troubleshooting and analytical need, Smart Building Central employed the use of three products. The first was Secure Network Analytics (SNA). Secure Network Analytics, with its ability to collect NetFlow traffic from across the network, can indicate where the traversal of traffic, containing a source and destination for the traversal, does not make it to its destination. This is based on observing the expected path and whether the packet makes it to the final device within that flow. Should a PC, for example, attempt to communicate to a digital signage device directly, the flow record would indicate that the communication between the two devices was dropped at the switch to which the digital signage device was connected due to an unauthorized flow occurring according to the TrustSec matrix. This failure could then be logged to the SIEM and analyzed to determine whether the attempt to access the device was in error, as indicated by a one-time access, or whether it was a pattern of access attempts, such as a scan of the network or an attempt to write nefarious information to devices as found in the packet contents.

In addition, both the Key Masters and the IT operations group used Secure Network Analytics on an ongoing basis. Try as they may to ensure that the culture of Smart Building Central was changed, allowing only pre-authorized and approved purchase devices onto the network, plenty of resources within Smart Building Central were still attempting to purchase or bring devices into the building without getting authorization first. In the spirit of adherence with policies written, the device would still be authenticated with the user's credentials, documentation provided when the device was found to be unauthorized, and information provided to IT operations. A device owner would still need to provide the type of device and its business relevance to the network, as well as justification relating to why the device was never properly onboarded through the proper processes. Most of these requests cited "timelines to success" and indicated a slow process of changing company culture.

For the first few months of Smart Building Central's existence, the IT operations teams, while attempting to educate staff into the proper processes, would utilize Secure Network Analytics to dynamically determine what resources endpoints needed to communicate to while allowing them to remain connected to the switchport that they would be allocated. This effort came in the form of statically quarantining devices that were unauthorized, providing them minimal access to the network, and then analyzing them on the fly to create proper authorization policies for them. This practice was discontinued after the first quarter of Smart Building Central's business-as-usual period due to interference with other priorities IT operations held. The result was that users were forced to go through proper onboarding processes after the policy was well established.

The second major tool used within Smart Building Central to analyze traffic traversal was Cisco Secure Workload. Secure Workload was a requirement within the Smart Building Central premises for all physical and virtual servers deployed. The goal of Secure Workload was to analyze communications of the servers with endpoints in such a fashion that alerts could be generated for interactions that occurred that were outside of the expected behavior of consumption of resources from the server. For example, to prevent cross-site scripting or command injection into server communications, Secure Workload could fire an alert specific to the virtual server in question when such a behavior was observed. Due to the limitations of data center switches within the local main distribution facility of Smart Building Central, Secure Workload was also used to apply policy directly to the server, without relying on the switch to which it was connected. Secure Workload makes use of IP tables present on the server to modify its communications to those communications that are strictly required as applied from a policy server, the Secure Workload Management Center. This made for easy application of policies down to the port and protocol level for physical servers within the premises.

The reliance of mobile phones on cloud services for navigation and ordering of elevators within the Smart Building Central premises was also a major use of Cisco Secure Workload. Much of the resources required to be done in building navigation, as well as the server-side application processing for interaction with elevators, smart lighting, and similar building services, was hosted in a major public cloud provider. While groupings based on allowed ports and protocols could be allowed and associated with the cloud servers, understanding which devices were interacting with these servers and enforcing policy related to these interactions was a major concern of Smart Building Central. Deployment of Cisco Secure Workload provided this visibility, enforcement, and analytical capability, comparable to physical servers, through the modification of IP tables.

The final analytics engine used within the Smart Building Central deployment was Cisco Thousand Eyes. With the building reliant on critical IOT systems that could have an impact on the health and safety of occupants of the building, Smart Building Central had a major goal of preventing the network administrators' favorite complaint of "my endpoint's connection is too slow!" Cisco Thousand Eyes was implemented to constantly measure the connectivity indicators within the building as well as to the cloud for indications of high latency and downtime of the application or server. It was also used to measure the response time to more easily determine whether the endpoint was prevented from accessing the application, whether there was impact on response time, or whether the endpoint should be consulted to determine why it wasn't reaching out or processing information received from the application server in a reasonable amount of time.

Conclusion

With the success of Smart Building Central and the changes made to the organization to address limitations exposed in the planning phases of Smart Building Central, SBC Inc. decided that the Zero Trust model would be applied to all net-new building deployments, renovated buildings, and maintained real estate in that priority. Not all of the company's real estate was smart device integrated. There are, however, significant numbers of devices within every building that would not have been known to be connected until the identification phase occurred for that building.

By breaking up these steps utilized for Smart Building Central's success within its Zero Trust journey, SBC Inc. was able to create a roadmap and evaluation standard for progress and milestones applied to each of its other buildings. As opposed to the question "When will the building be secured?" the more value-aligned question "Which phase is the building at, and how far along?" could be used to determine progress.

Because of the journey that is Zero Trust, no single destination awaits the organization that pursues it; removing trust from a network is an ongoing and never-ending process. The mountain of Zero Trust, seen in Figure A-4, is most definitely a journey. However, for organizations that choose to pursue Zero Trust, a mindset of the value realized throughout the process justifies the investment and helps validate where the organization is within the journey, like a map.

The Journey of Zero Trust

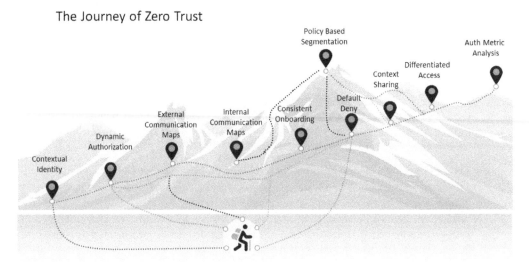

Figure A-4   *The Mountain of Zero Trust*

For Smart Building Central, that journey continues with new device onboarding, lifecycle management of devices that are at the end of support by their vendor, and a need to onboard replacement devices, while still providing them the access they require. Luckily, the principles of Zero Trust provided SBC with a roadmap of how to do exactly this, develop its own priorities for value realized, and maintain operation of one of the smartest and people-oriented buildings in the world.

Though the name of the organization has been changed, we hope that this real-life use case will assist organizations to understand, rationalize their own use cases, and then realize their goals to begin and achieve a successful Zero Trust journey.

Index

Numbers

802.1X, 17, 81–82

A

AAA (authentication, authorization, and accounting), 13, 31–32

access

access-focused security, 176–180

endpoint-based analysis policies, 180

malware prevention and inspection, 179–180

vulnerability scanners, 179

ACLs (access control lists), 18, 22, 67, 101–102, 125–126, 136–137, 265

external access requirements, 164–168

privileged, 35

accounting, 31–32

ACI Fabric Policy Model, 73

ACLs (access control lists), 18, 22, 101–102, 125–126, 136–137, 141, 265

acquisitions. *See* mergers and acquisitions, onboarding and

Active Directory, 32, 81, 146, 208–209, 216, 258

activists, cyber, 106

Address Resolution Protocol (ARP), 138

addresses

IP (Internet Protocol), 20, 67, 108, 123, 165–166, 212

MAC (media access control)

authentication with, 32, 36, 143

MAC spoofing, 154–155

OSI model and, 123–124

profiling with, 154

segmentation policy and, 108

Smart Building Central Inc. (SBC) use case, 260, 267

TrustSec and, 138

adds, 239

adoption of Zero Trust

organizational belief that firewall is enough

application security, 180–182

challenges of, 175–176

defense in depth and access-focused security, 176–180

B

E

F

J

W